SELL RESULTS

What Every Technology Salesperson Needs to Know

SELL RESULTS

What Every Technology Salesperson Needs to Know

by

Janice Lawrence

Learning Solutions Press
Fort Collins, Colorado

For more information about this book and other products to help you sell technology solutions, please visit our website: www.sellresults.com

Second Edition

Published by
Learning Solutions Press
420 West Mountain Avenue Suite 102
Fort Collins, CO 80521
www.SELLRESULTS.com

Library of Congress Catalog Number: 2004091727
ISBN:0-9753199-1-4
Printed in the United States of America

Contents

Chapter 1

Sell Results

Become a Sales Superstar

Late at night, when everyone is sitting around the bar at the national sales meeting, sales legends are told. Tales of early wins and dramatic closes. Salespeople who closed big deals against terrific odds. The competitive upset. The first million-dollar deal.

These stories reflect the soul of a technology company's culture. These salespeople are heroes. They did what no one else could. They saved the day. They made a difference.

If you listen to enough of these stories at different technology companies, patterns start to emerge. One interesting commonality is that there are so few sales heroes. In the early life of a company, there is often a sales force of 20-30 people, yet there are only one or two 'superstars' who outsell all the rest. These 'sales superstars' so dramatically outperform the rest of the sales organization that their feats become legendary.

What makes these exceptional salespeople so special? Why can they close deals before anyone else can? How do they sell the solution before the product is even built? How do they outwit the competition? What do they know that you don't know?

The exceptional salesperson sells results.

The Nine Secrets of Sales Superstars

1. Be in the right place at the right time. Markets are dynamic systems that create the energy required to fuel change. When you harness this energy, you can use the forces of evolution to drive market adoption of your technology.

The ability to find the sources of market energy – emerging business strategies, pent up frustration with legacy systems, increasing desire for what the new technology enables – is one of the things that distinguishes exceptional salespeople. They know they can't generate enough momentum on their own to sell an emerging technology, so they channel the energy caused by market change and use it to energize the sales process.

Top sales performers pay attention to the market. They are the first people to see the link between the new technology and emerging business strategies. Therefore, they are also the first to bring these new ideas and opportunities to their customers. First they sell the vision. Then they follow up on their early successes by subtly transforming their message in response to the evolving buying preferences of the maturing market. They know how to apply technology adoption theory to help them find the early adopters, build market acceptance of their technology, and cash in the fabulous opportunities caused by the geometric growth rates that drive technology markets. They know how to be in the right place at the right time.

2. Use logic to build emotional commitment. In theory technology purchases are governed by a rational decision making process that includes technical evaluations, risk analysis, and professional negotiating. In reality, most technology investments are made because someone on the customer's executive team believes that the new technology will give them a competitive edge. The ability to create that belief is a core competency of the exceptional salesperson.

Most technology salespeople sell functionality – what the technology does. The exceptional high tech salesperson sells value –the results the technology enables. Value links the technology solution to the customer's business success by showing how the technology enables them to achieve their strategic goals faster, better and cheaper. It links the technology decision to more important, strategic decisions that have already been made.

Building value-selling strategies is a logical process that links the customer's business strategies to the unique functionality of the technology solution in a way that compels the customer to buy. Value selling creates a logic chain between what is happening in the market, the customer's business strategy, their technology needs and operational issues, the technology's features and benefits, and the economic value of the solution. The logic of this thought process satisfies the customer's rational needs; the value built by the process creates an emotional desire for the results the technology enables. You need both logic and emotion to close the sale.

3. Sell business results to the executive. Solutions transform technology products and services into business performance. Customers buy solutions because solutions deliver strategic results – increased sales, improved productivity, competitive advantage, increased customer satisfaction, etc. Solutions create value; products don't.

Responsibility for the success of a core business strategy is rarely confined to one department. Furthermore, it is never the responsibility of a technologist or engineer. Most salespeople who sell technology-rich solutions let the IT or Engineering departments reduce them to the role of vendor. Great technology salespeople are masters of selling to the people who count. They become the CXO's coach. They change the rules of the game.

4. Use competitive energy to build value. A competitive sale is supercharged with energy.
Many more people are investing resources, time, and ideas into the decision-making
process than in a noncompetitive situation. It is hard for a sale to get stalled when
several aggressive salespeople are doing whatever it takes to motivate the customer
to make a choice.

The average salesperson tries to avoid competition. Exceptional salespeople
seek it out. They encourage their customers to consider all options carefully, so
they will feel more comfortable making their decision. They know how to use the
unique aspects of their solution to differentiate themselves and build the customer's
perception of the value.

Master salespeople are aggressive and subtle competitors. They use non-
confrontational suggestions to lay competitive traps that entice the customer into asking
competitors embarrassing questions. They create competitive issues, so they get a
chance to showcase the superiority of their solution. They build personal credibility
by inviting competitive comparison. They know how to play the competitive game.

5. Find the executive who cares. Prospecting is the process for finding and attracting the
attention of the people who are most likely to buy your technology solution, NOW!
Prospecting is usually the most unproductive step of the sales cycle. Because most
salespeople don't have the information they need about the market, buying process,
and business potential of the technology applications, they tend to prospect randomly.
They generate lots of vague interest and expect to lose a lot of prospects over the
course of the sales cycle.

Sales superstars do the opposite. They apply their knowledge about the
market, the technology's value proposition and the customer's buying preferences to
find and approach high potential accounts in a way that builds strategic advantage.
They apply technology adoption theory to find the customers who are ready to buy.
Then they approach them with personalized value propositions that directly link their
technology to the customer's business success.

Furthermore, exceptional salespeople map their account development
strategy before they approach the account. They find the business executive
responsible for the success of the business strategy and approach him directly. After
they win him over, they borrow his political power to penetrate the account. So often
they are selling several levels higher in the organization than their competitors, who
have approached the account through the IT or engineering department.

6. Focus on the best opportunities. Exceptional salespeople are excellent qualifiers. They ruthlessly evaluate the customer's intention as quickly as possible. They take a hard look at how applicable their technology is to the customer's situation. If they can't build extraordinary value, they walk because they know they can find better opportunities elsewhere. They are only looking for win-win deals.

Effective qualification is the key to sales productivity. There are only so many deals you can sell profitably. The average salesperson makes the mistake of trying to sell too many deals at once, so he doesn't have the time or resources to focus on the best ones.

Exceptional salespeople use the qualification process to find the highest potential deals. They look for opportunities where they have a unique competitive advantage, so they can easily outsell the competition. They test their ability to negotiate with the customer to verify their willingness to collaborate. They estimate the potential ROI the solution will create. They go beyond the traditional qualifiers of time, problem and budget to evaluate the intangible factors that drive the customer's sense of urgency and value.

Once this information is gathered and evaluated, the exceptional salesperson will make a conscious decision whether or not to invest the time and energy required to develop the account. They focus their energy. Consequently they win much more often than the salespeople who spread themselves too thin. Average salespeople tend to let opportunity drive their behavior. Exceptional salespeople drive the opportunity.

7. Build value and sell solutions. Once an exceptional sales team has committed to developing an opportunity, they give it all they've got. Their discovery process is rigorous. They engage the customer in a collaborative process so that by the time the solution is built the customer believes it is the only viable alternative. They uncover issues and solve problems. They escalate issues to upper management. By doing so they increase their control over the buying process, so they can negotiate a fair price, ensure a successful implementation, and close the deal.

Discovery is conducted through a series of conversations during which the sales team asks compelling questions that build the customer's perception of value. Each question has a purpose – to build the customer's awareness, to solve problems, to raise pain, to set a competitive trap, etc. Exceptional salespeople knows how to build questioning scripts that increase the customer's sense of urgency and commitment. They know the right questions to ask.

8. Take control of the account. Sales superstars use the proposal process to increase their control over the customer's buying process. Average salespeople write proposals too early in the sales process. The customer asks for a proposal and they deliver one. This gives the customer license to negotiate additional services for the same price, let competitors drive the evaluation, and the power to say no.

Exceptional salespeople never deliver a proposal until they completely understand the customer's needs and the scope of the solution. They understand how submitting a proposal changes the dynamics of the sale and use this insight to their advantage. They break the proposal process down into a series of events designed to win strategic, functional approvals and build sales momentum. During the proposal phase of the sales cycle, the sale intensifies – buyers focus on what could go wrong; competitors fight dirty, politics run rampant. The sales superstar knows how to take control of this emotionally charged environment and lead the customer through the closing process, so they win the deal.

9. Create momentum and negotiate success. Exceptional salespeople are great closers. Most salespeople aren't effective negotiators because they are too willing to do whatever it takes to make the sale. They are so attuned to serving the customer that they let professional negotiators walk all over them. Sales superstars realize that negotiating is a game that they must win for their customer to succeed. They play hard and fast, and they win.

Closing a deal is all about power. Sales superstars know how to use power – their own, their coach's, their decision maker's – to negotiate a win-win relationship. They don't discount their price. They don't let the customer cut corners in a way that will jeopardize the successful implementation of the solution. They know when to escalate issues to get them resolved, and they know when to walk away from an unprofitable deal.

Exceptional salespeople take the initiative to plan and lead the negotiating process. Their intimate knowledge of the customer's needs and how the technology works, enable them to scale the solution on the fly. They know what they can give up and what they can't, and they have a backup plan. The exceptional salesperson's deals are always successfully implemented. Their customers are always satisfied, so they become loyal, repeat customers.

THE NINE SECRETS OF SALES SUPERSTARS

★ Be in the right place at the right time.

★ Use logic to build emotional commitment.

★ Sell business results to the executive.

★ Use competitive energy to build value.

★ Find the executive who cares.

★ Focus on the best opportunities.

★ Build value and sell solutions.

★ Take control of the account.

★ Create momentum and negotiate success.

So, if it is this simple, why aren't there more sales superstars?

If we know what makes the exceptional salesperson successful, why are there so few of them? The answer is simple. Most salespeople don't have the information they need to sell, and most technology companies don't understand what kind of information helps salespeople sell.

Technology-enabled solutions are intangible sales. People don't buy the machine; they buy what it enables. Average salespeople tend to perceive technology as a tangible, so they focus on the functionality. Exceptional salespeople understand that customers only care about the results the technology enables, which are intangible. This difference in perception about the nature of technology is the fundamental factor in determining a salesperson's success.

Technology is the actualization of abstract theories. The more theories that are actualized, the more powerful the technology is. _For example, there is a computer chip in my car that makes me a better driver. The computer chip senses the car beginning to skid on a patch of ice much faster than I can. It automatically sends messages to the anti-lock brake system so the car responds to the changing road conditions before I am even aware there may be a problem._ This simple application is the actualization of theories that span the disciplines of physics, mechanical engineering, human perception, and computer software. It would take a long time to explain how it all worked. *As a car buyer, however, I only care about the fact that it makes me a safer driver.*

The more sophisticated the technology is, the greater the abstraction. Selling abstractions is more than just relating benefits. It is about linking the functionality of the technology to the desired end result, which is the intangible promise of the technology. *I can only appreciate the value of the car's computer controlled anti-locking device when I understand how it improves my driving. If the salesperson just explains anti-locking brakes, I don't perceive the benefit. If she tells me that I will be a better driver, but doesn't explain how, then I won't believe her.* She must help me understand the relationship between the how the technology is applied and the results that are important to me before I will value the technology.

The translation of abstract theory into useful applications that deliver strategic benefits is the essence of selling value. Value is created when the customer believes the technology solution will help them accomplish their objectives. To develop the customer's conviction, you must integrate their learning process with their decision-making process. The salesperson must provide the customer with the right information at the right time. Furthermore, it must be done in a way that increases the customer's perception of need, urgency to buy, and appreciation for the value contribution of the solution.

The information puzzle gets even more complex as we incorporate the relentless rate of change associated with any computer-based technology. As the technology evolves and its applications expand, it becomes practically impossible to stay current and informed about the solution. The body of information that the salesperson draws upon to sell a technology solution is constantly evolving. Products mutate. New technologies replace old ones. Competitors' products change. Markets accelerate. Each change has multiple implications for how customers buy and the best ways to sell the solution.

Keeping current about all the factors that influence a technology sale is not easy. It is hard enough to keep track of the ever-changing information. The fact that you must synthesize this information into strategically sequenced, customer learning experiences that build credibility and value greatly increases its complexity. No wonder the superstars make so much money!

What do you need to know?

Selling technology requires a unique blend of expertise – business, product knowledge, technology, engineering – skills – consulting, teaching, coaching, selling, negotiating, – and attitudes – partnering, 'win-win', service. If you are reading this book, you probably have already mastered many of these skills. However, you rarely have all the information you need. Why? Because it is too hard to find, maintain, and integrate into the sales process.

What you really need is accurate, current and insightful information about the technology you are selling and how it helps your customers accomplish their business strategy, which is what this book is all about.

Sell Results: *What Every Technology Salesperson Needs to Know* is about the information you need to become a technology sales superstar. In this book you will learn how to gather and analyze information about the market, your technology, and your customer's business, so you can sell more productively. More importantly, you will learn how to apply this information to the steps of the sales process, so you close more deals.

Section One explains what technology salespeople need to know and why. In each chapter a strategic thought process essential to selling technology is discussed:

- In **Chapter 2: Harness Market Energy** you will learn how technology markets evolve and what information you need to find emerging opportunities, so you will be in the right place at the right time.

- In **Chapter 3: Build Value** you will learn how to logically build the customers' perception of value by showing them how your technology enables their business strategies, so you can logically build the customers emotional commitment to your solution.

- In **Chapter 4: Sell Solutions** you will learn how to sell business results to the executive, so you have better control over the account and close deals faster.

- In **Chapter 5: Compete Strategically** you will learn how to use competitive energy to build the customer's perception of value.

In **Section Two** these strategic thought processes are applied to the technology sales process, so you can use this information to your advantage throughout the sale.

- In **Chapter 6: Prospect for Energy** you will learn how to enter new accounts strategically and find the business executive who cares about the value of your solution, so you prospect more efficiently.

- In **Chapter 7: Qualify Potential** you will learn how to use your understanding of value to qualify opportunities, so you focus on the best opportunities and improve your sales productivity.

- In **Chapter 8: Discover Solutions** you will learn how to use the needs analysis process to heighten the customers' perception of value, corroboratively build solutions that work, eliminate competitors and create momentum, so you close more deals faster.

- In **Chapter 9: Propose Value** you will learn how to use the customers' buying process to build commitment to your solution, so you can gain control over the account.

- In **Chapter 10: Close Fast** you will learn how to create momentum and negotiate a successful deal for both you and your customer, so you build ongoing, profitable relationships with your customers.

Finally, in **Chapter 11: Make it Happen** you will learn what you have to do to implement the processes in this book in your company. It will provide you with an overview of how to use content management and competency management to manage the process of building and maintaining the information you need to be a superstar.

Why does this book have all the answers?

There comes a time in every successful company's growth, when they need to build a sales team. Fast. Usually this moment comes when the market is accelerating, and the company is desperate to get 'feet on the street' before mass adoption occurs. There is so much market demand that the growing company can't respond fast enough. Resources are stretched to a breaking point.

At this moment of incredible tension created by promises of double-digit growth, massive hiring campaigns and aggressive sales quotas, our company gets called in to help the VP of Sales figure out how to get the new sales team up to speed. Yesterday. Often, the company doesn't really understand why all of a sudden it is successful. So they lock us in a room with their sales superstars for a few weeks and together we figure out what is causing their success.

We have been through this exercise with over fifty, very successful companies – Apple, Amdahl, Cisco, Commerce One, General Electric, General Motors, Oracle, Procter & Gamble, Sun, Sybase, to name a few. Although each situation has been unique, over time we have discovered the common factors that create sales success. This book is the result of thousands of hours of collaboration with some of the most successful and perceptive sales executives who have ever sold. Over the past twenty years we have worked with hundreds of sales superstars. This book distills what we have learned down to the essence of what these exceptional sales professionals know and do.

Who should read this book?

If you sell technology solutions, this book is for you. It will help you figure out what you don't know and provide you with a process to guide your information gathering efforts. It will also help you figure out how to apply the information to the steps of the sales cycle. Consider this your cookbook to become a sales superstar. Try out the recipes for strategic thinking. Learn how to spot emerging opportunities (Chapter 2), build value (Chapter 3) and outwit the competition (Chapter 5.) Then try applying these methodologies by using the techniques described in Section 2 to a new account. At first you may feel uncomfortable selling to executives or negotiating for customer resources on your second call. But try it. You will be surprised by how well these techniques work!

If you manage a sales team, this book will help you improve their sales productivity. It provides you with frameworks and processes that integrate technical, market, and sales data into useful, practical sales tools that will accelerate the learning process of your sales team. Use the maps and exercises in Section One to educate your sales team about how to sell new products and services. Build a Competitive Map at your next regional meeting (Chapter 5). Leverage the insights of your best sales team by asking them to write Value Building Questioning Strategies for everyone else to use (Chapter 3). Review the sales competencies found in each chapter of Section Two. They will help you determine what you need to do to build a team of sales superstars.

If you support a sales organization and create information for the sales team to use, this book will help you understand what salespeople need to know and how they use the information you create. It is chock full of templates and guidelines for sales tools that have proven to work at companies like Cisco, Oracle, GE and many other great technology companies. Use the **'What You Need to Know...'** sections in the Section One chapters to create a master list of content that you need to create. Then refer to the **'Take Action'** sections in Section Two to find models for synthesizing and packaging this information into useful sales tools that the field will love.

Finally, if you are a CXO, this book will help you direct your sales and marketing organizations, so you can accelerate the successful implementation of your new business initiatives. Use this book to create a practical plan around how to implement your upcoming strategic initiatives. Ask marketing to gather the information the field needs to 'sell the story'. Everything they need to know is listed in the chapters found in Section One. Then challenge sales to implement the sales techniques found in Section Two. Use this book to change the rules.

WHO SHOULD READ THIS BOOK?

Salespeople ➤ Learn what you need to know and do

Sales Managers ➤Accelerate your sales teams' learning process

Marketing & Training ➤Improve the quality and utility of your information

Executives ➤Learn how to accelerate your company's success

How should your read this book?

Applying a 16th century technology, book printing, to the needs of the 21st century salesperson is a challenge. Books assume that the reader has long uninterrupted spans of time that can be devoted to exploring ideas. This is a luxury that most of us don't have. So this book has been designed to satisfy the needs of three kinds of readers – the net-it-out scanner, the thought leader, and the practical doer.

If you are a net-it-out scanner, then look for pictures and notes that are separated from the text by vertical black bars. All of the critical concepts, questions, and recommended actions are summarized in these call outs. You also might want to read the **'Conclusions'** sections of each chapter because they summarize each chapter into a single page of cogent bullets. Then, if you want to do something with the knowledge, refer to the **'Take Action'** sections that can be found at the end of each chapter. If you really are the 'net-it-out' guy you think you are, you should master this book in less than 90 minutes.

For the thought leader, this book gathers and presents a wide range of theories in a new light. You will most likely want to spend some quality time reading the chapters in Section One and trying to build the **'Maps'** described in each chapter. In order to do so, you will need to gather the information you need, which is outlined in detail in the **'What you need to know…'** sections of each chapter in Section One. These are 'shopping lists' of the information you need to become a sales superstar. Since you will probably want to share your insights with your peers, refer to the **'Take Action'** sections of each chapter for ideas of how to use the maps you have created to find better opportunities, accelerate the sales cycle, and close more deals.

Most salespeople, however, are paid to execute. So **for the practical doer** who is looking for guidelines on what to do, Section Two applies the strategic thought processes to the steps of the technology sales cycle. In these chapters you will learn how to use the theories and information gathered in Section One to sell more productively. These chapters also provide you with useful tools and templates, **'Take Action,'** that will help you implement your ideas faster. Since you probably don't have enough spare time to do everything this book tells you to do, pass it along to someone whose job it is to support you. Highlight the information that you need. Circle the sales tools that you would use. Underline what you need others to do to help you get the job done. Use this book to tell your management, marketing group, training department, etc. what you need.

And you will become a superstar…

Exceptional sales performers do a better job than the rest of us because they know what information they need and how to get it. They are not necessarily more intelligent than the rest of us. However, they are fast learners. They know the right questions to ask. They have the capacity to become 'instant experts.' They use social and cognitive frameworks to help them make sense of a fast changing world. They continually update their perception of the market with new information and are capable of using these insights to find and develop new opportunities.

Exceptional salespeople are also good at generalizing their experiences into principles to guide their actions. They can relate what they experience in one situation to another. They are very creative in applying what they learn to a wide network of potential customers. They think 'outside of the box.' Once they understand the fundamental value proposition of a new technology, they are very good at finding ways to apply the technology to new business applications.

Sales superstars are good networkers. They know who to call to help them think through opportunity scenarios and how to engage visionary executives in a way that builds a sense of excitement around the new technology's potential. They are also good communicators. Once they understand the capabilities of the new technology, its value proposition, and how it can be applied to support business strategies, they are very good at succinctly getting their message across. They can 'net it out.'

These are probably all competencies you already have – the ability to learn quickly, network, communicate ideas, think out of the box. You just need the right information organized in ways that you can put it to use. The purpose of this book is to help you do it. So, go for it!

Section One

What You Need to Know

Sales superstars know how to gather and process the right information so they can find the best opportunities, sell productively, and close fast. The reason they don't waste any time is because they focus on results. In this section of **Sell Results**: *What Every Technology Salesperson Needs to Know*, you will learn how to think like they do. Strategically. Efficiently. Smart.

Exceptional high-tech sales people have a profound understanding of who their customers are; what customers are trying to accomplish, and how their technology enables the customer's success. They know how to read the market to find emerging opportunities. They help the customer build solutions that deliver strategic business results. They know who to call on and how to navigate political currents, so they can get to the decision maker faster. They defeat the competition before they even get up to bat.

Sales superstars do these things because they know how to think about their business. They use strategic thought processes to gather and organize information about the market, the customer, the technology, and the competition into strategic account development plans. In the following chapters, you will learn how they do it.

■ **Learn how to read markets so you can be in the right place at the right time.** By learning how to channel the energy caused by market evolution, you will be able to find high potential opportunities, approach them when they are ready to buy, and build sales momentum, so, you can close deals faster and sell more efficiently. When you build a Market Energy Map, you will see how market trends drive technology adoption. You will figure out which companies will adopt first and why they will, so you can focus your prospecting. You will also be able to predict how quickly the market is developing, so your forecasting will be more accurate and your company will be ready to take advantage of the incredible opportunities caused by mass adoption.

■ **Learn how to build value so you can link your solution to your customer's business success.** By logically showing customers how your technology enables them to accomplish their strategic business goals faster, cheaper, and more productively, you build their emotional commitment to buying your offer. Therefore, you are more likely to close a profitable deal quickly. When you build a Value Map, you trace the connection between the customer's successes and how your technology works. This increases the intangible value of your solution by making its benefits tangible. Furthermore, you document the financial return on the technology investment, so your customer understands the incredible value it can contribute to their business.

■ **Learn how to sell the economic value of your solution to the business executive**. When you sell business results to line executives, you can change the rules of the technology buying process to your advantage. This enables you to build more control over the account. When you draw a Solutions Map, you uncover who has the power to help you. You will discover non-traditional routes to the decision maker, so you won't get stuck in the IT or engineering department. You will also develop a better understanding of the customer's buying process, preferences, and style. This information helps you figure out how to sell your solution the way your customer wants to buy it. It makes your job easier and accelerates the sale.

■ **Learn how to build competitive advantage by differentiating your solution.** Competitive differentiation builds the customer's perception of the unique value contribution of your solution, which motivates them to make the buying decision and increases their commitment to implementing it successfully. When you build a Competitive Map, you will find your 'sweet spots' of opportunity, prospects where you have an inherent advantage, so you are more likely to win. You will also discover the unique differentiators that will help you build the customer's perception of value, which drives how much you can charge and how quickly you can close. Discover how to lay competitive landmines that blow up in your competitor's face when they least expect it. Play to win.

No one said this was going to be easy.

Good content is very difficult to develop. It is really hard pry relevant information out of an engineering team. We have stayed up all night trying to translate a company's value proposition into words an executive can understand. We realize that writing Value Building Questioning Strategies is an art. Although this book tries very hard to simplify the complex process of strategic selling, we know that this is not easy. To simplify the process we have broken each of these strategic thought chapters into sections designed to make the content development process easier to do.

■ The first few pages summarize the concept – **'What is…'** defines the process and **'Why is understanding … important** helps you understand why mastery is critical to successful selling.

■ Next comes the **'How to...'** section. This is an overview of the strategic thought process and the relevant theories that explain why it works the way it does. This section is the meat of the book. Chew it carefully, and it will nourish you. Throughout this section we have sprinkled questions to ask yourself or your customer to help you apply these theories to your job.

■ The **'What you need to know...'** sections help you identify the information you need to gather to use the process. These are not laundry lists. They are the results of years of trying to take shortcuts and finding out that you can't be successful without this information.

■ The **'How to use...'** sections apply the content to the various stages of the sales cycle so you can see how to use the information to move the sale forward. This section should whet your appetite to read Section Two, which expands on these ideas.

■ **Take Action'** offers you ideas and sales tools that will help you apply the strategic thought process to your job.

■ The **'Conclusions'** section summarizes the key points and the mapping process into a few pages. Hopefully these will be pages you turn to often in the future as you integrate these ideas and techniques into your personal sales process.

If after reading this book, you find that you want to explore these ideas in greater depth, then visit our website: **www.sellresults.com**. You will find many more examples of the tools and ideas presented in this book and useful sales tools that you can use to help you become a sales superstar.

Chapter 2

Harness Market Energy

Be in the Right Place at the Right Time

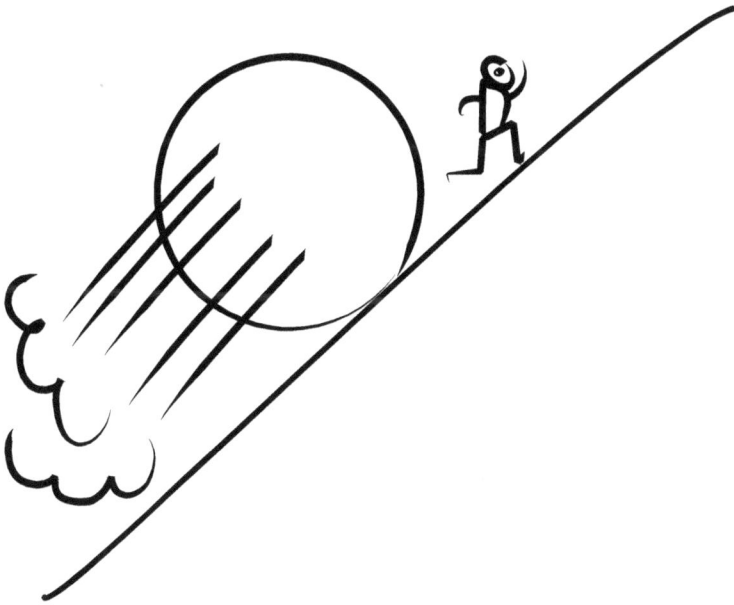

HARNESS MARKET ENERGY

What   Use market evolution to drive the adoption of your technology.

Why   Harnessing market energy ensures you will be in the right place at the right time.

How   1. Find market energy, so you can use market momentum to find high potential prospects and increase sales.

            2. Segment the market, so you find emerging opportunities faster and develop accounts earlier.

            3. Forecast market adoption, so you can forecast accurately and set realistic expectations.

So What?   Learning how to channel the energy caused by market change helps you find high potential opportunities, approach them when they are ready to buy, and build sales momentum, so, you can close deals faster and sell more efficiently.

WHAT IS MARKET ENERGY?

Market energy is the momentum created by mass adoption of a new technology. To harness this energy, you need to understand how the new technology is causing the market to evolve. You use market energy to find new opportunities; position your solution, and drive the sales process.

Technological innovation creates new markets. *The internal combustion engine created the automotive industry.* It also refreshes existing markets by offering improved capabilities. *The automatic gearshift made driving easier, so more people drove cars.*

Technology is not an end in itself; it is a means to an end. *You don't buy a car engine because it is a brilliant example of energy conversion; you buy a car engine because it gets you places...*

Because technology must be applied to create utility, the development of technology-driven markets is neither an automatic, nor straightforward, process. It takes a lot of smart people playing around with a new technology before its potential usefulness is crystallized into solutions. Usually it takes a "killer app" to create enough demand to build a new market. *Personal computer technology had been around for a few years before Visicalc, the first electronic spreadsheet, showed everyone how useful a PC could be.* Even with incremental innovations, the market doesn't build momentum until the first applications of the technology are successfully implemented and its potential benefits are proven.

WHY IS UNDERSTANDING MARKET ENERGY IMPORTANT?

To sell technology-enabled solutions successfully, you need to understand how technology markets develop. Market energy drives the dynamics of your target market – how fast it will grow, who will be the first adopters, how large the market will become, etc. This knowledge helps you find emerging opportunities early, sell consultatively and set realistic expectations.

- **Get into accounts early.** When change happens; it happens fast. A market perspective ensures you will be ready for change when it occurs. In this chapter you will learn how to anticipate market growth and development, so you can approach prospects with a compelling business solution before everyone else does.

- **Sell high.** Early in the technology adoption life cycle, the risks of implementation are very high. The technology is full of bugs, and the results have yet to be proven. It is definitely not in the IT or engineering departments' best interest to be a guinea pig. The best person to champion a new technology-based solution is a business executive responsible for delivering strategic results. The techniques in this chapter will help you figure out how to capture the executive's attention.

- **Sell consultatively**. Market energy causes change that directly impacts your customer' business. Providing your customers with insightful advice about the market and how to take advantage of emerging opportunities help them run their businesses more successfully. It encourages them to trust you.

- **Create demand**. As you refine your ability to predict market evolution, you will find new opportunities to present to your customers. If you can approach your customers before they approach you, you can become their partner, which is a far superior relationship than that of a vendor. Creating more opportunity for them means more opportunity for you.

WHY HARNESS MARKET ENERGY?

★ Be at the right place at the right time.

★ Propose business opportunities to executives.

★ Mine your existing accounts for new opportunities.

★ Improve your ability to read your customer.

★ Improve your forecasting accuracy.

- **Anticipate and understand customer behavior**. As markets evolve, buying behavior changes dramatically. If you know how rapidly the market is maturing, you will anticipate shifts in buying behavior better than your competitors. In this chapter you will learn how to adapt your selling style and value proposition to the changing buying preferences of your prospects, so you can build competitive advantage.

- **Improve your forecasting**. Forecasting is an important business process. It enables management to plan effectively and productively manage resources. The more accurate the sales forecast is, the more profitable the company. You are the core of the forecasting process. If you don't understand the market and the factors that are driving market growth and development, then you aren't going to be able to accurately forecast your sales. As you develop a market perspective, you get better at predicting when the market will expand and contract, so your forecasts are more accurate.

HOW TO HARNESS MARKET ENERGY

To harness market energy you need to develop a market perspective, which is the ability to understand and predict how emerging markets adopt new technology solutions. You develop a market perspective by understanding why customers need to adopt your new technology; logically segmenting the market, and forecasting the timing and urgency of market adoption.

The core of any technology market is the **technology's value proposition** – how it enables companies to increase their wealth. It explains why people will change their behavior to integrate the new technology into their work and lives. By applying the Harness Market Energy Process to your target market, you will be able to find early adopters and create activities to encourage technology adoption. This process also helps you predict when the 'tipping point' will occur, so you are ready to reap the benefits of mass adoption.

HARNESS MARKET ENERGY PROCESS

1. Find Market Energy.

   ➤ Define the market trends driving its growth.

2. Segment the Market.

   ➤ Logically group buying behavior into high potential market segments.

3. Forecast Adoption.

   ➤ Predict who will buy and when.

STEP 1: Find Market Energy

Markets create energy because they are dynamic. They are constantly evolving in response to changes in the economic, political, and technological environments. Understanding what causes a market to evolve helps you predict where opportunities will emerge; how fast they will develop, and when and whether mass adoption will occur. If you can capture this energy, you can use it to drive the sales process.

Dynamic systems create energy. If left unchecked, any systemic change tends to grow. *A snowball rolling downhill gets bigger.* Growth creates momentum. *As the snowball grows bigger, it goes faster.* Momentum creates energy. *The faster the snowball rolls; the bigger it gets; the harder it hits the tree.* Energy drives change.[1]

You can use the energy sources created by an evolving market to motivate prospects to buy your solution. Persuading people to try out a new technology is an uphill battle. You have to invest a lot of your precious energy – sales resources, capital, technical expertise, etc. – into convincing prospects they can benefit from using your technology to support their business. However, if you understand what is driving market change– *an increasingly mobile work force, higher need for personal security, faster access to global markets* – then you use the energy created by the market to motivate prospects to buy. Thus, you need to invest fewer of your own resources, and you can sell more productively and efficiently.

Technology markets create abundance.

There are two laws that explain why technology-enabled markets generate extraordinary amounts of energy. Moore's Law predicts that technology is going to improve in the future and cost less. Metcalf's Law states that technologies become more useful as more people use them. The combination of these two laws creates an economy of abundance that is unique to technology markets. As Moore's Law predicts an endless supply of ever-increasing resources and Metcalf's Law promises that innovations will be quickly adopted, the nature of the economy changes.

The implications of Moore's Law are that every 18 months technology is going to cost half as much and be twice as powerful. Moore's Law has held true for over 30 years. Previous economies were based on the laws of scarcity, where you have a limited amount of resources, and value is based on how scarce they are – *gold, oil, land, etc.* The more you use up the resources, the less energy you have.

A technology-based economy is based on the laws of abundance. According to Moore's law, there will always be cheaper resources tomorrow. This ever-increasing pool of resources enables customers to implement new business strategies. If it isn't possible today, it will be possible tomorrow. Improved technology is constantly fueling the market, creating energy.

---

[1] Senge, Peter. *The Fifth Discipline*, Currency. 1994

MOORE'S LAW

"Every 18 months processing power doubles while the cost
holds constant."

Gordon Moore
Founder, Intel

Furthermore, thanks to this simple formula, technological obsolescence is always only a few months away. Customers can never afford to sit still for fear that a competitor will be able to leapfrog ahead of them if they don't adopt the next generation of technology . This anxiety is another powerful source of energy that you can use to drive your sales.

Metcalf's Law also has a powerful effect on developing markets. It explains that the more people use a technology, the more useful it becomes. *If there was only one fax machine in the world, it wouldn't be useful. With two fax machines you can send mail back and forth faster and cheaper than if you send it through the post office. With 2,000,000 fax machines, you never have to wait in line at the post office again.* According to Metcalf a technology's usefulness equals the number of users squared. *If two people use a fax, it is four times easier than using the postal system. If 20 people use the fax machine, it is 400 times easier.* This creates a geometric increase in the technology's utility, which is just another way of saying why customers would want to buy it. *So if 2 people want to buy a fax machine today; 4 people will want to buy it tomorrow; 16 people will want to buy it the day after tomorrow; 256 people will want to buy it next week, and 2,147,483,648 will want to buy it by the end of the month.* That is a lot of potential customers lining up to buy your product, which is what market energy is all about.

METCALF'S LAW

"New technologies are valuable only if many people use
them... the utility of a network equates the square of the
number of users. "

Robert Metcalf
Founder, 3Com Corporation

Abundance creates demand for your technology. Since technology markets create abundance, they are not subject to the constraints of scarcity. They have unlimited growth potential and consequently unlimited potential to create wealth.

Value potential defines markets.

Technological innovation creates new markets by enabling organizations to create incremental wealth. Value is created when a new technology is applied through innovative business strategies to improve productivity, increase revenues, lower costs, etc. A market develops as the value of the applied technology grows.

At the core of a new market is the technology's value proposition – how it enables companies to create wealth. To define a new market you clarify:
- The value proposition of the new technology;
- How the technology will be applied to enable emerging strategies;
- How people will change their behavior as a result of what the new technology enables;
- The incremental wealth that will be created.

This information explains how the new market will create energy. The more powerful the technology's value proposition is; the greater the promise of new wealth becomes. The pursuit of this wealth causes companies to apply the technology to create useful goods and services, which in turn motivates people to adopt the new technology. The dynamics of this systematic conversion of technological capabilities into utility creates market energy.

How markets adopt.

Established markets resist change. *In 1900 a lot of people owned horses and buggies.* Most technological innovations require people to change their behavior to embrace the benefits of the applied technology. Markets don't grow until people believe the potential benefits of the new technology outweigh the risks and effort of change.

The more "discontinuous" an innovation, the longer it takes the market to adopt it. Discontinuous innovations are new ideas, products, services, etc. that require us to change our current behavior to something very new and different – *the automobile, telephone, or personal computer.* By contrast, continuous innovation doesn't require a change of behavior, because it is merely a better way of doing what we are already doing – *the automatic gearshift, the cell phone, or the next generation of word processing programs.* A new technology representing a discontinuous innovation is one that has the greatest potential to create wealth. It is also the hardest kind of innovation to sell because it means you have to convince people to dramatically change their behavior.

The laws of physics teach us that it takes a lot of energy to overcome inertia. Human inertia is what keeps people from adopting your new technology. It takes a lot of energy to get people to change their behavior, so if you want to sell into an early market, you must find and use market energy. The S-curve adoption model helps you figure out who will adopt when, so you can focus your sales efforts and harness the energy created by market evolution. It also helps you find new opportunities and approach prospects before your competition does.

S-curve adoption theory has three principles:

1. **Traditionally, innovations move very slowly into niche markets, then mushroom into the mainstream.** Early markets often develop slowly – the more "discontinuous" the innovation, the harder it is for people to figure out how to apply it. *The car was around for 30 years before you saw very many on the road.*

2. **It typically takes the same amount of time for a product to reach 10% acceptance as it does to reach 90% acceptance**. Widespread market adoption often happens very quickly. *In the fourteen years between 1914 and 1928, household adoption of the automobile grew from 10% to 90%.*

3. **Once a new technology reaches 50% market penetration, it starts to noticeably impact the economy and productivity.** *Propelled by the incredible productivity of the assembly-line revolution pioneered by Henry Ford in 1914 and by installment financing offered by General Motors in 1920, the wide-scale adoption of the automobile fueled the booming economy of the Roaring Twenties.*[2]

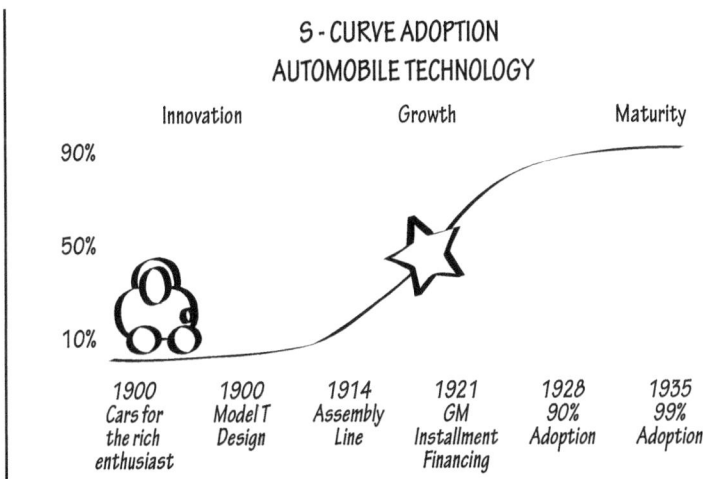

S - CURVE ADOPTION
AUTOMOBILE TECHNOLOGY

| Innovation | Growth | Maturity |

90%

50%

10%

| 1900 Cars for the rich enthusiast | 1900 Model T Design | 1914 Assembly Line | 1921 GM Installment Financing | 1928 90% Adoption | 1935 99% Adoption |

[2] Dent, Harry. *The Roaring 2000's*, Simon & Shuster. 1998

DEFINE MARKET

Ask Yourself:

? What does the new technology do? What new business strategies or organizational capabilities does the new technology enable?

? Who will benefit directly from the technology? What will they be able to do with the technology that they can't do now?

? How does the current market satisfy current needs that will be better satisfied by the new technology? How aware are people of their current needs/problems that will be satisfied by the new technology?

? What is the technology's value proposition?

? What is the estimated value of the new market today? When it reaches maturity?

Since technology markets tend to consolidate as they grow, early market share is very important to the long-term viability of your solution and your company. As technologies mature, the market tends to weed out many of the smaller players in favor of one or two major alternatives. This helps the market to standardize on one approach, which makes using the technology much easier. Once the market has chosen a market leader – *Microsoft Office, Cisco Routers* - it is almost impossible to unseat them. The benefits of market leadership are longer product life cycles, repeat business, and economies of scale, all of which serve to reinforce market dominance over time.

Identify market drivers.

Once you understand the promise of the new technology, you analyze the market to uncover the trends that are creating the need for new business strategies. The convergence of key trends creates high potential market segments – group of prospects who have an increasing need for your technology solution. Market Drivers are trends, innovations, and other factors that change the way a market operates. Market drivers create change. In emerging markets, these changes are often subtle and difficult to recognize. When developing a market perspective, you want to identify the market drivers that will drive people to change their behavior, which will consequently force companies to change their business strategies.

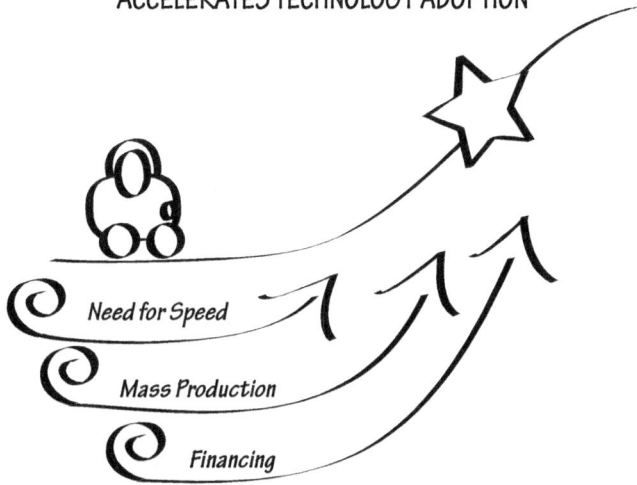

CONVERGENCE OF MARKET TRENDS ACCELERATES TECHNOLOGY ADOPTION

Need for Speed

Mass Production

Financing

The automobile enabled us to get places faster. However, it didn't develop into a market until several trends converged – lower manufacturing costs and increased availability due to mass production techniques, increasing urbanization of the general population – to make it a practical alternative to riding horses.

Market drivers can be:

- Economic trends – *falling interest rates, rising transaction costs, market globalization;*
- Social trends – *increased desire for personalization, aging of the population;*
- New laws or government regulations – *more stringent pollution controls, the ability to pay taxes over the Internet;*
- Technological breakthroughs – *human genome sequencing, miniaturization of computer chips.*

Market drivers can also be caused by increasing frustration with the current environments, such as:

- Legacy investments – *railroad tracks, pre-existing data bases, landlines;*
- Business processes – *outsourced tech support, paper-based accounting systems;*
- Human factors – *informal social networks, union contracts, sexual discrimination.*

Although it is easy to identify market drivers, it is difficult to pick out the two or three factors that will create enough change to drive mass adoption of a

MARKET DRIVERS CAUSE CHANGE

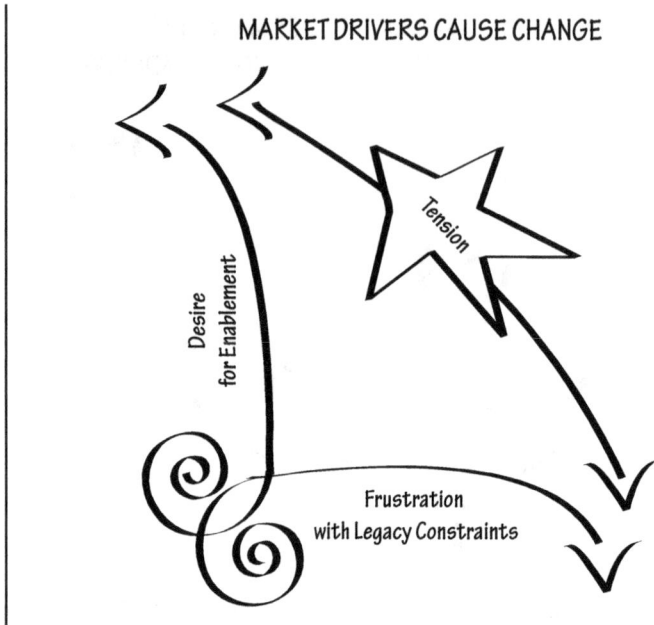

discontinuous innovation. You need to look for trends that when combined create a lot of tension. It is the conflict between a desire for what the technology enables and the frustration with current alternatives that create enough energy to motivate people to change their behavior. It is easy to get overwhelmed by the multitude of factors that could be shaping the market. Fortunately, as a salesperson, all you have to do is find the factors that are impacting your territory. Narrowing your focus makes the job much easier.

IDENTIFY MARKET DRIVERS

Ask Yourself:

? Which trends are driving market change?

? How are market drivers interacting to create tension?

? What are logical groupings of customers? By industry type? By vertical? By customer's business strategy? By consumer demographics?

? Assuming the interaction of two factors is defining critical change, how do they segment the market into groups of companies with similar needs or problems?

FINDING EMERGING MARKET SEGMENTS
WIRELESS TECHNOLOGY

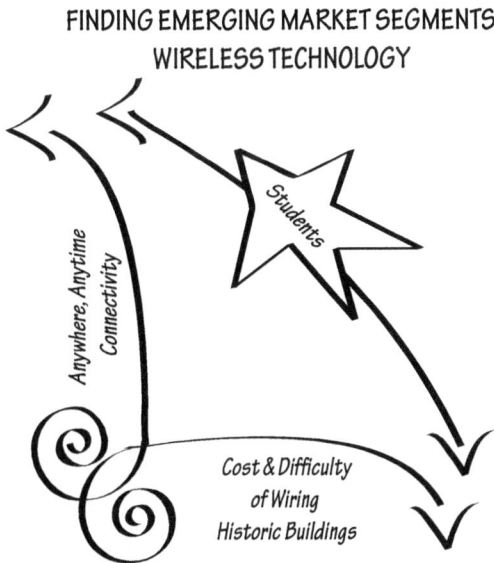

A salesperson for Aironet, a wireless technology company, had a large quota, but few prospects were interested in talking to him. It was too early in the market for people to understand how wireless technology could improve their lives, so he asked himself: "Who wants to be connected to the Internet all the time, but can't?"

One answer was students, who used email as a way to make dates and find their friends as they roamed around campus. A college campus is a very hard environment to wire because it is filled with old brick buildings. Thick, solid walls are very expensive to wire. The salesperson recognized that the college was a high potential opportunity because it was caught in the energy field created by two conflicting trends – an increasing desire to be connected to the Internet all the time and the high cost and difficulty of wiring historic buildings.

STEP 2: Segment The Market

Once you have identified market drivers, you need to figure out how they work together to create high potential market segments. Market segmentation defines logical groups of potential buyers who exhibit similar buying behavior because they share common needs, problems, business strategies, etc. Segmenting the market helps you see behavior patterns that you can use to find and develop accounts in your territory.

High potential market segments are the ones where the combination of market drivers is creating enough tension to convince people to try out new solutions. It is usually the combination of an increasing desire for enablement –the need to connect –with an increasing frustration with legacy constraints – buildings that are expensive to wire – that creates enough pain to motivate people to change.   A Market Energy Map can help you visualize logical market segments.

FINDING HIGH POTENTIAL MARKET SEGMENTS

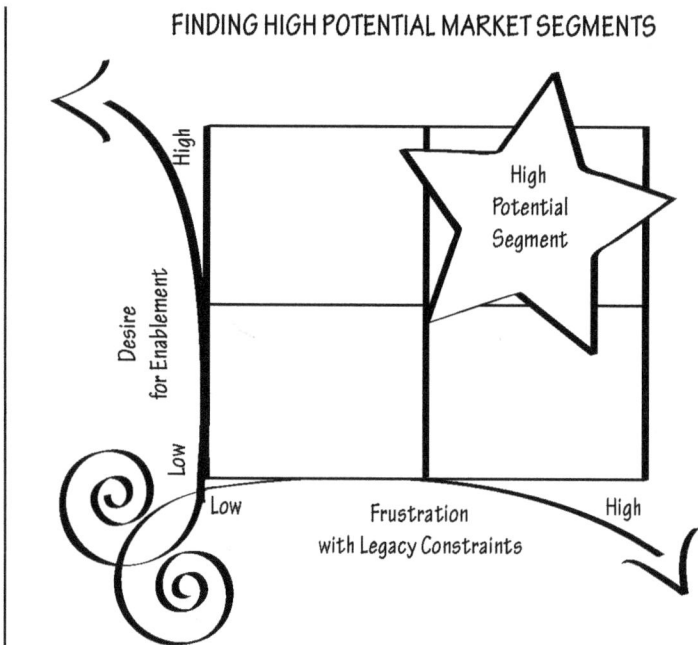

HOW TO BUILD A MARKET ENERGY MAP:

1. Identify two trends that when combined are creating tension in the marketplace.
2. Draw a square where the X and Y axis represents a scale of the increasing intensity of each trend.
3. Divide the square into quadrants.
4. Describe how the combined impact of the trends is causing people to change their behavior in each quadrant.

There are many ways to segment a market. Market analysts prefer traditional market segmentation, such as company size, industry segments, geographic regions, etc. However, in early markets you may find that it is easier to find prospects when you segment the market using less traditional factors, such as changing consumer behavior, emerging distribution channels, or evolving technology adoption profiles.

Defining emerging market segments helps you make sense out of what is happening in your territory, so you can find opportunities. There are many sources for insightful information about market trends and emerging customer needs – business and trade magazines, newspapers, and market research reports, etc. Look

Unfortunately, the wireless technology salesperson only had one university in his territory, so while it was an early win, it didn't provide him enough prospects to make his quota. However, by using the same market drivers – a need to connect to the Internet and historic buildings that were expensive and difficult to wire – he was able to identify the capital building, the bank, the local stockyard, and the hospital. In each case the end user had an increasing need to be connected to the Internet all the time, and the costs of wiring the buildings were prohibitive. He had uncovered a high potential market segment – old buildings.

FINDING HIGH POTENTIAL MARKET SEGMENTS
WIRELESS TECHNOLOGY

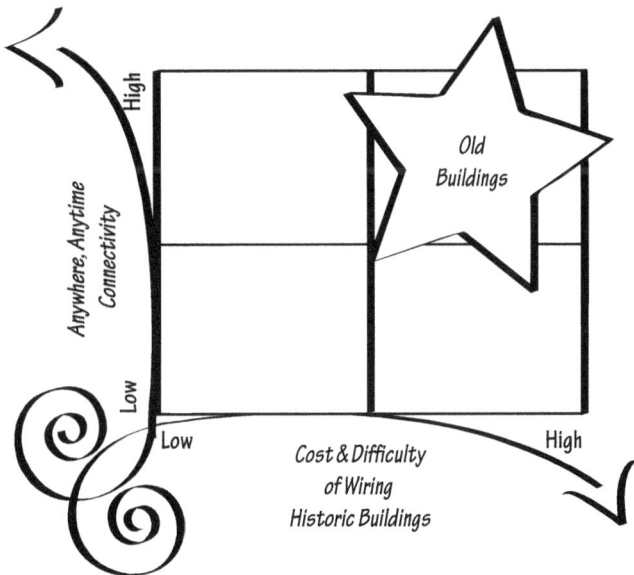

for patterns in the information to figure out how the energy of the market drivers is causing segments to emerge.

No self-respecting marketing department would identify old buildings as a high potential market segment. After all, it crosses multiple verticals – higher education, local government, financial services, food processing, and health care. It doesn't make analytical sense, yet it makes practical sense. It took a frustrated salesperson to see the commonality of need and recognize it as a market segment with enough prospects to create market momentum in his territory.

Marketing departments segment markets so they can use mass advertising and promotional techniques to create interest. Salespeople segment the market to find a few, high potential accounts, so the two functions may end up with very different pictures of the market.

Why buy?

Why would someone want to buy your technology solution? As companies try to capture the opportunities created by market change, they implement new business strategies. Since your technology promises to help them implement these strategies faster, better, or cheaper, they consider buying it. This is the primary motivation for technology adoption.

Identifying strategic motivations for technology adoption further refines your market segmentation. To clarify the impact of change on the emerging market segments, analyze your Market Energy Map to figure out how motivations for adopting your new technology solution differ by quadrant. Generally a prospect located in the upper left quadrant of the Market Energy Map is a company focused on building its business. In the upper right quadrant prospects are usually looking for ways to create strategic advantage in the marketplace. In the lower right quadrant, the prospect is likely to focus on projects designed to improve productivity and relieve the frustrations caused by legacy systems. In the lower left quadrant you will find a more price conscious prospect, whose main concern is reducing costs.

Using these general guidelines, you can further refine your understanding of why people will adopt your technology by considering the strategic, economic, operational, and technological reasons they need the new solution.

STRATEGIC MOTIVATIONS FOR TECHNOLOGY ADOPTION

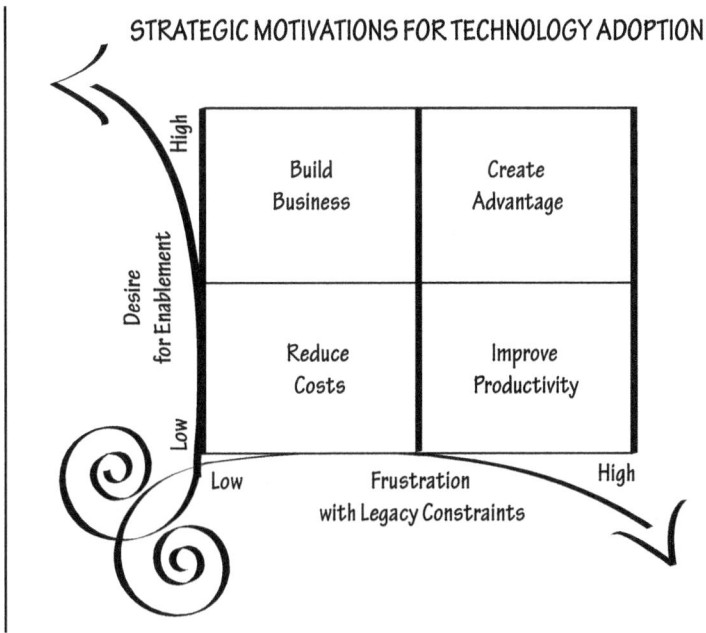

First, consider the strategic motivations for adopting a new technology solution. How can the new technology enable new business strategies, create competitive advantage, or dramatically improve performance?

Next consider the economic motivations of adoption. What are the financial benefits of implementing the solution? Consider the 'above the line' benefits – incremental revenues and increasing market share – companies can reap from applying the new capabilities to emerging customer needs. Also, think about the 'below the line' cost savings that happen when new technologies enable you to improve operational efficiency or increase the productivity of other resources.

What are the operational motivations for adoption? How could the new technology improve manufacturing processes, increase capacity without incremental capital investment, lower inventory carrying costs, etc.? Think about the many operational problems the new technology can solve.

Finally, consider the technological advantages of adopting the new solution. Many times your very first buyers will be other techno-savvy people who are motivated by the engineering brilliance of your new, more elegant solution. What are the key technology problems that your new solution solves? The answer to this question also helps you identify the legacy constraints that are creating tension in the marketplace.

Evaluate each potential prospect in your territory, and identify what might motivate an account to consider your solution. Use these account motivations to locate each prospect on your Market Energy Map. Align what you know about their business strategies and technology needs with the motivations you have identified in each quadrant. This exercise tells you why they will buy your solution.

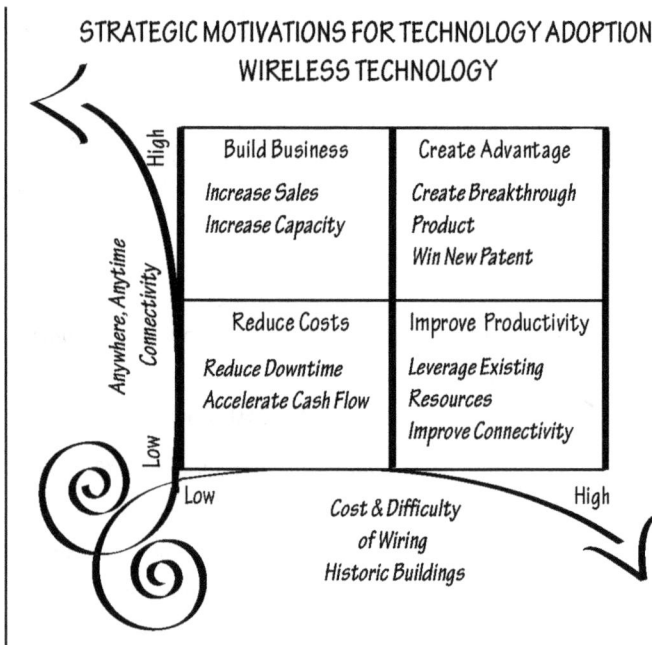

STRATEGIC MOTIVATIONS FOR TECHNOLOGY ADOPTION
WIRELESS TECHNOLOGY

Anywhere, Anytime Connectivity (High)	**Build Business** *Increase Sales* *Increase Capacity*	**Create Advantage** *Create Breakthrough Product* *Win New Patent*
(Low)	**Reduce Costs** *Reduce Downtime* *Accelerate Cash Flow*	**Improve Productivity** *Leverage Existing Resources* *Improve Connectivity*

Low   **Cost & Difficulty**
of Wiring
Historic Buildings   High

Identify emerging business strategies.

A strategy is how a company responds to market change in a way that improves its business. Ideally, strategies use the momentum created by market drivers to exploit emerging opportunities. *A sociological trend of increasing mobility of the work force might cause a company to initiate a business strategy to provide wireless access to its intranet.* The results of a business strategy — *increased productivity, increased efficiency, greater employee satisfaction etc.* — are the prospect's compelling reason to buy a new technology solution.

You need to understand your prospects' strategy, so you can figure out how your technology can help them achieve their result faster, better, or cheaper. To anticipate a prospect's business strategy, refer back to your Market Energy Map. Using the adoption motivators you have identified, brainstorm specific business strategies that prospects might implement in response to the market.

EMERGING BUSINESS STRATEGIES

	Build Business	Create Advantage
High (Desire for Enablement)	Mass Customization Multi-channel Distribution Provide Web Services	Compete Globally Build Customer Loyalty Participate in Value Chains
Low	**Reduce Costs** Consolidation Strategic Sourcing Outsoucing	**Improve Productivity** Reduce Cycle Time Demand Driven Forecasting 1-to-1 Marketing

Low — Frustration with Legacy Constraints — High

STEP 3: Forecast Adoption

Now that you understand why a company would buy your solution, you need to figure out when they will buy it. As a technology market matures, Metcalf's Law dictates that it will grow exponentially. Emerging technology markets balance the promise of enablement with the risk of adopting a new solution. However, in every market there comes a time when it is easier to adopt the new solution than resist change. This moment is called the tipping point; when it is reached, market behavior changes dramatically.

To anticipate behavior in technology-driven markets, you need to understand Technology Adoption Lifecycles, a theory explaining how people incorporate technological innovation into how they work, play, and live. *If you create a better mousetrap, does everyone run out and buy it today? No. It takes time for people to hear about it; they need to see it work; they need to have a mouse in their house, etc., before they will buy one.* There are going to be some people who will want to buy it as soon as they hear about it; they are 'early adopters.' Other, more cautious people will wait until they see how well it works; they are 'early majority buyers.' Others are too cheap to buy it until they can buy it at the discount mall; they are 'late majority buyers.' These human responses to new ideas and the changes they bring are the essential concepts behind technology adoption.

TECHNOLOGY ADOPTION LIFECYLE PROFILES

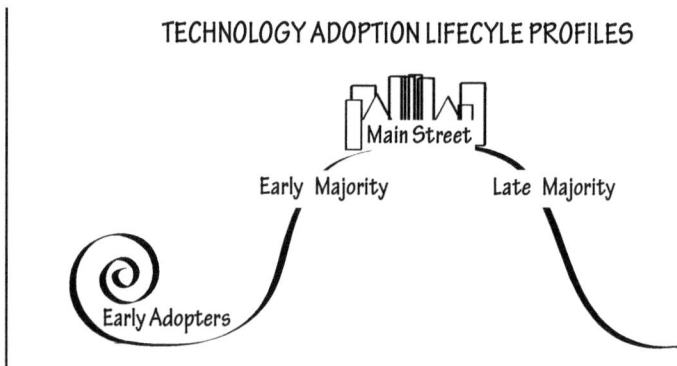

Understanding how people integrate new technologies to improve their business processes, personal life-styles, etc., is the essence of selling technology solutions. As a technology salesperson, your success depends on your ability to find the early adopters, so you can establish the successful track record you need to build credibility as the market matures. Early success captures the attention of the broader market and provides proof that your solution works. Like the snowball rolling down hill, your solution builds the momentum required to establish a dominant market position.

Find early adopters.

Early adopters are critical to the long-term viability of your technology solution because they help you build your track record. If you want to be considered a serious contender as the market adopts, you need early competitive wins. Early adopters are customers who are willing to risk the inevitable hassles of trying to implement a new technology in exchange for being the first ones to enjoy its benefits. Early adopters are the key to any technology success story. They teach you why customers will buy your solution. They are a reality check for your value proposition. From them, you learn about what customers really need, not what you think they need. You also learn the issues that can stall the sale or the successful implementation of your solution. By paying close attention to the buying behavior of your early adopters, you learn what future customers really value.

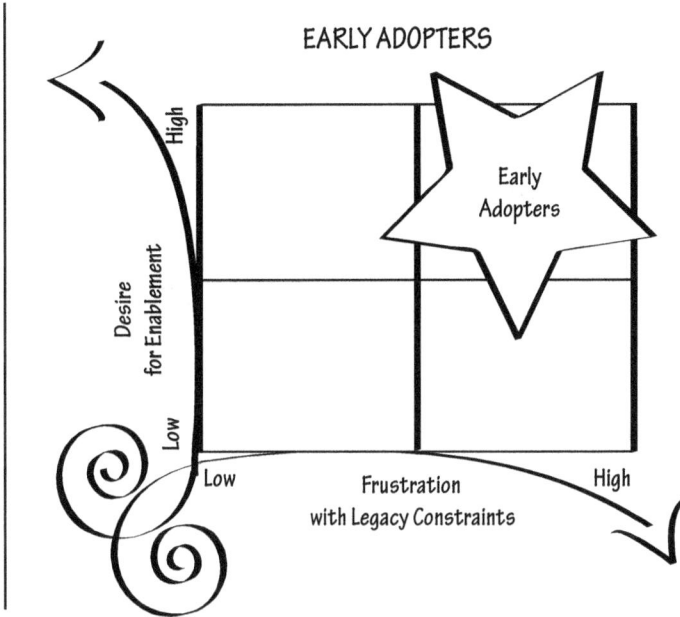

EARLY ADOPTERS

Early Adopters

Desire for Enablement — High / Low

Frustration with Legacy Constraints — Low / High

To find early adopters, look for prospects who want to create unique strategic advantage. Look for pockets of tension in the marketplace. Who wants to change and is really frustrated by the status quo? Early adopters like to shake things up. They have a lot of energy and want to use it to make a difference.

One of the challenges of prospecting for early adopters is that you don't really know who you are looking for. Finding and working early adopter accounts is an iterative process. You will learn something new every day. You have to constantly revise your theories and be open to new ideas, even if they don't fit in with your existing frameworks. Because you only have the limited perspective of your territory, it is difficult to see key trends and identify emerging business strategies. This means you need to set up a communication network that supports a collaborative learning process between field and staff organizations. Develop a network with your peers in other territories, and pick the brains of the "closers," who are working with other salespeople, so you can keep current on fast-breaking news about new accounts, market shifts and the competitive environment.

FIND EARLY ADOPTERS

Ask Yourself:

? How discontinuous is the innovation? What are the risks and benefits of adoption?

? How compelling is the technology value proposition? What new business strategies does it enable?

? What are the compelling needs that represent the increasing desire for what the technology enables? How does the technology create competitive advantage?

? Which prospects depend on being first-to-market to build competitive advantage? Who are managers that thrive on taking risks?

? What are the costs of legacy constraints? How does the new technology eliminate them?

Forecast the early majority.

Like people, markets learn from experience. Once they see early adopters enjoying the benefits of the new technology – *University enrollment doubles, but thanks to their wireless LAN, they don't need to build new buildings* – a new set of companies start to consider adopting it, too. This next generation of prospects is the early majority. Early majority buyers are more pragmatic and concerned about the risks of adoption. Fortunately, you have your early adopters to use as proof sources for this new set of customers.

Early majority prospects are likely to be found in the quadrants adjacent to the highest potential market segment. The customers in the upper left quadrant are more likely to focus on new opportunities because they have a high desire for potential incremental revenue applications that your new technology enables. *The professor who wants to run virtual seminars.* The customers in the lower right quadrant are more interested in improving productivity because they are frustrated with legacy constraints. *The senator who wants to watch the discussion on the house floor from his office, so he doesn't miss the vote.*

MARKET ADOPTION
WIRELESS TECHNOLOGY

	Anywhere, Anytime Connectivity (High → Low)	
High	Early Majority *Virtual University* *Professor*	Early Adopters *University* *Student Services*
Low		Early Majority *Senator*

Low — *Cost & Difficulty of Wiring Historic Buildings* — High

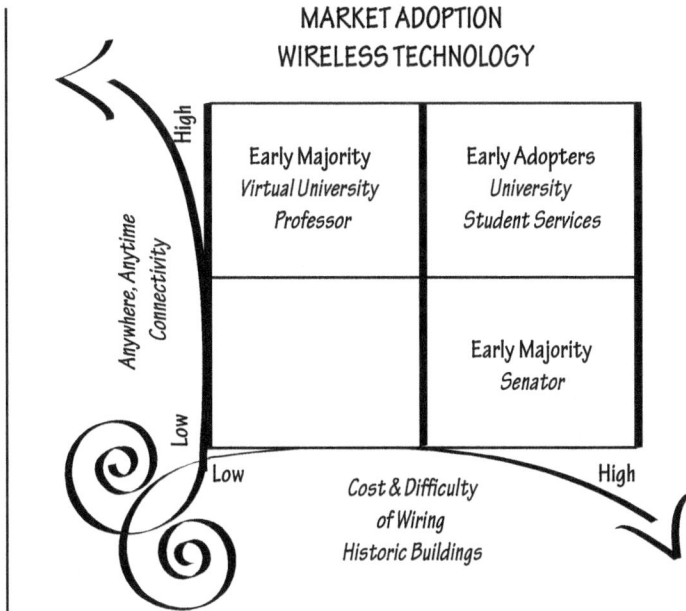

Forecast the tipping point.

As more and more companies adopt the new technology, market momentum starts taking on a life of its own. At this point you want to be able to forecast when the tipping point will occur, so you will be well positioned to take advantage of it. The tipping point is when the benefits of adopting the discontinuous innovation overcome the pain caused by not adopting it. It is the moment in time when adoption becomes inevitable, and anyone who doesn't adopt will be left behind.

In his fascinating book, *The Tipping Point*, Malcolm Gladwell makes three key points about what causes people to change, which has important implications for selling up the technology adoption curve.[3]

1. **Change is contagious**. Once people see the early adopters enjoying the benefits of a new technology, they are going to want to enjoy them, too. Ask your early adopters for testimonials describing the superiority of your solution. Many early adopters expect a lot of special services. They know that your success depends on their satisfaction, so they use it as leverage to get you to do a lot of extra work for them for free. Make sure that in return they will write you testimonial letters and allow you to bring other customers to see the successfully implemented solution. A reference base will be critical to your success when the market takes off.

---

[3] Gladwell, Malcolm . *The Tipping Point*, Little Brown & Company. 2000

2. **Little causes can have big effects.** The market drivers that cause the market to accelerate can often be small changes that happen at the right time. Thanks to your market perspective, you are more likely to recognize the little causes that end up tipping the market. Market analysts rarely pick up little causes. You have to be close to the customer to figure out the real reasons that cause the new solution to work. Once you do recognize them, use them to map how the market will evolve, so you can anticipate each new wave of prospects.

3. **Change happens in a hurry.** When the market takes off, you want to be ready. Ideally you will be actively working accounts before your prospects start their decision making process. If you have anticipated who needs the solution correctly, you might be the first one to approach the prospect with the technology's value. Being first is a big advantage, especially as the market develops and becomes more competitive.

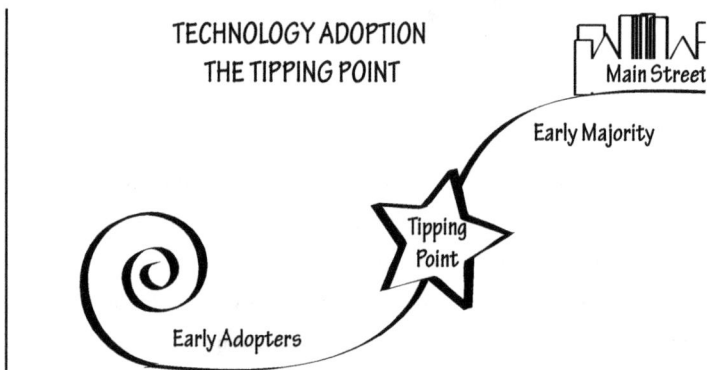

TECHNOLOGY ADOPTION
THE TIPPING POINT
Main Street
Early Majority
Tipping Point
Early Adopters

In *Inside the Tornado,* Geoffrey Moore describes this stage of market development as "when demand dramatically outstrips supply and a huge backlog of customers appears overnight... It represents a massive sales opportunity in and of itself; it also represents an even larger follow-on market opportunity." [8] In other words, it is an extraordinary sales opportunity that you don't want to miss because you aren't ready for it.

Market analysts make their living predicting the future, so they are a good source for statistics about market adoption. However, a more practical and reliable source of information may be the observation of your prospects' behavior. As the market evolves from visionary early adopters to the more practical and pragmatic early majority buyers, you are getting closer to the tipping point. As prospects' adoption motivators change from building competitive advantage or developing new markets

[4] Moore, Geoffrey. *Inside the Tornado* HarperCollins. 1995

to improving productivity and performance, the market is gaining momentum. When prospects start asking you more questions about where your solution has been successfully implemented and the measurable results it produced, you can be sure that the tipping point is drawing closer.

FORECAST THE TIPPING POINT

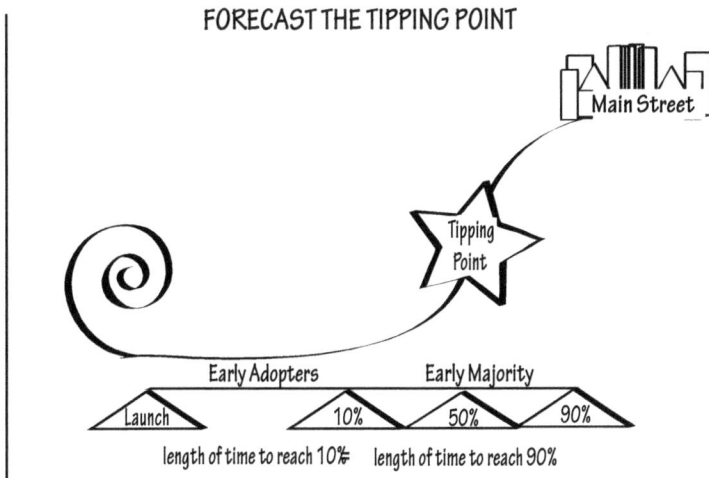

To forecast the tipping point, you estimate how long it will take for your early adopters to implement their first projects successfully. Then you project the same amount of time into the future and divide by two. This should give you a rough estimate of the tipping point for your solution.

FORECAST MARKET ADOPTION

Ask Yourself:

? Who will be the early adopters? How long will it take them to implement the technology solution? How long until the early adopters will reap the benefits of early adoption? What are the financial benefits of early adoption?

? Who will be the second set of adopters? Why will they adopt? What is the risk of not adopting?

? What are the market trends most likely to accelerate adoption? How far along are industry standards?

? What will happen to companies that don't adopt? How long will it take them to feel the impact of not adopting on their business operations and results?

? When will the market begin to 'tip?' When will 50% of your accounts be actively involved in the buying process?

WHAT YOU NEED TO KNOW TO HARNESS MARKET ENERGY

A market perspective is more than facts and figures. If you are going to use market energy to drive the sales process, you need a profound understanding of why people will change their behavior and adopt your technology-enabled solutions. Although estimated market size and growth projections are important things to know, the qualitative information about what is motivating customers to change is often more useful. A market perspective is information that helps you understand the fundamental causes driving technology adoption and market evolution. It is a "big picture" perspective of the market today and in the future.

INFORMATION ➤ PERFORMANCE

Technology Value Proposition ➤ Understand how technology creates new markets and wealth.

Market Drivers ➤ Understand what is causing the market to evolve and create energy.

Emerging Market Segments ➤ Find high potential market segments and opportunities faster.

Emerging Strategies ➤ Identify how the technology enables business strategies.

Adoption Drivers ➤ Focus your prospecting.

Profiles of Early Adopters ➤ Score early wins and build market credibility.

Market Forecasts ➤ Forecast the tipping point to maximize your potential market share.

Information required to harness market energy.

■ **Technology Value Proposition** – A definition of the technology; its potential applications; what people do currently to satisfy fundamental needs; how the technology will cause people to change their behavior; benefits users can expect from adoption, and how it will create incremental wealth, **so you understand how your technology solution will create new markets and wealth.**

■ **Market Drivers** – A definition of the economic, demographic, regulatory, and technology trends causing the new market to develop; quantification and descriptions of the increasing desire for what the technology enables, and quantification and descriptions of the costs of legacy constraints, **so you understand causes of market evolution and how it creates market energy.**

■ **Emerging Market Segments** – Explanation of how the market drivers are interacting to create change; the impact of these changes on consumer and organizational behavior, and emerging business strategies designed to support these new behaviors, **so you can identify high potential market segments and find opportunities faster.**

HARNESS MARKET ENERGY PROCESS SUMMARY

What	How	Information Required
1. Find Market Energy Define market trends driving growth.	1.1 Define the market	Technology Value Proposition
	1.2 Identify market drivers	Market Trends - economic, demographic, regulatory, and technological Frustrations with legacy contraints
2. Segment the Market Group buying behaviors into high potential market segments.	2.1 Hypothesize high potential market segments	How market drivers are interacting to drive change Impact of market changes on consumer/customer behavior Emerging busness strategies that capitalize on change
	2.2 Define strategic motivations for adoption	Strategic, economic, operational and technological motivations for adoption
	2.3 Identify emerging business strategies	How the technology enables new business strategies to capture emerging opportunities
3. Forecast Adoption Predict who will buy and when.	3.1 Find early adopters	Profiles of Early Adopters How early adopters applied the technology Early results
	3.2 Forecast the tipping point	Description of the fundamental causes of adoption Market Forecasts

■ **Emerging Strategies** – New business strategies that enable companies to respond to the market change and capture new opportunities, including how the strategies work; what they accomplish, and expected results, **so you can create demand.**

■ **Technology Adoption Drivers** – A definition of strategic, economic, operational, and technological motivations for adoption, including how the technology enables new business strategies; increases profits; improves productivity, and enables new capabilities, **so you can focus your prospecting.**

■ **Profiles of Early Adopters** – Descriptions of early adopters; why they bought the new technology; how they applied it to build competitive advantage, and early results and benefits, **so you can score early wins and build market credibility.**

■ **Market Forecasts** – S-curve analysis of the market evolution; description of the fundamental causes of adoption; forecast of 50% market adoption milestone, and evolution of new customer's compelling reasons to buy, **so you can forecast the tipping point and maximize your market share potential.**

HOW TO USE A MARKET PERSPECTIVE TO SELL BETTER

■ **Find opportunities faster.** A market perspective helps you **prospect** more effectively because it builds your understanding of how market drivers are interacting to create change. Change causes problems, which in turn create opportunities for your new technology. Prospecting early in the technology adoption lifecycle can be very frustrating. Often you are looking for opportunities that do not exist. A market perspective helps you recognize pockets of increasing tension, which are usually where the first opportunities materialize.

■ **Improve sales productivity.** A market perspective also improves your ability to quickly **qualify** an account. The faster you determine the customer has a viable need, budget, and a sense of urgency, the more productive you will be. An insightful understanding of the market is invaluable early in the sales process. The primary goal of your first sales call is to establish your credibility and earn the right to develop the account. If you can intelligently discuss how market trends are impacting the prospect's business and suggest ways to take advantage of emerging opportunities, it is likely that you will be invited back to discuss your ideas with senior executives. However, if you are not knowledgeable about the prospect's business, it is unlikely you will ever be invited out of the technical departments. Finally, the better you understand the market momentum, the better you will be able to gauge the customer's urgency. An important part of forecasting is being able to predict when the customer will buy. A market perspective helps you understand the market drivers that can cause an account to move slowly or close quickly.

■ **Recognize issues.** Much of the information you gather and analyze while developing a market perspective can be used as you plan and implement your **discovery** process. Market drivers are excellent sources of potential issues around which you can build provocative questioning strategies. If you understand where the market is in its technology adoption life cycle, you know where to focus your account development strategy. Early in the market development, you will want to focus your discovery on the line executives who are interested in building competitive advantage. Later in market you will want to make sure that you include a wide range of functional and technical influencers in your data collection, so you can manage their concerns about risk.

■ **Focus your proposal.** A market perspective is critical to making a compelling **proposal**. It helps you balance conflicting customer needs into a coherent proposal that reflects the balance of risk and reward required to close the deal. When proposing a solution, use relevant market drivers to help the customer understand the inevitability of adoption. This will drive their urgency to buy the solution and implement it quickly.

■ **Negotiate Smarter.** The stage of market adoption determines the customer's compelling reason to buy. It also drives the urgency of the **closing** process. If a prospect wants to use the technology to build competitive advantage, then he has to move quickly. You can use this urgency to your advantage to negotiate a profitable deal. Fast.

TAKE ACTION

■ **Monitor market evolution.** As the market evolves, it changes. Sales strategies that work in early markets bomb as the market matures. You need to stay current with the market. Create a plan to help you monitor market evolution. Use this intelligence to drive your territory/account development plans and to figure out clever ways to encourage technology adoption.

■ **Do your homework.** Developing a market perspective requires a lot of research. Set up a system so you can be constantly monitoring the market and looking for indicators of emerging needs. Figure out how to incorporate market research into your territory development plan. Ask your customers, marketing gurus, and sales managers the questions in this chapter. Then draw a Market Energy Map, and compare it to those drawn by your peers. Use the Market Energy Map to drive your prospecting.

MARKET ENERGY MAP WORKSHEET

Technology Value Proposition _____

High

Build Business	Create Advantage
Reduce Costs	Improve Productivity

Low

Low   High

1. Write technology value proposition.
2. Identify market trends.
3. Identify strategic motivations for adoption.
4. Identify emerging business strategies that the technology enables.
5. Describe your early adopters.

■ **Identify likely suspects.** Use your Market Energy Map to identify likely prospects. Look at territory from the perspective of how the market changes are impacting your customers' businesses. Talk to your marketing and business development managers to find out how prospects could benefit from implementing emerging business strategies.

HARNESS MARKET ENERGY
TERRITORY PLANNING WORKSHEET

Technology Value _____
Proposition   _____

High	Build Business	Create Advantage
	Account 1 _____	Account 1 _____
	Account 2 _____	Account 2 _____
	Account 3 _____	Account 3 _____
	Reduce Costs	Improve Productivity
	Account 1 _____	Account 1 _____
	Account 2 _____	Account 2 _____
Low	Account 3 _____	Account 3 _____

Desire

Low   Frustration   High

_____

1. Write technology value proposition.
2. Identify market trends.
3. Identify accounts that can use the technology to help them:
   ★ Create strategic advantage
   ★ Build their business
   ★ Improve productivity
   ★ Reduce costs

■ **Time your prospecting.** Predict the tipping point for your new solution. Estimate how long it will take for the early adopters to buy the solution, and demonstrate its value. Use this information to predict the length of the sales cycle, when early majority buyers will start their buying decisions. Plot the technology adoption curve, and calculate the tipping point.

FORECAST TIPPING POINT WORKSHEET

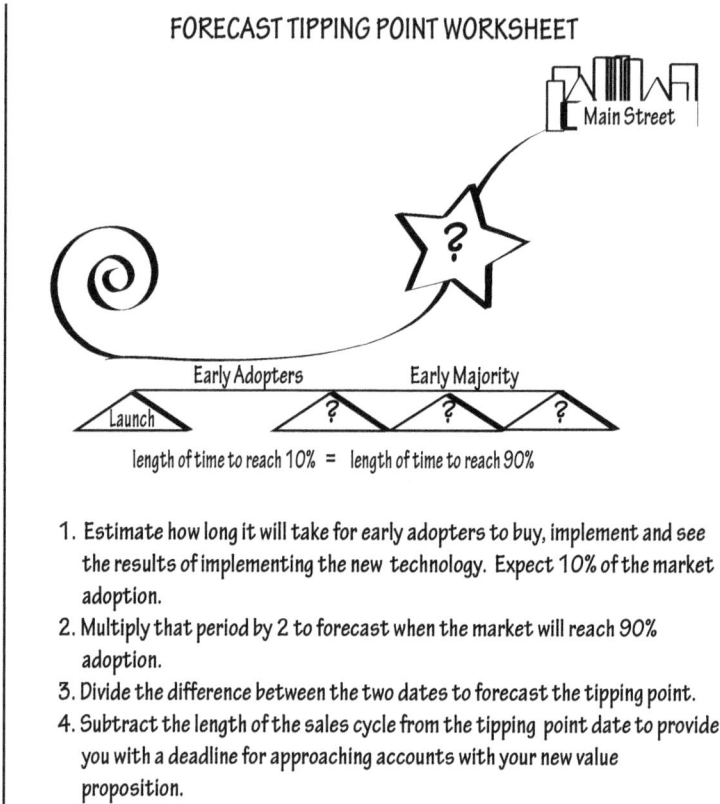

Main Street

Early Adopters   Early Majority

Launch

length of time to reach 10% = length of time to reach 90%

1. Estimate how long it will take for early adopters to buy, implement and see the results of implementing the new technology. Expect 10% of the market adoption.
2. Multiply that period by 2 to forecast when the market will reach 90% adoption.
3. Divide the difference between the two dates to forecast the tipping point.
4. Subtract the length of the sales cycle from the tipping point date to provide you with a deadline for approaching accounts with your new value proposition.

■ **Set up a network.** Don't be a lone wolf. Even wolves know that they get better results hunting in packs. Set up a network of your peers, and share information on a regular basis what you are seeing on the street . You can't see trends unless you have a lot of data. The discussion process will help you spot trends and patterns in customer behavior that you need to identify prospects and predict the tipping point.

CONCLUSIONS

- **Markets create energy.** Markets are dynamic systems that create the energy required to fuel change. If you can harness market energy, you can use it to drive your sales and build market share.

- **Technology creates wealth.** The enabling properties of technological innovation create new resources and demand, which in turn create new sources of wealth. Technology markets are unique because they are based on the economics of abundance, not scarcity.

- **The greater the change, the greater the wealth it creates.** The potential value of the new market depends on how innovative the new technology is. The more "discontinuous" the innovation, the greater the potential value of the market.

- **Change happens fast.** Technology adoption theory explains how new markets develop. Markets tend to develop slowly in niches and then mushroom into the mainstream. It takes as long for a market to reach 10% adoption as to grow from 10% to 90% adoption.

- **Why is more useful than how much.** For salespeople, qualitative market information that explains why customers will buy your technology solution is more useful than quantitative data about the market.

- **Segmentation focuses you on energy sources.** Defining market segments into logical groups of buying behaviors helps you find high potential prospects.

- **Markets are microcosms.** Market trends, adoption motivations, and market segmentation vary by territory. You can't count on marketing to be right about what may be happening in your territory or accounts. The ability to develop a Market Energy Map and use it to identify prospects is a critical sales skill.

- **Early adopters count.** Early adopters are critical to the long-term viability of your solution because they help you establish a credible track record early in the market. This credibility is critical to building market share as the market evolves.

- **The tipping point is the bull's-eye.** You can use technology adoption theory to help you forecast the market tipping point. Applying this time line of market development optimizes your prospecting efforts and increases the likelihood that you will be in the right place at the right time.

Chapter 3

Build Value

Use Logic to Build Emotional Commitment

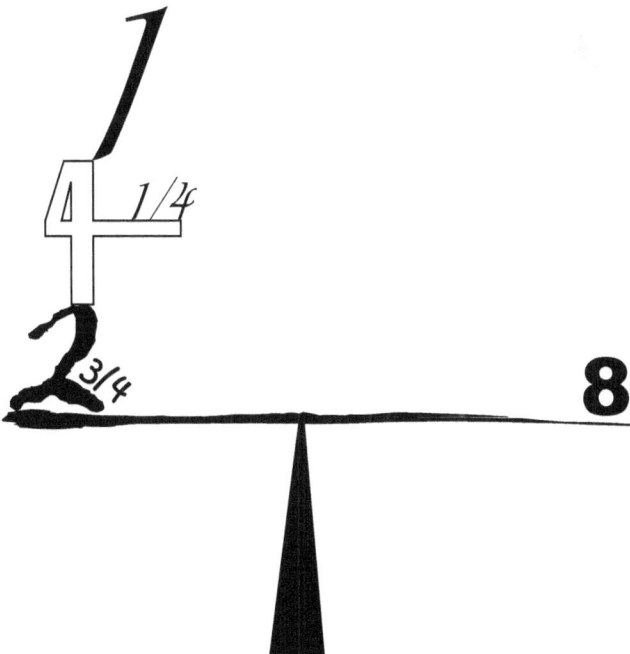

BUILD VALUE

What Show how your technology enables your customer's strategy.

Why   Building value links your solution to your customer's success.

How   1. Define emerging strategies, so you have more control over the buying process and earn the right to call higher.

     2. Create solutions, so you can build the credibility of your promises.

     3. Sell value, so you can close faster, charge more, and negotiate a better deal.

So What? By logically showing customers how your technology enables them to accomplish their strategic goals faster, cheaper, and more productively, you build their emotional commitment to buying your offer. So, you are more likely to close a profitable deal quickly.

WHAT IS VALUE?

Value is the customers' perception of the benefits they will reap by using your technology to implement their strategies.

Value links your solution to your customer's success. To build value you need to understand how your solution enables customers to implement their business strategies faster, better, and cheaper. Value helps you sell higher, increase your control over the account, and close faster. Selling value creates trust and builds your credibility.

Building value starts with an understanding of how market drivers are changing the way people live, work, and play – *Widespread adoption of the Internet means that we book our vacations over the Web instead of calling up a travel agent.* As the market changes, new opportunities are created, and old ways of making money disappear. Companies need to constantly reinvent themselves through new business strategies to continue to grow and prosper.

Understanding how your technology helps customers implement strategy – *lower costs through strategic sourcing* – and consequently reap its benefits – *smaller inventories, lower raw material costs, faster response to changing demand* – is essential to defining its value. Customers only care about how your technology can help them. They do not care about the technology itself. *Business executives don't care that your strategic sourcing software application's API's use open standards; they only care about being able to getting a better deal when they buy components.* This simple fact of life is often a rude awakening. *After all, it isn't easy to build an open, standards-based application that enables inter-company visibility.* To build value you need to shift your focus from what you do, to what your customer wants to do.

WHY IS BUILDING VALUE IMPORTANT?

The customer's perception of value is the driving force behind the sale. It determines how much they are willing to pay, how quickly they will buy, and how much risk they will take in the buying and implementation process. Value is built through effective selling.

Value is always subjective. Someone's sense of value is dependent on many factors. It changes as you move from account to account. Although we try to set the customer's expectations for value through pricing, the value of the solution is ultimately determined by how much customers believe the solution will enable them to implement their strategies successfully.

WHY BUILD VALUE?

★ Drive the customer's sense of urgency.

★ Get to the decision-maker faster.

★ Build competitive advantage.

★ Sell more profitable deals.

★ Build sales momentum.

■ **Close faster.** Selling value creates momentum because it links your solution to what is happening in the market. The market doesn't wait for the customer to make up his mind. *The Internet is not going away...* In this chapter you will learn how to use value to link the customer's buying decision to the successful implementation of a market-driven strategy, so you can close more deals faster.

■ **Sell higher.** Value captures the attention of the decision-maker. Most sales are exercises in climbing the organizational chart until you finally reach the person who has the budget to buy your solution. This climb is usually slow and painful. In this chapter you will learn how to build value, which greatly improves your chances of getting to pitch directly to the people who count.

■ **Improve your competitive positioning.** Value determines your competitive strength, both within an account and in the marketplace. Early in the technology adoption lifecycle, the ability to convince customers of the superior value of your solution enables you to win the strategic deals you need to establish market credibility for your solution. Later in the technology adoption curve, value helps you build market momentum. Learning how to build the customer's perception of the value of your solution increases the chance that your company will end up being the market leader.

■ **Sell profitable deals.** Value enables premium pricing. As the market matures, more alternatives emerge. Greater choice erodes your competitive advantage, and, consequently, your ability to charge a premium for your solution. The ability to continually evolve your value proposition protects your solution from becoming a commodity.

■ **Build sales momentum**. Value is the only thing that builds belief. Features and benefits build points in your favor. Solving problems builds confidence that your solution works, but value builds the customer's belief that they will be successful. In this chapter you will learn how to use the customer's belief in the value of your solution as a powerful source of energy to drive the sale.

HOW TO DEVELOP VALUE

You build value by linking your technology solution to what the customer expects to achieve through the successful implementation of their strategy. You do this by analyzing your customers' strategy within the context of the market environment and determining what kinds of technology solutions they need to implement it successfully. Throughout this process you help your customer anticipate problems, so you can show them how your solution solves them. Satisfying needs and solving problems build the customer's appreciation for your technology and their trust in you.

Value links the need satisfaction sales process to what is happening in the marketplace. It channels market energy directly into your sales process to create sales momentum, so you can close the deal faster.

BUILD VALUE PROCESS

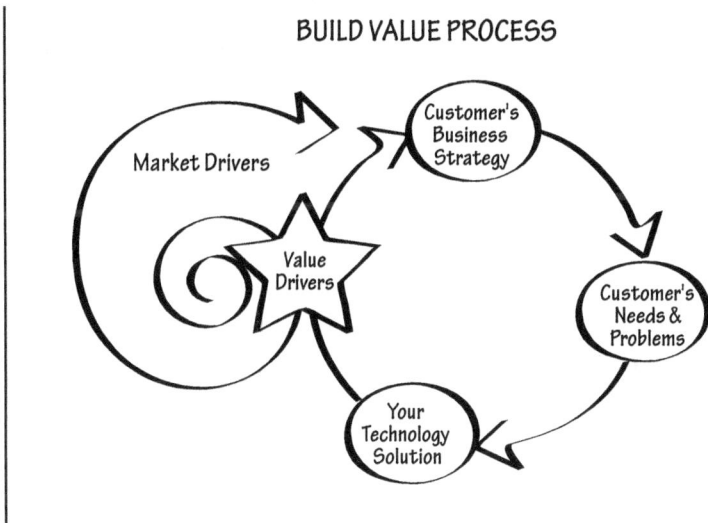

BUILD VALUE PROCESS

1. Define Emerging Strategies.

    ➤ Link the customer's need for your solution to market-driven opportunities.

2. Create Solutions.

    ➤ Translate strategies into specific needs you can satisfy and problems you can solve.

3. Sell Value.

    ➤ Link your solution to the customer's success.

STEP 1: Define Emerging Strategies

Technology enables companies to implement new business strategies so they can capture opportunities created by changes in the market. This is the essence of every technology value proposition. To build value around your solution, you need to understand how market change is impacting a customer's business and how your technology solution can help them manage the change to their advantage.

To define the impact of changing market dynamics on a customer's business, you need to start with an understanding of the market drivers causing the change – *rising transaction costs.* Then you refine this general information into specific descriptions

DEFINE MARKET IMPACT

Ask Yourself:

❓ What are the key trends that are impacting the customer's target market? Economic? Technological? Demographic?

❓ What is the financial impact of the changing market environment on the company's performance? Profits? Revenues? Market Share?

❓ What new opportunities are emerging? What new capabilities does the customer need to capture these opportunities?

❓ How quickly is the market changing? Which market drivers are fueling the customer's urgency to buy?

of how the market change is creating both new opportunities and new problems for your customer. *Rising transaction costs are eroding the customer's profit margins.* The more specifically you explain about how market drivers are changing the customer's business environment and the potential impact of ignoring them, the better. *Rising transaction costs caused by the increasing complexity of Internet-enabled global competition are increasing the cost of raw materials by 7% per year, which translates to a 2.5% decrease in your gross profits each year.*

Uncover customer's strategy.

You need to understand your customers' strategies, so you can figure out how your technology can help them achieve results faster, better, or cheaper. As discussed in the previous chapter, a strategy is what an organization does so it can benefit from the changes caused by market evolution. Smart companies use technology to help them respond productively to change. *An economic market trend of rising transaction costs coupled with improved eTrading technologies might cause a company to initiate a business strategy to lower costs through strategic sourcing, which is an automated approach to managing the purchasing process.* The results of the customer's strategy – *increased revenues, lower costs, improved productivity, increased efficiency, etc.* – are their compelling reasons to buy the new technology-enabled solution.

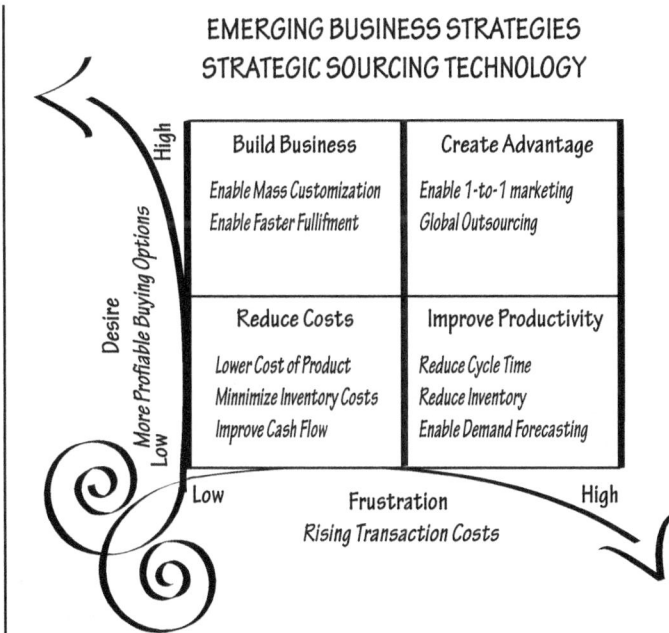

EMERGING BUSINESS STRATEGIES
STRATEGIC SOURCING TECHNOLOGY

	Build Business	Create Advantage
High	Enable Mass Customization Enable Faster Fullifment	Enable 1-to-1 marketing Global Outsourcing
Low	Reduce Costs Lower Cost of Product Minnimize Inventory Costs Improve Cash Flow	Improve Productivity Reduce Cycle Time Reduce Inventory Enable Demand Forecasting

Desire — More Profitable Buying Options

Low   Frustration   High
Rising Transaction Costs

If you use emerging business strategies to guide your early conversations with customers, you will develop a clear understanding of what they want to do and why.

UNCOVER EMERGING STRATEGIES

Ask Your Customer:

? How is the current market trend "X" impacting your market sector?

? Are these changes threatening your ability to reach your strategic business goals? Revenue targets? Profit predictions? Market share? Stock price?

? What new business strategies are you considering in response to the changes in the market?

? What is your vision for the successful implementation of this strategy?

? What are your concerns about implementing this strategy?

Identify the compelling reason to buy.

Once you understand a customer's strategy, you will be able to identify his compelling reason to buy – *lower costs through improved sourcing of raw materials and components.* This is important because, if the customer doesn't have a compelling reason to buy, he won't.

Compelling reasons to buy evolve as the market develops. Early adopters buy new technologies to increase revenues and gain market share. They are looking for discontinuous innovations that "enable new strategic capability that enable dramatic competitive advantage."[1] Their business strategy is to leapfrog the competition by being first to market, so they are looking for fast results. They value being first to market. So you build their perception of value by showing them how your solution will enable them to speed their time to market, improve their responsiveness to market change, and create innovative products and services. You need to show them how your solution will produce strategic results, such as accelerating their growth, increasing sales, and opening up new markets.

The early majority customer's compelling reason to buy is to "radically improve productivity on a well-established critical success factor."[2] Early majority

---

[1] Moore, Geoffrey . *Crossing the Chasm*, HarperCollins. 1991

COMPELLING REASONS TO BUY

Improve Productivty

Incremental improvements
Improve performance
Improve responsiveness

Fast results
Speed time to market
Breakthrough solution

Build Competitive Advantage

buyers are more pragmatic. They have experience implementing change, and they know how hard it is to do. They are interested in 'evolution, not revolution.' The ability to prove that your solution reliably delivers what you are promising becomes very important. Therefore, your ability to build value around the features and functionality of your solution become more important to your success.

Customers' compelling reason to buy is dependent on their business strategies, so use your Market Energy Map to identify the compelling reasons to buy your solution for each potential strategy.

DREAM CABINS BUSINESS STRATEGY

Let's say your customer has the bright idea of selling semi-customized, factory-built vacation cabins over the Internet. "Enjoy your dream cabin in 60 days..." In order for this bright idea to be a profitable one, the Dream Cabins company needs to organize and manage the purchasing of pre-built subcomponents from a wide range of suppliers around the world. To implement this business strategy using a conventional purchasing process would be unfeasible and cost prohibitive, because there would be too many vendors to manage. But with a state-of-the-art, strategic sourcing application, Dream Cabins would be able to manage their component inventory productively.

For each different strategy there will be a different compelling reason to buy. *If a customer's business strategy is to reduce her costs by cracking down on inefficient buying of office supplies, then the compelling reason to buy a automated purchasing system would be to control and consolidate*

---

[2] Moore, Geoffrey . *Crossing the Chasm*, HarperCollins. 1991

EMERGING BUSINESS STRATEGIES
DREAM CABINS BUSINESS STRATEGY

Create Advantage

Strategy: Sell semi-customized,
factory-built vacation cabins over the Internet
Compelling Reason to Buy:
Be able to profitably buy components from
a wide range of global suppliers

Desire
Profitable purchasing from
many suppliers

High

Low

Low   Frustration   High

Prohibitive cost and logistical nightmare
of buying from many suppliers

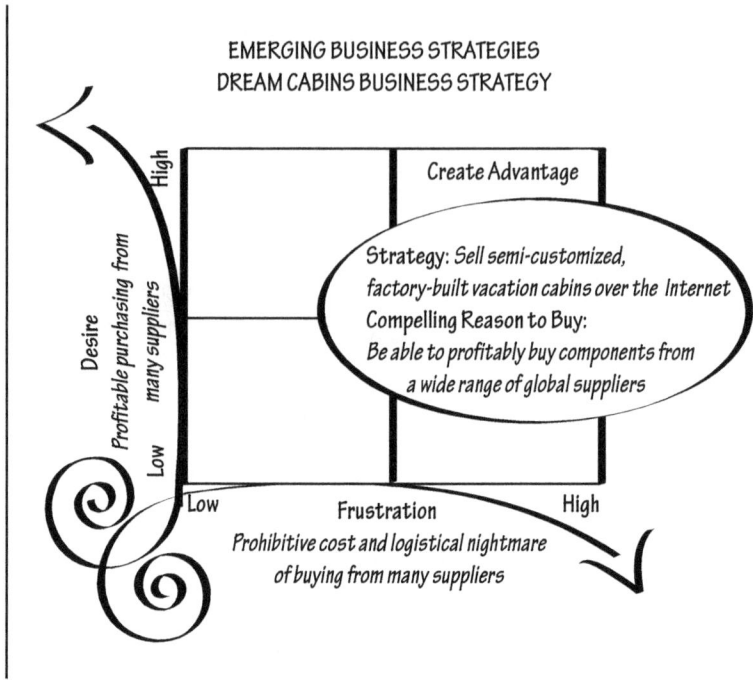

the purchasing of paper clips. This is a very different motivation from the strategic reasons compelling the CEO of Dream Cabins.

In each account the customer's compelling reason to buy is going to be different. To win the account you need to prove to the customer that your solution is the only way she will be able to achieve the results she wants. When your solution is unique, you create value. *Other strategic sourcing solutions promise to reduce costs, but your solution has unique functionality that enables global auctioning by product specification. You can promise Dream Cabins that they will be able get the best deal on authentic elk horn chandeliers. Knowing they won't be surprised by a cheap plastic set of antlers when they open the box is valuable to Dream Cabins' management.*

Furthermore, when you can quantify the benefits of your solution and prove measurable economic results, the customer's perception of value soars. You quantify the economic benefits by showing how your solution either increases revenues or reduces costs — *Since your strategic sourcing solution enables Dream Cabins to offer its customers increased personalization, it helps them sell more cabins. Your on-line auctioning functionality minimizes the costs associated with offering greater choice and carrying multiple product lines.*

COMPELLING REASONS TO BUY
STRATEGIC SOURCING TECHNOLOGY

	Low Frustration High	

Desire — _More Profitable Buying Options_ (Low to High)

Build Business	Create Advantage
Strategy:	Strategy:
Enable Mass Customization	_Global Outsourcing_
Compelling Reason to Buy:	Compelling Reason to Buy:
Access to More Suppliers	_Better Intercompany Planning_
Reduce Costs	Improve Productivity
Strategy:	Strategy:
Reduce Cost of Product	_Reduce Inventory_
Compelling Reason to Buy:	Compelling Reason to Buy:
Conduct On-line Auctions	_Increased Control Over Vendors_

Low — Frustration — High
Rising Transaction Costs

IDENTIFY COMPELLING REASONS TO BUY

Ask Your Customer:

? How will this new business strategy build competitive advantage? Are your competitors already using technology to accomplish the same goal? What are the rewards and risks of being the first company in your market segment to offer this kind of solution?

? How will this new business strategy improve your productivity? What are the critical success factors you will use to measure its success? How will this new capability impact profitability?

? How will this new business strategy build your business? What kind of economic results do you expect to deliver? Improved profits? Increased revenues?

STEP 2: Create Solutions

Organizations are focused on achieving their objectives. To figure out customers' compelling reasons to buy, you must understand what they are trying to accomplish. Helping customers translate their business objectives into a set of clearly articulated, technology-enabeled needs is an important part of your sales process. Without this information, you can't build a solution.

There are four categories of objectives you need to explore with a customer to gather the information you need to build value. Strategic objectives energize the organization. They are the organizing logic that connects all the other kinds of objectives – *to enable landowners to easily build a dream vacation home.* Economic objectives quantify the financial benefits of achieving the strategic objectives – *to make a 20% profit on every cabin sold.* Operational objectives explain how the strategy will work – *to provide extensive customization at factory-built prices.* Technological objectives define how the technology will enable the business strategy – *to use eTrading technology and Internet sourcing to minimize costs.*

Strategic objectives are the primary sources of value creation because they focus the business on the future. Strategies are designed to guide the organization towards an ideal vision. Strategic objectives usually define core business initiatives, such as establish market leadership, revolutionize a business process, or build breakthrough products.

UNCOVER STRATEGIC OBJECTIVES

Ask Your Customer:

? What are the performance goals of your business strategy?

? What are the projects your company is initiating to accomplish this strategy?

? What are the performance expectations of each project? How do they directly contribute to successful implementation of your strategy?

? How could these projects fail? What are the strategic consequences if any of these projects fail?

? Who owns each of the major projects? Are they involved in the decision-making process for this technology acquisition? In not, why not? If so, what is their role in the process?

Economic objectives are measured in money, such as increasing sales, reducing costs, accelerating cash flow, and minimizing risk. It is easy to see when you are making money and when you are not When a company is losing money, there is a lot of pain. There is also panic, because people often don't understand what is causing their problems. Your job is to help your customers sift through the symptoms to find the cause of their financial problems. When you quantify the impact of the problems, customers are motivated to spend their precious cash on your solution.

UNCOVER ECONOMIC OBJECTIVES

Ask Your Customer:

? How will you measure the economic impact of the project? What is the upside potential of the project - increased revenues, improved profits, increased productivity per employee, improved customer satisfaction ratings, etc.?

? What is your target ROI for the project? What is the risk-to-return ratio you seek? What is your desired payback period?

? Will this new solution make existing systems obsolete? Have the current systems been fully depreciated? What is the possible negative impact to your ROI of buying the solution?

? Do you have cash flow concerns about funding the solution? Have you considered leasing your new solution?

Operational objectives balance the need for efficiency with the ability to respond to change, such as improving quality, increasing flexibility, ensuring capacity and building new capabilities. This is not easy. Most operations are like freight trains. They take a long time to get going and once they do, they are very hard to stop. Effective operations are ones that remain flexible and responsive while they are operating at peak capacity.

Operational problems are usually caused by change, but the only way to improve operations is to make changes. It's a paradox. Organizations must manage change carefully and monitor the impact of these changes. To sell a technology-enabled solution you must analyze their operational problems to determine what is causing them. Then you need to show the customer how your technology solution will solve them.

UNCOVER OPERATIONAL OBJECTIVES

Ask Your Customer:

? Have you considered the organization or operational changes required by the
new solution?

? Who will be responsible for implementing the change management programs?
What are their concerns? Are they on the buying committee?

? What is the opportunity cost of the new strategy? Will it negatively impact
employee productivity? Does it cannibalize existing or projected revenues?
Will it make your current product or services obsolete?

Technological objectives define an organization's technology environment –
all computers will have open systems architecture, all PC's will use Microsoft as their operating system, etc.
Technological objectives balance a company's need to enable increasingly complex
business strategies while protecting their legacy investment in hardware and software
systems. Considering the energy created by Moore's Law of innovation, this is a
constant struggle. Companies want to use emerging technologies so they don't become
obsolete. However, as soon as they do, the relentless pace of technology innovation
renders the purchase obsolete.

UNCOVER TECHNOLOGICAL OBJECTIVES

Ask Your Customer:

? What are your current technology standards? What platforms and
programs do you use for computing, data management, telecommunications,
networking, etc.?

? Who sets these standards? How flexible is the policy? How are exceptions
handled?

? Who owns the technology budget for new purchases? How does the IT
department work with the line of businesses? Is there a charge back for IT
services?

? How often to you upgrade your infrastructure equipment? Who owns that
process? Who owns that budget?

When selling technology-rich solutions, you need to show how your technology protects the customer from technical obsolescence. You do this by translating the customer's objectives into technology needs and then demonstrating how your solution satisfies them. Most successful technology companies do a good job at pulling this information together. However, it is usually presented in a way that is incomprehensible to anyone but an engineer. It is your job to translate this information so the decision-maker and operational stakeholders can understand it.

Linking solutions to strategies creates value.

A company's business strategy guides the organization towards its business goals. Strategies cascade down the organization from the top. At each level of the organization strategies are converted into tactical decisions. Successful tactics move back up the organization in the form of results.

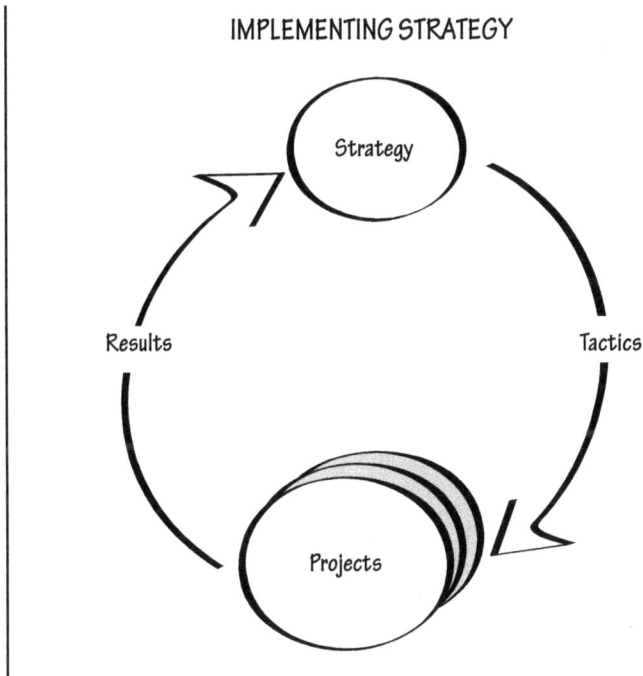

IMPLEMENTING STRATEGY

As you move down the organization, customer needs and problems become increasing specific. At each level, people are implementing strategy by making increasingly tactical decisions. These decisions are producing results that eventually roll up to deliver the CEO's promise to increase profits.

To build the value of your technology solution, you need to link the results your solution can deliver to the strategies that are driving the tactical decisions. You need to show how the technology satisfies the needs of not only the people that will use the solution, but the higher level executives who are responsible for the strategic results.

> The C.E.O. of Dream Cabins promised his investors that the company sales would turn a profit next year. According to the VP of Sales, the more customized the cabin, the greater the value of the offer. So, if Dream Cabins implements a mass customization manufacturing strategy, the VP of Sales has promised to deliver twice as many customers. The management challenge is to be able to offer a highly customized product profitably. To implement this strategy, Dream Cabins needs to quickly complete several projects – outsource the manufacturing of pre-assembled kitchen units; implement a strategic sourcing application to reduce costs, increase the number of component suppliers they can buy from, and improve the process for subcontracting installation of the cabins.

IMPLEMENTING STRATEGY
DREAM CABINS BUSINESS STRATEGY

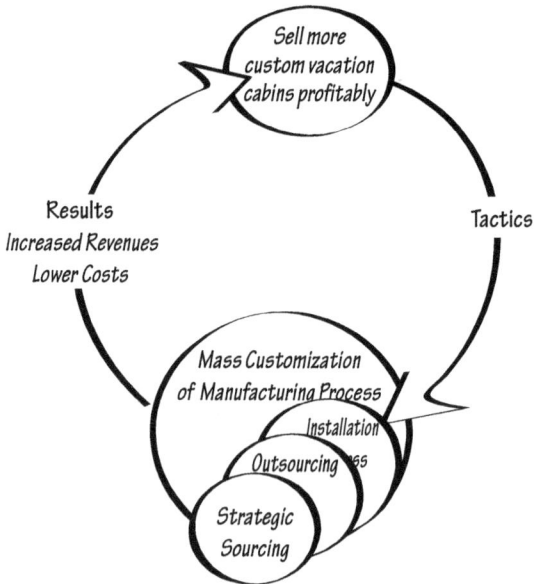

Sell more
custom vacation
cabins profitably

Results
Increased Revenues
Lower Costs

Tactics

Mass Customization
of Manufacturing Process

Installation

Outsourcing

Strategic
Sourcing

SELLING VALUE UP THE ORGANIZATION
STRATEGIC SOURCING TECHNOLOGY

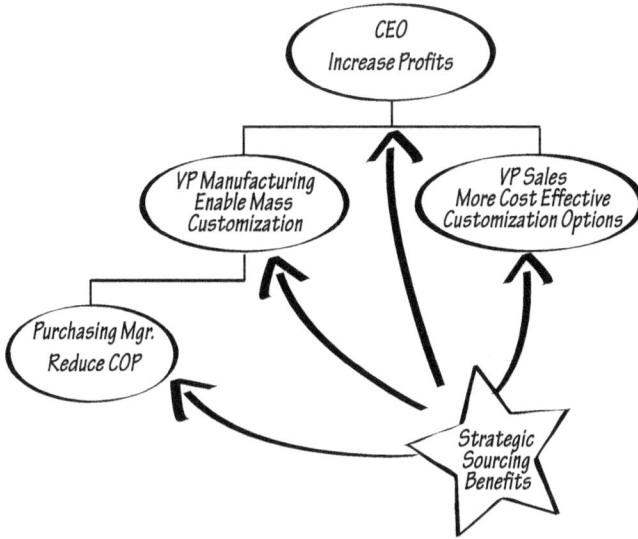

When you are trying to sell your strategic sourcing software application you want the Purchasing Manager to see how it reduces raw material and component costs; the VP of Manufacturing to see how it supports a mass customization manufacturing process; the VP of Sales to see how it enables Dream Cabins to offer a wider range of cost-effective, customization options, and the CEO to see how it contributes to their strategy to sell more custom cabins profitably over the Internet.

By helping each level of the organization see how they fit into the big picture you build the credibility of your proposal. By satisfying needs on every level and providing benefits that link the tactical results to the successful implementation of the business strategy, you strengthen the link between your technology and their success. Satisfying needs and solving problems by demonstrating features and benefits build the customer's appreciation for your technology. However, you don't actually create value in your customers' mind until you show them how these benefits directly impact the success of their business strategy. Making the link between your solution's benefits and the results generated by the successful business strategy is the key to selling value.

Identify needs.

A business strategy is going to generate a set of specific technological, economic, and operational needs. *To lower costs through strategic sourcing creates technology needs, such as visibility across the supply chain, multi-variable purchasing decisions, and integration of procurement with other business processes.* Uncovering, clarifying, and satisfying these needs drive most of your sales activities.

To translate your customer's business strategies into needs your technology solution can satisfy, you need to gather information about the tactical projects they will implement to accomplish their strategic objectives. The better you understand the customer's plans, the better your solution will be. As you invite customers to share their plans, make sure you document the results they expect from the successful implementation of the tactical projects and how they add up to quantifiable strategic results.

Uncovering your customer's needs is an iterative process. Start with your internal experts so you know the generic needs, and use them to figure out whom you need to talk to in the customer's organization. Talk to the company's technology experts, engineers, process consultants, functional managers, etc. Fortunately, the people who can articulate the tactical needs are easier to reach than the CXO's who drive the strategy. Furthermore, they are motivated to tell you about their needs because they want to make sure that new technology solution will make their jobs easier.

IDENTIFY NEEDS

Ask Your Customer:

? What are your expectations for the new strategy?

? What new capabilities do you need to accomplish this strategy?

? What approaches have you already considered?

? What do you need to successfully implement your strategy?

? What is your current technology/engineering environment?

? How open are you to changing your requirements?

Most likely you will find that each person you talk to will tell you only part of the story. Since you are dealing with multiple departments, they each color their assessment of the company's needs by their personal and functional needs. It is up to you to put together the pieces and figure out how they add up to the successful implementation of the customer's strategy.

Uncover issues.

Customer issues are problems, attitudes, misconceptions, or other factors that can stall the sale. *For a business strategy of lower costs through strategic sourcing, a potential issue might be a lack of inter-enterprise integration restricting information visibility.*

Generally customers won't make a decision until they have resolved all their issues. Helping the customer to resolve issues, either by solving problems or minimizing the impact of the issues, is a critical part of the salesperson's job.

UNCOVER ISSUES

Ask Your Customer:

? What are your concerns around the implementation of the new strategy?

? Does your current technology/engineering infrastructure support the business requirements for the new strategy?

? What are the business requirements for the strategy? ROI expectations? Time to market? Improved productivity?

? Will you need to change your current business processes to implement the new strategy?

? What are your executives' expectations for the scope and timing of implementing the solution?

As you uncover and resolve customer problems, it is very easy to get sucked into the political issues that drive the emotional sale. You may think you are building value by solving a technology issue only to find out that the resolution of the problem causes embarrassment to someone else. *Enabling Dream Cabins to make multi-variable purchasing decisions means that Purchasing Manager needs to learn more about the manufacturing process.* Pay attention to the decision-making process and roles as you resolve issues so you can optimize everyone's perception of the value of your solution.

The more your customer trusts you, the more issues you will uncover. Sales superstars are delighted when customers start to share their problems, because it gives them an opportunity to show how their solution can solve them. Since issues are barriers to the successful implementation of the business strategy, removing them creates a lot of value.

Build solutions.

Most technologies can enable a wide range of business solutions. In the value building process, you need to focus customers on the aspects of your solution that builds value by satisfying needs or resolving issues critical to the successful implementation of their strategic business initiatives. *A strategic sourcing solution that uses industry standards and open API's helps companies lower costs because it enables visibility across the supply chain and resolves the problems caused by a lack of inter-enterprise integration.*

Figuring out how to tailor your solution to optimize its value for the customer requires a team effort. Talk to your product marketing and technical specialists to find out how the solution can solve the needs and issues you have identified. Then confirm their ideas with the individuals who own the problems within the customer's organization. This process encourages the customer's acceptance of the solution before you make your final proposal and builds the commitment to making a decision in your favor. You also build their perception of value because you show them how the solution will enable their business strategy to adapt to the constantly evolving marketplace.

Value is created by the promise of results. Even if you are not selling the entire solution, you need to make customers aware of what the solution needs to include to produce the desired results. Then you need to show them how indispensable your part of the solution is to their ultimate success.

Early adopters will buy pieces of a solution and put them together. As the market matures, however, customers increasingly demand 'turn key' solutions. These are solutions that include everything the customer needs to achieve the results they expect – such as hardware, software, training, support, consulting, etc.

Even if you are only selling a part of the whole solution, you want to help customers define everything they need to successfully implement their business strategy. You are the expert. The customer needs your help in anticipating the scope of the project and the total cost and benefits of the solution. The benefit to you of giving customers this level of service is twofold:

- First, it gives you a great opportunity to explain how your technology fits into the big picture and how important it is to their success.
- Secondly, it builds tremendous rapport and encourages the customer to increasingly rely on your advice as a trusted advisor.

Embracing this level of service is especially important to people who sell infrastructure technologies – routers, servers, storage boxes, security software, etc. Since you are selling only part of the solution, it is easy for management consultants and engineering firms to capture the dominant mind share of the executive buyer. After all, most executives think of infrastructure as just 'plumbing.' However, if you take the time to educate the customer, you have the potential to develop a deep relationship based on a solid understanding of the importance of the infrastructure to the company's ability to quickly respond to change.

BUILD SOLUTIONS

Ask Your Sales Team:

? Given this need/issue, how does the solution work?

? What are reasonable expectations for performance once the solution is built and implemented?

? What are the benefits the customer can expect from this solution?

? What are the three most compelling reasons to buy? How do they drive technology needs?

? What are the features and benefits customers need? Why?

? What is the best way to prove each feature-benefit statement?

Building value with benefit statements.

At this stage of the value building process, you have gathered a lot of information about your customer needs and the details of your solution. You next step is to create feature/benefit statements that clearly articulate the value of the solution. Features and benefits alone don't build value because they don't relate to what the customer wants to accomplish. *Our strategic sourcing solution's open API's increases inter-company visibility.* When building value, you need to focus on what the customer is trying to accomplish, not what you are trying to accomplish. *Our strategic sourcing solution's open API's increases inter-company visibility, which means that more vendors can respond to your bids, so you will cut better deals.*

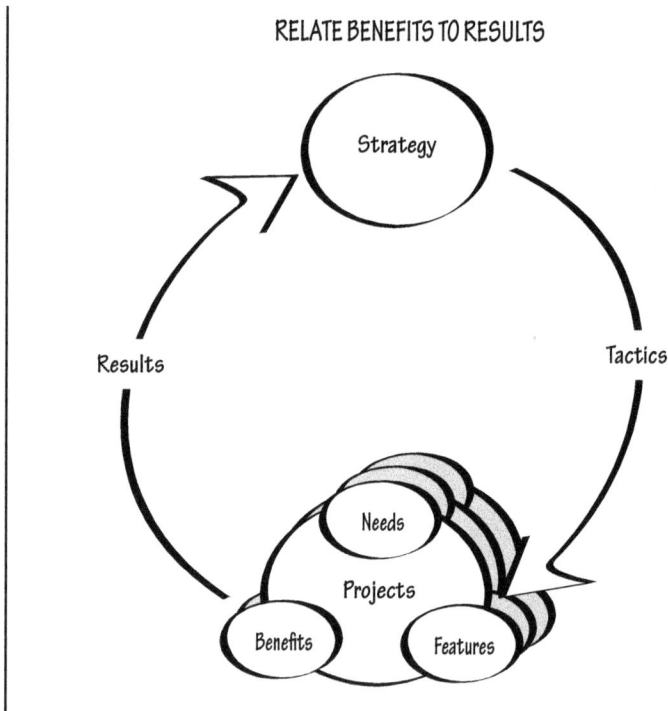

RELATE BENEFITS TO RESULTS

Strategy

Tactics

Results

Needs

Projects

Benefits

Features

Exceptional salespeople build value throughout the sales process. By consistently focusing customers on what they want to accomplish, they use value to drive the sales forward. Although they spend a lot of time explaining how the features of their solution will benefit the customer, they always present the benefits within the context of what the customer wants to do, which requires a crystal clear understanding of the essence of the technology solution's value proposition.

STEP 3: Sell Value

Building value is about shaping the customer's perception. Since each selling situation is unique, it is up to the salesperson to tailor the value selling process to every sale. This is a complex process because there are so many variables that can affect the customer's perception of value, which is influenced by decision-making role, the stage of the sales cycle, and the technology adoption profile.

Value is dependent on the role someone plays in the decision-making process. Decision-makers are responsible for bottom-line results, so they value how quickly and efficiently your technology solution will enable the company to achieve its strategic objectives. Stakeholders tend to value how the unique differentiators of the technology will improve the company's productivity and efficiency in the functional areas they represent. Coaches value how the solution resolves issues, satisfies needs, and delivers new capabilities. Since gatekeepers want to ensure that the decision is well balanced, they tend to value how your solution minimizes risk.

VALUE IS INFLUENCED BY DECISION MAKING ROLE

Feature	Role	Benefit	Value
Open API's based on industry standards	Decision Maker	Ensures that your strategic sourcing solution can be built quickly	So you can reap the economic benefits - increased revenues and lower costs - of your strategic sourcing initiative sooner.
	Stakeholder	Makes it easier to integrate your strategic sourcing solution with your current and future trading partners.	So you will be able to capitalize quickly on emerging market opportunities.
	Coach	Enables a flexible eTrading application that can evolve as your business needs change.	So you will be able to trade with the widest range of vendors today and in the future.
	Gatekeeper	Ensures that your strategic sourcing solution can be built quickly and cost effectively.	So you will minimize the risk of a long, complex implementation process.

Value is dependent on where you are in the buying process. The customer's perception of value can change over the course of the sale. Early in the sale, when customers are trying to figure out what they need and are exploring various options, they tend to value the benefits of the technology and the advice they get from vendors. Later in the sale they tend to value how the solution can minimize risk. They become more concerned with the new solution's track record, how much it will cost to implement, and the potential for failure.

VALUE IS INFLUENCED BY THE BUYING PROCESS

Feature	When	Benefit	Value
Open API's based on industry standards	Early in the buying process- qualifying & prospecting	Ensures that your strategic sourcing solution can be built quickly.	So you can reap the economic benefits the strategic sourcing initiative sooner.
	Late in the buying process - proposing & closing	Ensures that your strategic sourcing solution can be built quickly.	So you will minimize the risk of a long, complex implementation process.

Another key factor influencing the customer's perception of value is the technology adoption profile of both the decision-making team and the various people that make up the team. Early adopters value innovation and change. Early Majority buyers value reliability and practicality.

VALUE IS INFLUENCED BY TECHNOLOGY ADOPTION PROFILE

Feature	Benefit	Technology Adoption Profile	Value
Open API's based on industry standards	More companies can respond to your bids	Early Adopters	So you can offer greater personalization options.
		Early Majority	So you have greater control over your vendors when managing inventory levels
		Mixed Audience	So you can offer greater personalization options, while still maintaining tight control over your inventory.

It is not unusual to be facing a decision-making committee made up of very different technology adoption profiles. This creates a lot of political issues that can complicate the sale. Experienced salespeople are able to tailor the value proposition to satisfy the needs of the various players, without creating inconsistency.

Since value is about perception, it is important to evolve your value proposition as the sale progresses. Learning how to write effective value propositions that you can use to develop questioning strategies, build your solution and structure your proposal is critical to your long-term success selling technology solutions.

Identify value drivers.

Value drivers are the tactical benefits that add up delivering strategic results. They close the value loop by explicitly telling customers how the your technology solution will enable their business strategies, better, faster and more productively than any other alternative.

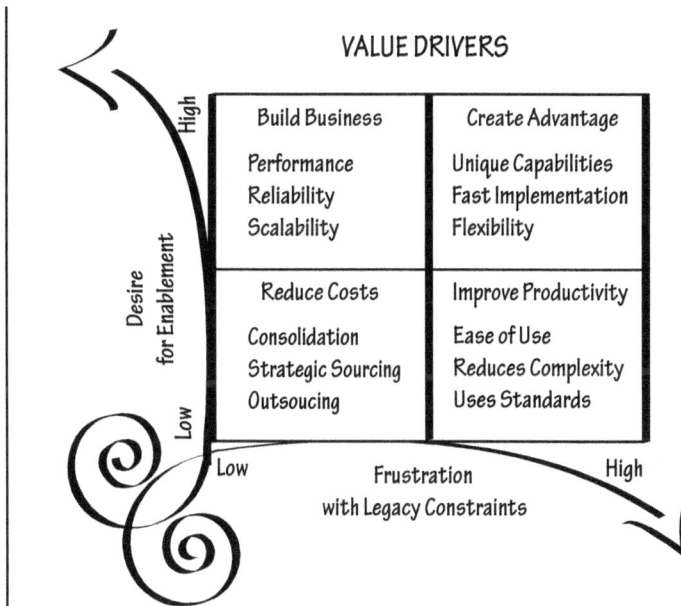

Although your strategic marketing organization spends a lot of time and money developing value propositions, it is up to you to find the one that crystallizes the value of the solution your are proposing to your customers. Value drivers are completely dependent on your customers' strategy, technical environment, and financial objectives. You need to know what the customer values before you can combine the appropriate value drivers into a value proposition that will win the deal.

IDENTIFY VALUE DRIVERS

Ask Your Customer:

? What are the results you expect to achieve by implementing your strategy?

? What are the key needs to be satisfied to enable the strategy?

? What are the key issues that need to be resolved before you can implement the strategy?

? How does the solution satisfy these needs and resolve the issues?

? What are the solution benefits that support the successful implementation of the strategy?

Once you have a clear picture of what is specifically driving the customers's perception of value, you need to create a Value Map to identify your most compelling benefits in light of your customer's strategy, and describe how their combined value adds up to significant strategic results. A Value Map clearly links the customer's strategy to the specific technology needs your solution satisfies. The value is created by the results the technology enables, which ultimately is the successful implementation of the strategy.

VALUE MAP

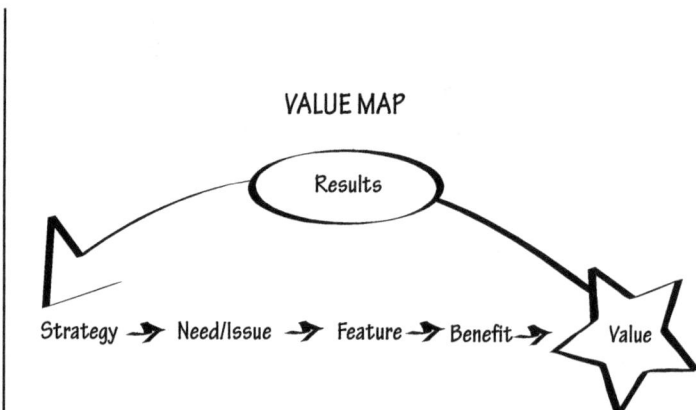

Results

Strategy → Need/Issue → Feature → Benefit → Value

Quantify value contribution.

You will greatly improve the impact of your value selling strategy by quantifying the results it enables. The value contribution of your solution is calculated by quantifying its impact on the customer's ability to produce strategic results. Impacts can be measured in quantities of time, money, new customers, market share, customer satisfaction rates, etc.

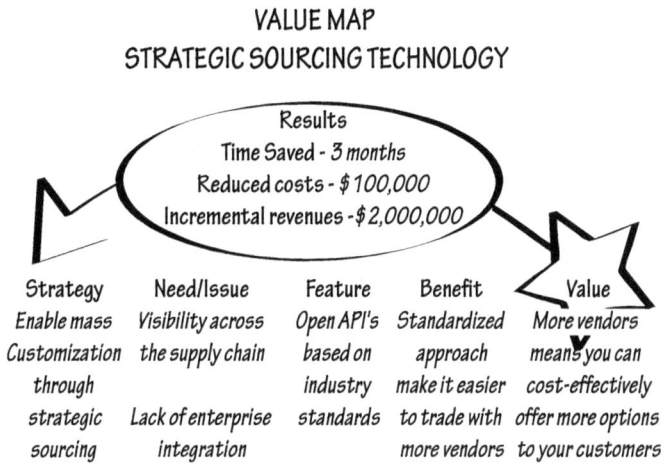

VALUE MAP
STRATEGIC SOURCING TECHNOLOGY

Results
Time Saved - 3 months
Reduced costs - $100,000
Incremental revenues - $2,000,000

Strategy	Need/Issue	Feature	Benefit	Value
Enable mass Customization through strategic sourcing	Visibility across the supply chain	Open API's based on industry standards	Standardized approach make it easier to trade with more vendors	More vendors means you can cost-effectively offer more options to your customers
	Lack of enterprise integration			

The openness of the eTrading application means it is easier to integrate the Dream Cabins'
purchasing process with their key trading partners, then you can quantify its benefits by
documenting

- *time saved when implementing the application – 3 months,*

- *reduced costs from better purchasing – $100,000,*

- *increased opportunity – projected incremental revenues of $2,000,000 thanks to the increased personalization options.*

Since you have already documented the business results the customer expects at both the strategic and tactical levels, showing the potential contribution of your solution on their ability to realize these results is merely a matter of quantifying how much faster, cheaper, or better they can do it with your solution.

Write a value proposition.

A value proposition is a simple statement that links the benefits of your solution to the benefits of your customer's strategy. Your value proposition identifies **who** the customer is, **what** the customer needs to do, **how** your solution helps them to do it, and **why** your solution is uniquely superior to other alternatives.

VALUE PROPOSITION
STRATEGIC SOURCING TECHNOLOGY

Who	*For companies who want to lower their procurement costs*
What	*Through more interactive trading with a wider range of vendors*
How	*Our Strategic Sourcing application enables a more flexible and responsive purchasing process*
Why	*The unique openness of this solution enables visibility and interactivity across the supply chain despite a lack of enterprise integration caused by legacy systems.*

Be succinct. A compelling value proposition is one that simply states what the customer can expect by accepting your proposal. Make sure it showcases how the value drivers will enable the business strategy and the quantifiable benefits of its successful implementation.

The definition of value is constantly changing.

The subjective nature of value means that it is constantly changing. As the sale progresses, as the market adopts, as the competitive landscape evolves, the definition of what the customer values changes.

In his book, *Crossing the Chasm*, Geoffrey Moore describes the transition between the early adopters to the early majority sales as 'the chasm.' The chasm is the epicenter of the fight for market share. Because technology buyers want to establish a market leader, the market tends to standardize on one technology solution. Standardization benefits customers because it makes it easier and safer to implement the new technology solution. [3]

---

[3] Moore, Geoffrey. *Crossing the Chasm*, HarperCollins. 1991

EVOLUTION OF
VALUE PROPOSITION

Pragmatic, Reliable, Evolution

Innovation & Radical Change

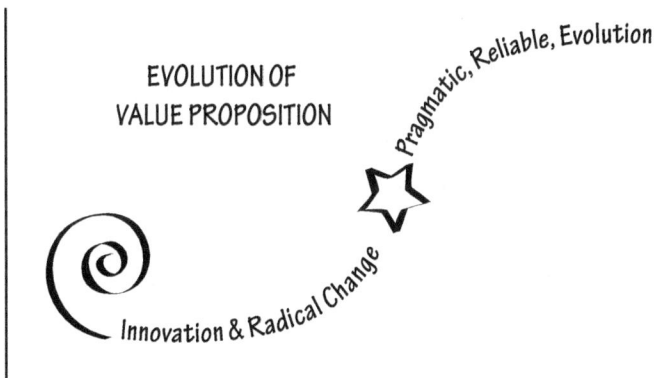

This is a very difficult time for technology companies because they have to transform a value proposition promising innovation and radical change into one promising pragmatic, reliable, evolutionary improvement. Evolving a message is a complex and dangerous process. Unless it is perfectly executed, customers hear conflicting messages about your solution, which undermines your credibility.

Maintaining your value proposition requires discipline. You must be sure that your value proposition reflects what is happening in the marketplace and in each of your accounts. As the market evolves, the essence of your solution's value will change from innovation and competitive advantage to risk management and productivity. As the sale progresses, your customers will value risk reduction over the promise of enabling benefits, so you need to be constantly revising your value proposition and how you apply it.

Develop value building questioning strategies.

People have to feel pain before they are motivated to do anything about it. It is human nature. Your job is to help your customers feel their pain. The more pain customers feel about their problems, the more motivated they will be to do something about them. In a perfect world, customers would always have a clear understanding of their needs, logically see how your product features satisfy them, and enthusiastically accept the benefits of doing business with you. The world is not perfect. Usually customers don't even know what they need. They are confused about their problems or discouraged because they don't know what is causing them. It is your job to help them understand their problems by applying analytical thought processes designed to solve them.

You have seen their problems before, and you have probably solved similar problems in the past. You could tell them what to do, but the odds are that they wouldn't listen. Why not? Well, even though you understand their problems, they probably don't. They need to become aware of the problem and its seriousness before they will be motivated to do anything about it.

Of course, no one likes having their problems pointed out to them. Telling someone directly that they are rapidly becoming obsolete usually doesn't win you any friends. You need to coach them so they discover their problems on their own. By asking them the right kinds of questions, you build their awareness of their problems and fuel their desire to solve them. Your questions help them define their needs and raise the issues they need to resolve. The process also builds their trust in you at the same time.

Technology salespeople use Value Building Questioning Strategies to help build the customer's pain, and subsequently their perception of value, around the critical factors required for the successful implementation of the business strategy. These questioning strategies are designed to help customers analyze their situation so they have a better understanding of how to use technology to accomplish their strategies. They also can be used to subtly build the customer's anxiety about the situation, so they are increasingly motivated to do something about it.

Value Building Questioning Strategies are solutions-specific questions that guide the customer through the value building process. Well-written Value Building Questioning Strategies combine logic and emotion into a provocative and compelling conversation. The purpose of a Value Building Questioning Strategy is to help the customer:

- **Discover** how the market is impacting their business and the importance of implementing new business strategies.
- **Build anxiety** around the impact of these problems to increase their sense of urgency around the need for a solution.
- **Analyze** the situation to uncover key problems, determine what is causing them, and link the problems to strategic issues.
- **Acknowledge** their tactical needs, and accept the benefits of your solution.
- **Realize** the value of how your solution supports the strategy by solving key tactical problems.

Writing a Value Building Questioning Strategy is the single most important thing you can do to accelerate the launch of a new technology solution. Technology salespeople are great conversationalists and smart people. But trying to figure out the logic flow that builds value is a hard thing to do, especially if you are unfamiliar with the product and market knowledge of a new solution.

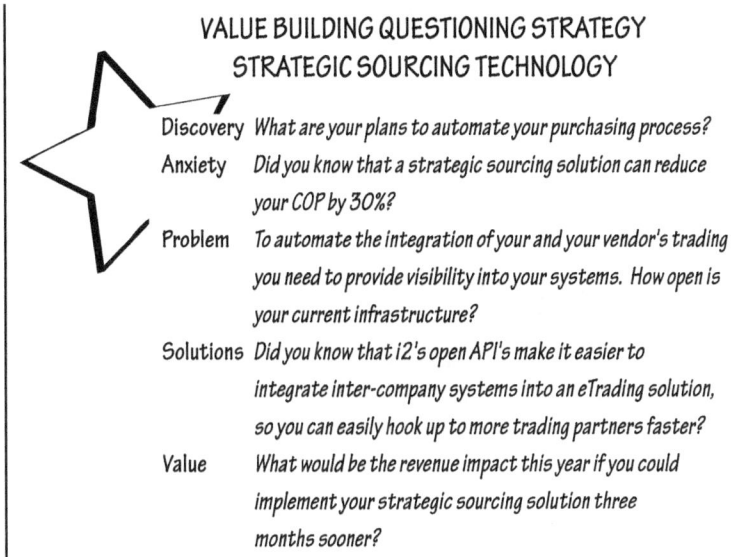

VALUE BUILDING QUESTIONING STRATEGY
STRATEGIC SOURCING TECHNOLOGY

Discovery	*What are your plans to automate your purchasing process?*
Anxiety	*Did you know that a strategic sourcing solution can reduce your COP by 30%?*
Problem	*To automate the integration of your and your vendor's trading you need to provide visibility into your systems. How open is your current infrastructure?*
Solutions	*Did you know that i2's open API's make it easier to integrate inter-company systems into an eTrading solution, so you can easily hook up to more trading partners faster?*
Value	*What would be the revenue impact this year if you could implement your strategic sourcing solution three months sooner?*

WHAT YOU NEED TO KNOW TO BUILD VALUE

Building a Value Map is a rigorous exercise in applying logic. To develop a value map you need to consult with market analysts to understand the market dynamics that are driving change; business executives to understand the emerging business strategies and economic and operational needs; technologists to understand the technology needs and issues, product marketing and sales engineers to understand how the technology solution's features and functionality can support the customer's needs and enable their business strategy.

Although it is not really hard to find this information, figuring out what is really important is challenging. Most likely, your corporate web site has lots of information about customer needs and multiple white papers discussing market trends. However, it is the rare marketing organization that synthesize this information into logical thought strategies that build value and creates useful sales tools so it is easy to apply them to your accounts.

INFORMATION ➤ PERFORMANCE

Market Drivers ➤ Understand what causes market change and opportunities to develop.

Emerging Strategies ➤ Understand what your customer is trying to accomplish.

Customer Needs ➤ Help the customer translate his/her strategies into tactical needs.

Customer Problems ➤ Help the customer anticipate problems.

Solutions ➤ Build the customer's confidence in your solution's results.

Value Drivers ➤ Build the customer's perception of value.

Information required to build value.

- **Market Drivers** – Trends \causing the new market to develop and why, **so you understand what is causing the market to change and new opportunities to develop.**

- **Emerging Strategies** – New business strategies that enable customers to respond to the market change and capture new opportunities, including how the strategies work; what they accomplish and expected results; the customer's compelling reasons to buy, and real-life examples of the strategies in action, **so you know what your customer is trying to accomplish.**

- **Customer Needs** – Tactical requirements to implement the business strategies including economic, operational, and technological needs, **so you can help the customer translate his strategies into tactical needs for your solution.**

- **Customer Problems** – Problems and issues arising from the implementation of the new business strategies; economic, operational, and technological impacts of the problem; causes of pain, and examples of how customer pains manifest themselves, **so you can help the customer anticipate problems and show her how your solution will solve or prevent them.**

- **Solutions** – Features and benefits of your solution; how the solution satisfies needs and resolves key issues; economic, operational, and technological benefits of the solution; ways to prove the benefits, and examples of successful implementations, **so you can build the customer's confidence that your solution will deliver the results that you are promising.**

- **Value Drivers** – How to combine benefits to demonstrate strategic results, and examples of linking the solution's benefits to expected results of the business strategy, **so you can build the customer's perception of value.**

BUILD VALUE PROCESS SUMMARY

What	How	Information Required
1. Define Business Strategy Link the customer's need for your solution to market-driven opportuntities	1.1 Identify emerging business strategies	Market Trends Emerging business strategies
	1.2 Identify compelling reason to buy	Technology Value Proposition Strategic motivations to buy
2. Create Solutions Translate strategies into specific needs you can satisfy and problems you can solve.	1.1 Identify needs	Tactical requirements to implement the business strategy
	1.2 Uncover issues	Problems and issues arising from the implementation of the new busienss strategies
	1.3 Build solutions	Features & benefits How the solution satifies needs and resolves issues Proof sources of successful applications
3. Sell Value Link your solution to the customer's success	3.1 Identify value drivers	Value drivers How to combine benefits to demostrate strategic results
	3.2 Quantify value contribution	Expected Results Estimated total cost of implementation
	3.3 Write value proposition	
	3.4 Write Value Building Questioning Strategies	

HOW TO USE VALUE TO SELL BETTER

You build credibility through consistent communications. Understanding what your customers value should shape all your interactions with them. When customers have a series of consistent experiences reinforcing their belief in the value you are promising, they become increasingly confident in their decision to buy your solution. If, however, the experiences are inconsistent – *if the sales engineer gives a generic demo after you have just led them through a perceptive assessment of their business strategy* – then the customer will doubt your sincerity and/or the ability of your company to deliver on your promises.

Doubt slows down the sale. A stalled sale is ripe for competitors, so make sure that everyone on the sales team understands the value proposition and that it is consistently communicated throughout the sales process.

BUILD VALUE THROUGH THE SALE

★ Use your value proposition to find high potential opportunities.

★ Use value to qualify the customer's needs, urgency, and budget.

★ Value drives your conversations with customers to uncover needs, issues, and competitors.

★ Value helps you define the application.

★ Value drives the logic of your proposal.

★ Value builds your negotiating power.

■ **Target the best customers.** Value helps you find emerging opportunities. Understanding value improves your **prospecting** because it explains why customers buy. Knowing how your solution enables emerging strategies will help you target companies that are the most likely to adopt early. Understanding value also helps tailor your pitch to the customer's business needs. This helps you break through the noise, capture the customer's attention, and earn the right to call on the customer. Value is the quickest way to open doors.

■ **Pick the winners.** If you can't create value, go somewhere else. Value helps you **qualify** accounts quickly because it helps you better determine the scope of the customer's needs. If a customer only has technical needs, it is unlikely that you will be able to build enough value to justify a premium price or urgency to drive to sale to closure. However, if you can link the technical needs to high-priority business strategies, you will be able to figure out how compelling your solution is to the customer. If there is a clear connection between what your solution enables and what the customer wants to do, you will be able to use value drivers to build momentum in the account. It also helps you assess the probability of closing the account and negotiating a premium price, other important account qualifiers.

- **Build value in every sales conversation.** The goal of the **discovery** process is figure out what the customer is trying to accomplish, translate his strategy into technical needs, uncover issues and suggest relevant solutions. You conduct the discovery process by asking questions and listening carefully to what your customer is saying. Value selling should guide every conversation your sales team has with the customer. Asking questions that build awareness and intensify pain is the art of selling. Value questioning strategies enable you to conduct consultative conversations that build your customer's trust and belief that your technology will be able to satisfy their needs, solve their problems, and enable their business strategies.

- **Propose value.** Value drives the logic of your **proposal**. The customer's perception of the value of your solution depends on how well you link your technology to their business strategies. Benefits are most powerful when they are presented within the context of the customer's needs and problems. A benefit that doesn't directly relate to the customer's perception of the situation is irrelevant. Value building strategies help you keep your proposal relevant. Furthermore, they provide a consistent logic to guide key sales events, such as the executive presentation, demo, and written proposal.

   The economic justification, a key element of the proposal, should also be built to showcase the value of your solution. By linking your solution to mission-critical business strategies, you are tying the decision to purchase your solution to other business decisions. Linking the purchase of the product to overall success of the strategy builds value because it associates the financial benefits of the technology purchase to the successful implementation of the strategy.

- **Negotiate with strength.** Value lets you play hardball. If you had built the customer's sense of value throughout the sales process, then you can use it as a negotiating tool during the **close**. Value makes your customer vulnerable and you strong. If the customer really believes in the potential value of your solution, he is more likely to pay more; be more committed to the implementation, and accommodate your needs. On the other hand, if the customer is not convinced of the value of your solution, most likely the decision will be made on price alone.

TAKE ACTION

■ **Use technology adoption profiles to interpret behavior.** Technology adoption theory explains a lot about customer behavior. Read the technology marketing classics by Geoffrey Moore – *Crossing the Chasm* and *Inside the Tornado* – to deepen your understanding of how markets develop and how technology adoption profiles influence the customer's buying process. Draw a technology adoption curve for your territory and use it to predict behavior.

COMPELLING REASONS TO BUY WORKSHEET

Improve Productivty

Build Competitive Advantage

1. List three unique ways your solution enables companies to build competitive advantage.
2. List three unique ways your solution enables companies to

■ **Research the market.** Identify the market drivers – economic, demographic, technological, etc. – that are changing the marketplace. Read up on how innovative companies are capitalizing on these changes by creating new business strategies. Use the *Wall Street Journal* or business magazines to better understand what is happening and why.

■ **Identify value drivers.** Apply your technology solution's value proposition to the various business strategies identified in your Emerging Strategies Worksheet to uncover what drives value in each market segment.

■ **Build a Value Map.** Work with your marketing and product engineering team to figure out how your technology supports emerging business strategies. Lead a multi-disciplinary team – account executives, business analysts, sales engineers, product marketing, product development engineers – through the value building process. Create a Value Map that you can use to create value propositions for each account.

VALUE DRIVERS WORKSHEET

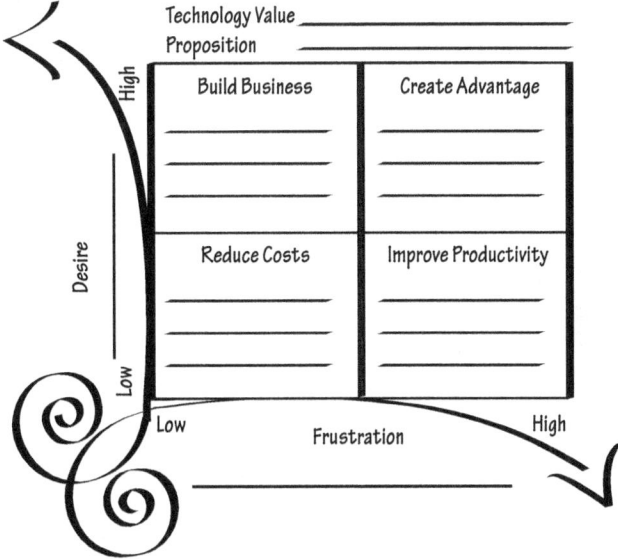

Technology Value _____
Proposition   _____

	Build Business	Create Advantage
High	_____	_____
	_____	_____
	_____	_____
Desire	Reduce Costs	Improve Productivity
	_____	_____
	_____	_____
Low	_____	_____

Low   Frustration   High

_____

1. Refer to your Market Map.
2. Identify how your technology solution creates value by enabling companies to create strategic advantage, build the business, improve productivity, & reduce costs.

VALUE MAP WORKSHEET

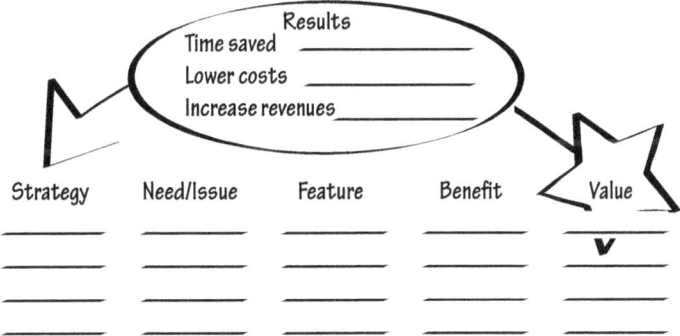

Results
Time saved _____
Lower costs _____
Increase revenues _____

Strategy	Need/Issue	Feature	Benefit	Value
_____	_____	_____	_____	_____
_____	_____	_____	_____	_____
_____	_____	_____	_____	_____
_____	_____	_____	_____	_____

1. Identify the customer business strategy.
2. Identify the key needs/issues to implement their business strategy.
3. Describe how the features of your solution satisfy these needs or resolve the problems.
4. Write the benefits of satisfying these needs or resolving the problem.
5. Explain the value of the benefit - how it enables the business strategy.

- **Develop Value Building Questioning Strategies**. Develop Value Building Questioning Strategies to help you get through the initial telephone calls and sales interviews. They ensure you focus on what the customer is trying accomplish.

VALUE BUILDING QUESTIONING STRATEGY WORKSHEET

Discovery _____

Anxiety _____

Problem _____

Solutions _____

Value _____

1. Write 2-3 open questions asking the customer to describe their business strategy and the results they expect it to achieve.
2. Write 2-3 questions that raise the customer's awareness about what will happen if they don't achieve these results.
3. Write questions to help the customer analyze their problems/needs. What do they need to implement the strategy successfully?
4. Write several questions that help you introduce the relative functionality of your technology solutions that satisfies the need or solves the problem.
5. Write several questions that help the customer visualize the value crated by the benefits of your solution.

- **Schedule a customer education meeting**. Propose an educational meeting with your customer. Use your value proposition to set the meeting agenda. If it is focused on the customer's business strategy and promises success, it will most likely grab the attention of the people who count. Then use your value building strategy to drive the meeting. Take chances, and aim high. Executives are always interested in new ways to improve their business. By using value as your guide, you will be speaking to them in a language they understand.

CONCLUSIONS

- **Link your solution to the customer's results.** Value links your solution to your customer's business success because it shows them how it will help them achieve their strategic goals faster, better, and cheaper.

- **Value drives the sale.** The customer's perception of value is the driving force behind the sale. It determines how much customers are willing to pay, how quickly they will buy, and how much risk they will take in the purchasing and implementation process.

- **Value is contextual.** The perception of value changes by decision-making role, the stage of the sales cycle, and the technology adoption profile. Maintaining your value proposition requires discipline. Since each selling situation is unique, it is up to you to tailor the value building process to every account.

- **Value is quantifiable.** You create value when you quantify the benefits of your solution and prove to the customer its direct contribution to the financial results they expect from the successful implementation of their business strategy.

- **Anxiety builds value.** To build value you have to build your customer's awareness of the consequences of not accomplishing their strategic objectives. You do this by linking the customers' technology problems and needs to the company's strategies.

- **Value is a moving target.** The subjective nature of value means that it is constantly changing. As the sale progresses, as the market adopts, as the competitive landscape evolves, the definition of what the customer values will change.

- **Pain causes momentum.** People have to feel pain before they are motivated to do anything about it. Technology salespeople use Value Building Questioning Strategies to help build the customer's pain, and subsequently value, around the critical factors required for the successful implementation of their business strategy.

- **Value creates energy.** Using value to drive a sale makes your job as salesperson much easier. Selling value is like riding a wave; the energy of the marketplace keeps moving the sale forward. If you don't sell value, then you have to create all the momentum of the sale by yourself, which is exhausting and rarely successful.

Chapter 4

Sell Solutions

Sell Business Results to the Executive

SELL SOLUTIONS

What	Sell the business results your technology solution enables.
Why	Selling the economic value of your solution to the executive builds strategic advantage.
How	1. Map the buying process, so you have more control in the account.
	2. Personalize the solution, so you make more compelling proposals.
	3. Resolve issues and build urgency, so you close deals faster.
So What?	When you sell business results to line executives, you can change the rules governing the technology buying process to your advantage, so you have more control over the account.

WHAT IS A SOLUTION?

Solutions integrate products and service to optimize a technology's value proposition. The value of the solution is greater than the sum of its parts.

Customers buy solutions because they believe the solution will enable them to achieve strategic results, such as improving operational productivity, building competitive differentiation, capturing new opportunities, increasing customer satisfaction, etc. The technology alone – *the computer, the software, the network, etc.* – does not deliver strategic business results. Technology must be applied, implemented, used, and supported to successfully deliver on its promise. This means that customers have to buy more than just the "box." They need to buy all of the intelligence required – *business process engineering, systems analysis, training, software, maintenance, administration, etc.* – to make the solution work.

One of the characteristics of emerging technology markets is that customers are willing to build their own solutions by assembling products and service from a variety of vendors. However, as the market matures, customers increasingly expect the vendor to put together the solution and guarantee the results. So, to successfully sell your technology, you need to evolve from a product to a solutions salesperson. Product salespeople sell features and benefits. Solutions salespeople sell results.

Selling strategic results is complex because you have to sell cross-functionally. A strategy is rarely contained in one department. *A strategy to enable multi-channel distribution means that the sales, customer service, and telecommunications departments need to collaborate.* To sell your solution, you need to appeal to everyone who is responsible for the successful implementation of the strategy. *You need to show the sales group how offering customers greater choice in how they interact with your company will increase sales; the customer service team how consistent, high-quality interactions across multiple channels – Web, phone, mail, etc. – increases customer satisfaction, and the telecommunications group how migrating to an IP telecommunications infrastructure will save them money in the long run.* You figure out who cares about the results your technology will enable; how they want to buy your solution; and resolve the issues that arise from the complexity of selling cross-functional capabilities. The solutions selling process helps you understand how cross-functional decisions are made and how to apply your sales methodologies, product knowledge, and business expertise to winning the deal. It helps you gather the information you need to build a wide base of support for your solution; create competitive advantage, and close deals faster.

WHY IS SELLING SOLUTIONS IMPORTANT?

People buy results, not functionality. Without insight into the business application, a technology sale is just a comparison between the features and functions of competitive products. In this situation, your product is a commodity. Most likely the lowest price determines who wins the business. There is little room for profit in sales like these. To get the price you deserve, you need to show customers how your solutions will help them implement their strategies faster, easier, better, or cheaper than other competitive alternatives.

WHY SELL SOLUTIONS?

★ Increase sales productivity.

★ Build value by selling cross-functional results.

★ Help the buying committee look good to the boss.

★ Solve problems to increase sales momentum.

■ **Sell strategically.** Solutions selling expertise improves your ability to plan your account development strategy. In this chapter you will learn how to figure out whom you want to talk to and what questions to ask, **so you sell more productively.**

■ **Build consensus.** A technology-enabled business solution almost always has an enterprise-wide impact, which means you have to sell your solution to many different functions. In this chapter you will learn how to personalize the benefits of your solution in order to build cross-functional consensus and establish a wide base of support.

■ **Sell up the organization.** When you understand the customer's buying process, you can get to the economic decision-maker faster. By selling solutions that solve problems and support strategic goals, you help the buying committee look good to the boss, so they are more likely to introduce you to him. This helps shorten the sale cycle and reduces the likelihood of a competitor stealing the business.

■ **Close more deals.** Ultimately, the ability to integrate your understanding of what the customer is trying to accomplish with how you sell the account increases your close rate. In this chapter you will learn how to use solutions selling to increase your control over the customer's buying process.

■ **Own the account.** When you sell solutions, the customer is buying results. When these results materialize, the customer doesn't remember all the vendors of all the products and services that made up the solution. She just remembers the person who put it all together for her. In this chapter you will learn how to sell the solution so you can 'own the customer' and reap the benefits of an intimate relationship – higher margins, repeat business, strategic opportunities, etc.

HOW TO SELL SOLUTIONS

Selling a technology-enabled business solution is a complex sale. Since the solution impacts many aspects of the customer's business, everyone wants to be part of the decision-making process. This means that many of the people you have to convince, including the economic decision-maker, are most likely not technologists or engineers, and they have a lot to learn before they can make a good decision.

SELL SOLUTIONS PROCESS

1. Map the Buying Process

   ➤ Define the buying process and figure out who is making the decision.

2. Personalize the Solution

   ➤ Tailor your value proposition so everyone can see how they will benefit.

3. Build Momentum

   ➤ Solve problems and build urgency to close.

Solutions selling is basically a process for managing the customer's learning process, with special attention paid to how the buying decision is made. It is your job to teach the right people what they need to know so they can confidently make a decision to buy your solution. This means figuring out who counts in the decision; what they need to learn about the solution, and the best way to manage their learning process.

In every account and for every solution, this solutions selling process is implemented slightly differently. No two accounts are ever exactly the same. Using a process helps you organize account and solutions-specific information into your sales strategy, so you do a better job at positioning your solution within the context of what is important to customer.

STEP 1: Map Buying Process

When selling solutions, you adapt your sales techniques and value propositions to how the customer wants to buy your solution. You map the buying process to find out how the customer wants to make the buying decision, the scope of the buying decision, who will be involved, and when it will happen. A better understanding of the customer's decision-making process, needs, and issues helps you position your solution within the context of what is important to them. It also helps you set realistic expectations so your forecasts are more accurate, and your account development strategies are more effective.

When selling a solution, you integrate your technology into a broader customer business initiative. Your technology is in some way enabling customers to do something that is important to their success. To sell a solution you need to define specifically what customers are trying to accomplish so you can figure out how to apply your technology in order to help them. This means you have to clarify their strategic objectives and define the scope of the current decision.

Decision-making – theory vs. reality.

In an ideal world, the decision-making process helps people work together to make the best choice to accomplish an explicit objective. A decision-making goal is agreed upon. Decision-making criteria are written and weighted in a consensus-building process. Alternatives are objectively evaluated against the criteria. Risks are identified and used to further evaluate the best alternatives,. Finally a choice is made that balances the risks against rewards of the alternative most likely to achieve the decision-making goal.

In the real world, this theoretical process is rarely applied consistently to technology decisions. In the early market, you may be the only game in town. A business executive wants to do something new. You show him how your technology can help him do it. The decision gets made. In later applications of the technology, the risk evaluation process greatly overshadows the potential rewards. Huge cross-functional teams all need to come to consensus. Decisions get bogged down.

As a salesperson, your goal is to help the customer make the best decision as quickly as possible. This benefits you because it optimizes your sales productivity.

DECISION MAKING PROCESS

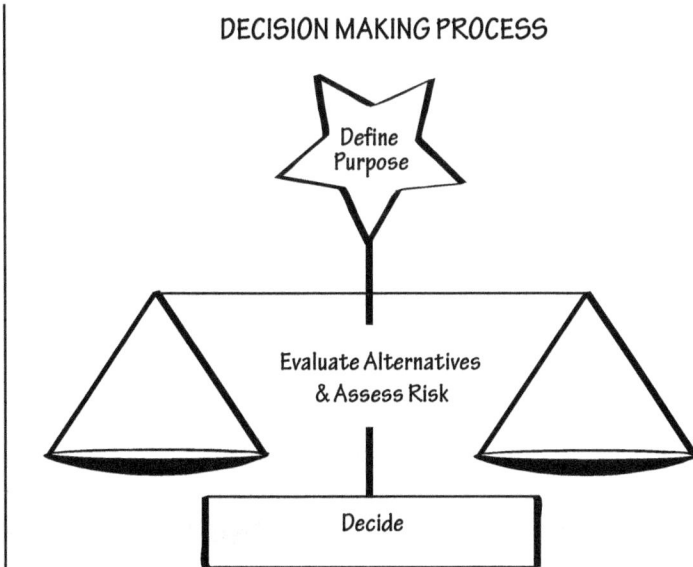

It also benefits your customers, because it accelerates the implementation of their strategy. To help them make the best decision, you need to encourage them to adhere to a rational decision-making process. Selling consultatively means that you help them clarify their decision-making purpose and the important decision-making criteria. For an early adopter that may mean scratching out some ideas on a napkin over lunch. For a 'Main Street' customer this same sales activity may mean consulting on RFP construction, running group brainstorming meetings, conducting extensive needs analyses, etc.

Ideally, you are also involved as the customer evaluates alternatives and assesses risks. In the informal decision-making process that characterizes the early adoption market, this may mean helping customers clarify their business strategies and inventing new products and services. In the more formal decision-making process of the 'Main Street' buyer, you may encourage your customer to set up competitive pilots in order to showcase the superiority of your solution.

Whether they choose your alternative or not, helping the customer make the best decision is your job. If you sell them a solution that fails, they will never forgive you. If you help them make the right decision, they will remember you the next time they are making an important technology decision, and there will always be a next time. Understanding the decision-making process and being able to adapt your selling style to facilitate it are paramount to your success.

Define the scope of the buying decision.

The first step in a rational decision-making process is to define the purpose of the decision, so everyone knows what decision they are making, its scope, and what they hope to achieve by making it.

One of the benefits of selling your technology solution within the context of the customer's strategy is that it makes the buying decision part of a larger, more important process. The customer has already decided to implement the strategy. By positioning your proposal as how they will get their job done, not whether or not it is a good idea, you can accelerate the buying process and eliminate a lot of issues that have supposedly already been resolved. It also serves to minimize the customers concerns about risk. After all, the company has already committed itself to the strategy. Furthermore, it maximizes the customer's perception of the solution's benefits because they can be associated with the results of the successfully implemented strategy.

To define the scope of the current buying decision, you must see it within the context of the decisions that have already been made. Think of all of the decisions made to implement the customer's strategy as a chain, and the current decision is one of the links in the chain. This helps you figure out both the relative importance of the technology buying decision to the big picture and who cares about its success. Placing the technology buying decision in the customer's decision-making chain is critical to mapping the decision; identifying buying roles and responsibilities, and building your strategic account plan.

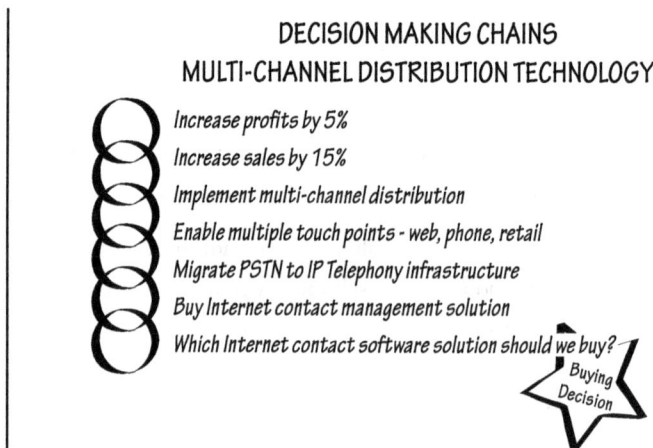

DECISION MAKING CHAINS
MULTI-CHANNEL DISTRIBUTION TECHNOLOGY

Increase profits by 5%
Increase sales by 15%
Implement multi-channel distribution
Enable multiple touch points - web, phone, retail
Migrate PSTN to IP Telephony infrastructure
Buy Internet contact management solution
Which Internet contact software solution should we buy?

Buying Decision

Since your technology is enabling a business strategy, it is a means to an end. By aligning your solution with much larger decisions that the customer has already made, the buying process for your solution becomes a subset of other decisions. This helps you figure out its relative importance, which provides clues about how high you will need to go in the customer's organization to find the decision-maker. It also helps you figure out who cares about the decision's success. This is important information because the IT group or engineering department is most likely your first point of contact. In most technology decisions these departments serve as gatekeepers. They may even think that they are the decision-maker. Asking questions that link the technical decision to the business decisions that have preceded them is a subtle way of funding out which other departments to call on without stepping on the gatekeeper's toes.

Asking the customer to clarify the purpose of the buying decision is the first step in establishing a consultative relationship. Questions that help clarify the relative importance and impact of the technology decisions expand the customer's perception of importance of the decision. Often executives consider the technology the 'plumbing' rather than the enabling infrastructure that ensures their success. By asking them the right questions, you expand their awareness of the potential benefits of the solution. Awareness is the first step of the learning process. The more aware the executives are, the more likely you will be able to capture their attention and sell them results.

DEFINE THE SCOPE OF THE BUYING DECISION

Ask Your Customer:

? Why are you considering "x" solution? What business strategy will this technology enable? Who owns the results of this business strategy? What is your relationship to this person?

? What is the scope of the technical decisions you plan to make?

? What are the business and technical decisions that have preceded this decision? Who made these decisions?

? What are some of the other operational decisions that need to be made to implement the strategy successfully? Who is making these decisions? Will these people be involved in this decision? If not, why not?

Identify decision-making style.

There are many different ways to make a decision. Some decision situations call for quick action. In others, everyone needs to vote in order to build her commitment to its success. Complex decisions need the perspective of a wide range of experts, but not necessarily their approval. Generally the decision-making process for buying technology solutions is driven by **urgency** – how quickly the decision must be made and **commitment** –the degree of organizational support and personal commitment required to successfully implement the decision.

Depending on these two factors, decisions are either made **unilaterally** by someone who has the authority to make the decision on his own; **consultatively** when the decision-maker elicits and considers the opinions of other people before he makes his decision, or by **consensus** where the decision is made by a group of people who all agree on the best course of action.

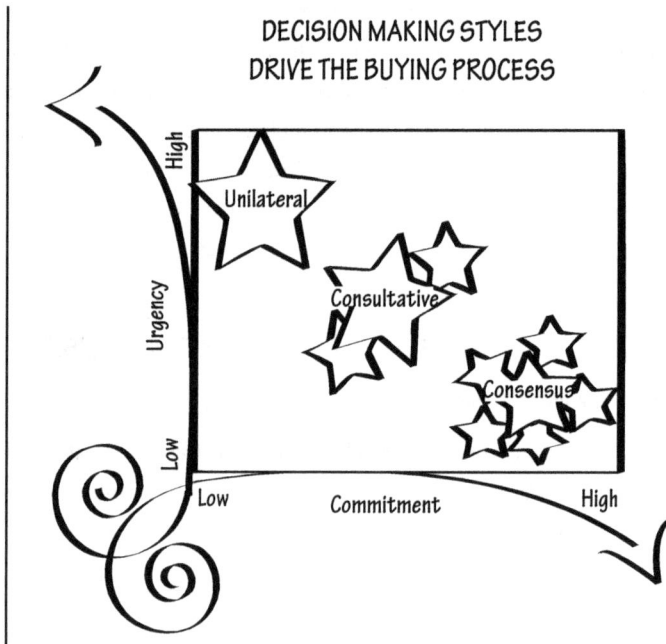

DECISION MAKING STYLES
DRIVE THE BUYING PROCESS

The trade-off between urgency and commitment is likely to be different in each account. However, it is important that you clarify the customers' preferred decision-making style early in the sale. It helps you anticipate how they will build their evaluation criteria, which increases your ability to influence them.

DETERMINE URGENCY VS. COMMITMENT

Ask Your Customer:

? When do you need to complete your project to support the successful implementation of the business strategy? What happens if your project is delayed? What will be the impact of the delay on expected performance?

? How quickly does the decision have to be made? Implemented?

? How much commitment needs to be built into the decision-making process to ensure its successful implementation?

? What is more important to the buying committee – a fast decision implemented quickly or a slower process that builds consensus and minimizes risk?

Identify decision criteria.

Once everybody has a clear idea about why they are buying a technology solution, those empowered to make the buying decision assemble a list of criteria that they will use to evaluate several alternatives. Often these criteria are called **requirements** in technology decisions.

As a salesperson, you want to have as much influence as possible over what these criteria are; their relative importance, and how they are written. The closer the decision criteria describe your solution, the more likely the customer will choose it over other alternatives. Developing decision criteria often takes a long time and involves a lot of consensus-building activities. Everyone has a different opinion on what is most important, and generally these discussions raise a lot of conflict that needs to be resolved in a positive way.

Once the criteria are set and approved, the customer usually asks several vendors to write them a proposal explaining how their solutions satisfy the needs expressed by the criteria. This process is usually governed by an RFP – Request for Proposal. If you have not been involved in the decision-making process before the RFP is finalized, the chances of winning the deal are very slim. Most likely, a competitor has already won the role of trusted advisor and influenced how the criteria were written. The deck is already stacked in their favor.

The buying committee reviews all the proposals and evaluates each one in terms of how well it satisfies the decision criteria. In theory, this is an easy process. Since all the people making the decision agreed on what was important, evaluating alternatives should be merely an exercise in sorting out which solution satisfies the criteria the best. In practice, however, this is never an easy job.

As the decision-making team learns more about the solutions and what they do, they start to reevaluate their criteria. The creative, evolutionary nature of the learning process take over the rational decision-making process. This is a point in the buying process when you can overcome an entrenched competitor with a superior solution. It is also when, if you have sold "wide and high," you can use the power of the line and functional executives to open up the decision-making process and modify the decision criteria to your advantage.

Once the buying committee has chosen the top few solutions, they become increasingly concerned about the risks of making the wrong choice. Nobody wants to make a mistake, so the decision-making team starts to focus on potential risk factors. At this point, if you have made **the short list,** you will be asked to make a closing presentation. If you have built your credibility during the sales process by helping the customer identify and solve the problems associated with the implementation of the solution, you will have, most likely, instilled enough confidence in your solution to win the deal.

IDENTIFY DECISION-MAKING PROCESS

Ask Your Customer:

?   What will be the steps of the decision-making process?

?   Who will create the decision-making criteria? Does the entire buying committee need to approve the criteria?

?   Do you expect to evaluate many alternatives? Have you already chosen the alternative solutions you want to consider?

?   Will there be an RFP? Have you already written it?

?   How many vendors will make it to the short list?

Identifying the decision-making process early in the sales is critical to closing the deal. You may not always have the luxury of competitive advantage. Someone else may already be working the account. Someone else's solution may be better than yours. However, if you understand how the customer will be making the decision, then you will be able to find the fleeting moments of opportunity when the competitor is vulnerable, and the customer is ready to listen to your ideas.

The decision process evolves as market adopts.

Most technology decisions are made by consensus because the impact of adopting the new technology crosses functions and requires the cooperation of many different kinds of people working together to make it a success. However, the importance of building consensus varies depending on the stage of the technology adoption process.

Early in the technology adoption life cycle, the buying decision is basically a business decision. The decision-maker is usually an executive with bottom-line responsibility. She is trying to build competitive advantage by being the first player in her marketplace with the enhanced capabilities offered by a technology solution. In the early stages of adoption, the visionary executive drives the buying decision with an authoritarian style. The decision is made quickly. Unfortunately, this decision is often made in response to unrealistic promises based on unproven technology. Visionaries are by nature risk-takers, so you can sell them an immature solution as long as you promise that your company will "do what it takes to make it work." Your management lets you do this because they are so thrilled that anyone actually closed a deal that they are willing to make technical support employees work around the clock to rack up early successes.

As the market matures, the decision-making process slows down and focuses increasingly on the pragmatic issues of implementation. The early majority buyer is more cautious, so the preferred decision-making style becomes more consensus-driven. This means that the customer will rely heavily on the rational decision-making process. Decision goals and selection criteria will be discussed and written down. Alternatives will be analyzed and potential risks closely evaluated. Many more people will be involved in the decision-making process, and consensus among the key influencers will most likely be required. This makes the sale much more complex and political. However, the benefits of this slower process are that better decisions are made, and there is more commitment to the successful implementation of the technology solution.

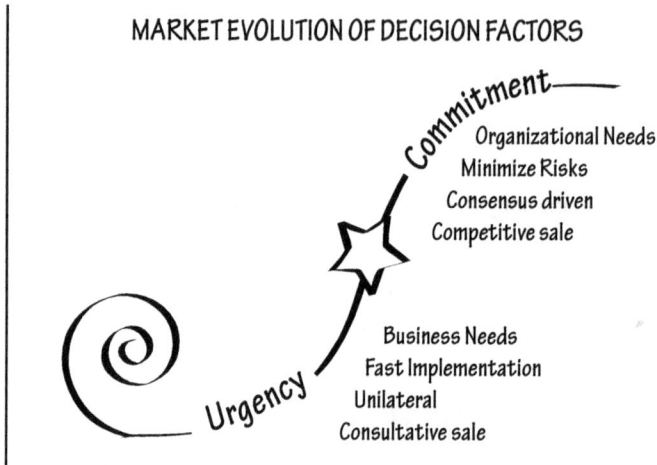

MARKET EVOLUTION OF DECISION FACTORS

Commitment

Organizational Needs
Minimize Risks
Consensus driven
Competitive sale

Urgency

Business Needs
Fast Implementation
Unilateral
Consultative sale

In the early majority sale, the sales process becomes more formal, and your role is to help the buying committee work together to make the best decision. Most likely the sale will be very competitive, as early majority buyers like to compare alternatives. The ability to prove that your solution reliably delivers on its promise becomes very important, so references, proof sources, and benchmarking pilots are critical sales assets. Early majority buyers are also more price conscious, so your ability to build value around the features and functionality of your solution becomes more important to your success.

Adapting your selling style to the changing dynamics of the decision-making process helps you successfully expand your customer base as the market matures. During the transition period between early adopters and the early majority buyers, you will often find yourself facing customer decision-making teams that include both pragmatists and visionaries, who generally hate each other. Visionary buyers are executives that want to get things done and shake up the status quo. As a result, pragmatists feel that the visionary neither recognizes the importance of the existing infrastructure, nor respects the value of their experience. It gets personal. Pragmatists see the visionary's new ideas as disruptive and short-term. Visionaries see the pragmatists as people who are getting in their way. Your job is to make them all feel valued and happy. The only way that you are going to be able to do this is to convince them your solution will produce the strategic results they both want. No one ever argues with results!

Identify decision-making roles and responsibilities.

To sell solutions, you apply your understanding of the technology solution's value proposition to helping your customers accomplish their strategic goals. This means you need to figure out who is responsible for the successful implementation of the strategy and convince this person – the decision-maker – and the people he relies upon – stakeholders, coaches and gatekeepers – that your technology will help them implement these new business strategies faster, better, or cheaper.

This implies that, unless you are selling a well-established solution to a 'Main Street' buyer, the decision-maker is probably not a technologist. CIO's and engineers very rarely have bottom line responsibility for strategic results. Although they often claim to be decision-makers, in reality they aren't. They may be responsible for the performance of the technology as part of the strategy, but they are not responsible for the outcome of the business strategy itself.

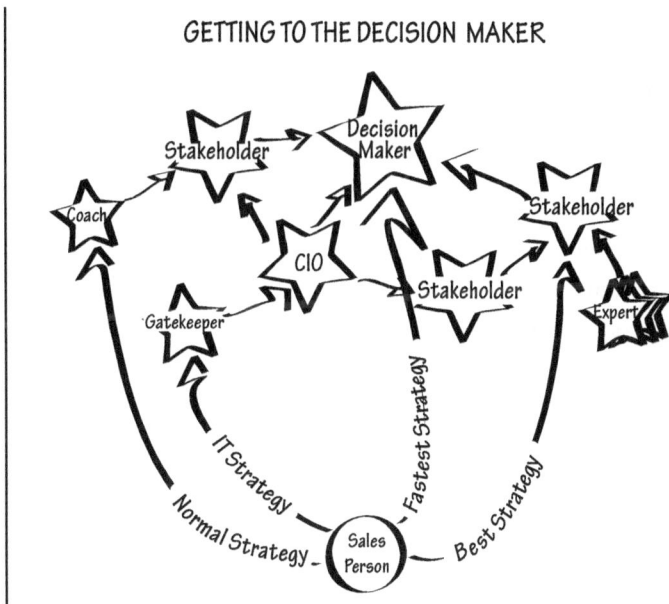

GETTING TO THE DECISION MAKER

The person who is responsible for the business results is the ultimate decision-maker. Unfortunately, this person often perceives the technology as merely 'plumbing.' In most technology sales it is difficult to engage with the real decision-maker. However, developing a direct line of communication with the decision-maker is key to winning the deal and controlling the account. The decision-maker is potentially your greatest ally because he is most likely to appreciate the business value of your proposal.

Most high tech purchases are made by committee. Since the cost is high and the impact of adopting new technologies crosses many departments, important technology decisions are made by cross-functional teams high up in the organization. These decision-making teams usually include the following roles:

- **A decision-maker**, who owns the budget and has the responsibility for the economic or strategic results of the technology implementation. Decision-makers are usually business executives who have bottom line responsibility – *the CEO, COO, or line of business (LOB) executives.* The decision-maker cares about how your technology enables the company to implement its strategy and how quickly he can expect to see results.

- **Stakeholders**, who understand various technical and functional implications of the decision and advise the decision-maker on the best course of action. Stakeholders care about how your solution will impact productivity and efficiency in the functional areas they represent. They may be technical – *a CIO, Director of Engineering, Chief Scientist, etc.* or functional – *a Plant Manager, VP of Marketing, Controller, VP of Sales, etc.* Although stakeholders can't say yes, they can say no, so it is important to include them in the sales process.

- **Coaches**, who champion your solution because they believe that the decision is important, and your alternative is the best choice. Coaches can be anyone. However, in technology buying decisions they are usually technically savvy. It is because they understand the potential value of your solution that they are willing to become your internal advocates.

- **Gatekeepers**, who manage the decision-making process to insure that the decision is a well-balanced one. Gatekeepers, *the CFO, CIO or Purchasing Manager* are often more concerned about managing the process that the final results of the decision are expected to produce.

The relative power of the various decision-making roles tends to change as the market evolves. In the early market, decision-makers tend to have more power and make more unilateral decisions. They care less about building consensus around the technology decision because they perceive it merely as a means to an end. Buying the technology solution is just one in a series of decisions, *such as building a new plant, starting a new division, or floating a new corporate bond.* Although they listen to their internal stakeholders and gatekeepers, they are equally as likely to make their decision based on the advice of external consultants, like you.

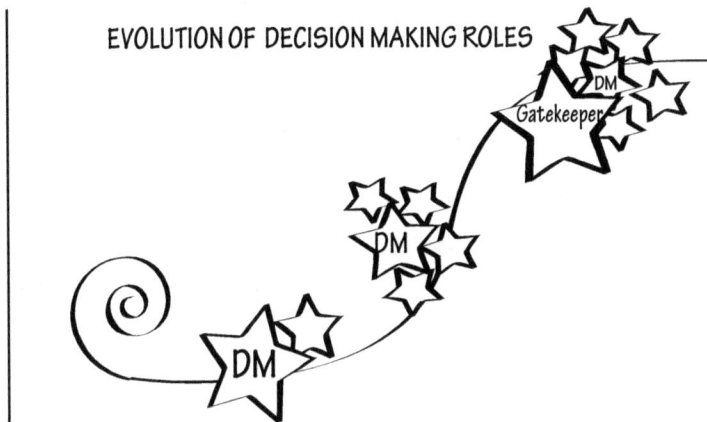

EVOLUTION OF DECISION MAKING ROLES

In more mature markets, it becomes increasingly hard to develop a direct relationship with the decision-maker because the decision-making process becomes increasingly consensus-driven. As the novelty of the innovation wanes, the decision becomes more interesting to the functional executives responsible for productive operations and less interesting to the visionary executive who is trying to capture new market share. The role of key influencers and gatekeepers grow in importance, and your coach becomes an invaluable resource. Mature technology solutions sales tend to be very complex and political. However, they also are bigger and more likely to result in profitable repeat business.

Follow the money.

Once you understand how the decision will be made, you need to find out who specifically will be making it. The most important person to identify is the decision-maker. One would think this is a simple thing to do, but it isn't. Usually someone who reports to the actual decision-maker will tell you he is the decision-maker, but he is not. However, you can't afford to anger this person by challenging his authority, so you need to subtly explore the power structure in the organization to uncover who the real decision-maker actually is.

To uncover the players in the game, start by figuring out who is responsible for the economic, operational, and technical objectives that support the business strategy. These stakeholders may not be directly involved in the buying process, but they are the people who will be influencing the decision. Most likely these executives will have delegated this task of participating in the decision-making process to someone who reports to them. These people are usually the project leaders of the various initiatives the company is implementing to actualize the strategy.

IDENTIFY DECISION-MAKING ROLES AND RESPONSIBILITIES

Ask Your Customer:

? Who will be managing the decision-making process? What is this person's decision-making style? What is this person's relationship to the decision-maker?

? Who is the ultimate decision-maker? What economic results does s/he expect from the implementation of this solution? How involved will s/he be in the actual decision-making process? What is his/her decision-making style?

? What are the decision-maker's expectations for when the decision will be made? When it will be implemented? When s/he will start reaping the benefits from the investment?

? Who will the decision-maker turn to for advice? Will these key influencers all have to agree on the decision? Can any one of them veto the decision? How will the decision impact their span of control?

? Who are the people that have the highest motivation to make the decision? Why do they think this decision is important?

? Who is responsible for evaluating the return on investment of this decision? Who is responsible for evaluating the risks of implementing the solution?

? Who is the gatekeeper in the decision? Who does the gatekeeper report to? What are the key relationships between gatekeeper's organization to the decision-maker's organization?

Then move up the organization one level above the stakeholders to the person who owns the business results of integrating these functional objectives into a strategic objective. That is most likely the business executive who approves the recommendation made by the buying committee. This is your decision-maker.

There is a good chance that you will never meet the decision-maker face to face. There is an even better chance that he will never read your proposal. However, this is the person you need to convince that your solution is the best choice. Since you may never get a chance to pitch him personally, you need to make your case through the mouths of the buying committee and stakeholders, which means you'd better do a really good job of teaching them why your solution is the best.

STEP 2: Personalize the Solution

Organizations don't make decisions; people do. Therefore, you need to show each person involved in the buying decision how your solution satisfies his needs and solves his problems. When you personalize your solution's benefits, you encourage stakeholders to support the decision by helping them understand "What's in it for me?"

Map the solutions impact.

In Chapter 3: Build Value we discussed how business strategies are implemented through a series of tactical projects. Each tactical project produces results that eventually add up to strategic results. When you personalize your solution, you figure out who is responsible for each of the tactical projects, and you show them how your technology solution supports their initiatives in a way that accelerates or augments its positive contribution to the strategic results.

To do this you need to treat every related project as a mini-sale within the larger sale. You need to interview the project manager and the executive responsible for its results about their objectives, so you can understand how their project fits into the overall strategy. Then you use their objectives to create a personalized value proposition that explains:

1. How your technology will enable them to achieve their objectives
2. How all the objectives add up to the successful implementation of the overall business strategy.

TAILORED VALUE PROPOSITION
VP CUSTOMER SERVICE
MULTI-CHANNEL DISTRIBUTION TECHNOLOGY

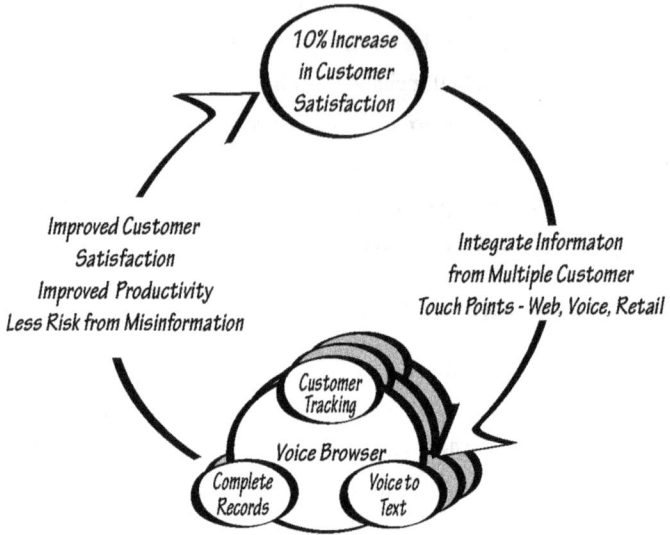

The benefit of breaking your strategic value proposition down into more specific, functional ones is that it links all of your sales activities to the customer's strategic business objectives. It is very easy to forget the strategic benefits of your solution when you are in the middle of a demo discussing the finer points of your

SOLUTIONS MAP
MULTI CHANNEL DISTRIBUTION TECHNOLOGY

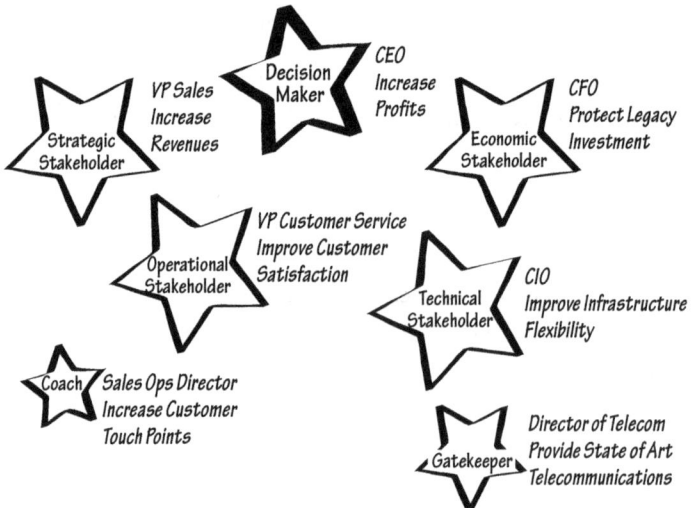

technology's functionality. By having a structure that organizes all of your solutions selling content within the context of the customer's strategic intent, you ensure that you are constantly building the customer's perception of value. Furthermore, you will constantly reinforce the link between the decision to buy your solution to the decision the customer has already made, which is to implement the business strategy your technology enables.

MAP THE SOLUTION'S IMPACT

Ask Your Customer:

? What is your role in the decision to purchase this technology solution?

? How does the success of your project depend on the technology solution?

? What could go wrong with the implementation of the technology solution?

? How would this impact your project's implementation? Results? Contribution to the successful implementation of the business strategy?

? What do you think are the most important criteria in ensuring a good decision?

? How important is it that new technology integrates into your existing IT infrastructure?

Tailor the value proposition.

To tailor a value proposition to a specific buyer, you need to write a simple statement that clearly shows how your solution links the success of the tactical project to the overall business strategy. It should identify **whom** you are addressing, **what**

PERSONALIZED VALUE PROPOSITION
VP CUSTOMER SERVICES
MULTI-CHANNEL DISTRIBUTION TECHNOLOGY

Who	Ms. VP Customer Service
What	By implementing a Multi-Channel Distribution strategy
Results	We have estimated that you will be able to increase your customer satisfaction ratings by 10% over the next year.
How	Our unique voice browser ensures that the all customer interactions, including voice messages, are automatically documented and entered into the appropriate customer file.
Why	So that no customer is lost.

the project is, how the **results** of the project support the customer's strategy, **how** your solution uniquely enables the desired results, and **why** this benefits him or her.

In most technology sales, the buying committee represents a wide range of functional and operational interests, so you need to tailor your value proposition to satisfy each stakeholders compelling reason to buy. To do this first you need to identify who cares about your solution and why on your Market Energy Map.

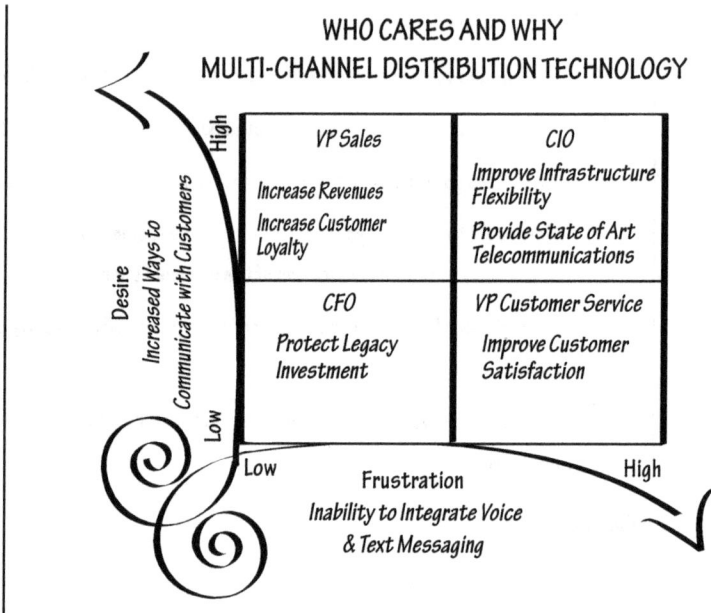

WHO CARES AND WHY
MULTI-CHANNEL DISTRIBUTION TECHNOLOGY

	VP Sales Increase Revenues Increase Customer Loyalty	CIO Improve Infrastructure Flexibility Provide State of Art Telecommunications
	CFO Protect Legacy Investment	VP Customer Service Improve Customer Satisfaction

Desire Increased Ways to Communicate with Customers (High / Low vertical axis)

Low ————————— Frustration ————————— High
Inability to Integrate Voice & Text Messaging

You need to modify your core value proposition to the specific concerns of each stakeholder. *For example, if you are trying to sell an Internet Contact Center solution, you need to appeal to the:*

- *VP of Customer Service by showing how it will increase customer satisfaction.*
- *VP of Sales by showing how it will increase sales revenues.*
- *CIO by showing how it will improve the quality of service of the infrastructure.*
- *CFO by how it will protect legacy investments.*

Furthermore, you will need to support each of these functional value propositions by translating them into technology needs and issues and developing role-specific benefit statements and proof sources.

- *So, Ms. VP Sales, what if I could show you how our Internet Contact Management Software would provide a consistent customer experience across multiple channels, including phone web and retail, resulting in an estimated 30% increase in your revenues next year?*

- *So, Mr. VP Customer Service, what if I could show you how our Internet Contact Management Software improves customer satisfaction by ensuring that all customer interactions are tracked and stored for future use?*

Also, when tailoring your value propositions, don't forget how technology adoption profiles influence someone's perception of your proposal. Early adopters like to hear words like new, breakthrough, revolutionary, fast results – *Our revolutionary voice browsing software is a breakthrough in the integration of web and voice technologies providing you with a chance to be first to market with a truly integrated customer experience.* Early majority buyers like to hear words like improved, integrated, proven, reliable, cost-effective – *Our voice browsing software has been proven in the marketplace to provide the most reliable and cost-effective approach to providing customers with a consistent shopping experience.* Even when presenting similar value propositions, tailor them to the technology adoption preferences of your audience, so you can be sure you are heard.

TAILOR THE VALUE PROPOSITION

Ask Your Customer:

? Will the new technology enable you to accomplish your strategic business goals faster, better, or cheaper?

? Will the new technology help you become more profitable, either by reducing costs or increasing revenues?

? Will the new technology make you more productive or efficient in managing your core business?

? Will the new technology help you deliver better service and greater benefits to your end users/customers than your current technology does?

STEP 3: Build Momentum

As people get closer to making decisions, they become more concerned with the risks, which slows down the buying process. No one wants to make a mistake.

Building momentum helps reduce the customers' sense of risk and increases their desire to get the benefits. You build momentum by solving problems and building credibility, so the customer becomes confident enough in the potential success of the decision to make it. The more problems you solve, the more credible you are. Solving problems helps you show customers you care about them and that you are committed to their success.

Solve your customers' problems.

Problems are often what prompt companies to make technology decisions. As a consultative salesperson, your job is to help customers analyze their problems and turn them into opportunities. Research studies conducted by The Rackham Institute show "that successful consultative salespeople focus most of their attention on the early stages of the acquisition cycle, in particular the recognition of need stage. This is the point where the seller can create the most value by helping customers gain new insights into their problems and discover new solutions that will give superior value."[1]

Most stakeholders involved in the buying decision don't evaluate technology

SOLVE PROBLEMS

Ask Your Customer:

? Have does your project contribute to your organizational goal of 'x'?

? What results does your project need to deliver to support the organizational strategy? Are you confident that you will be able to produce them?

? Are you concerned about getting the project done on time, on budget?

? How dependent is your project on the successful and timely implementation of the technology solution?

? What happens if your project fails? What will be the impact of its failure on the overall strategy?

? What if I could show you how our solution could prevent the problems that could cause your project to fail?

? What would be the incremental benefits for the strategy if our solution accelerated or augmented your project's results?

[1] Rackham, Neil. *Reinventing the Sales Force,* McGrawHill. 1999

solutions for a living. Their real jobs are running the plant or closing the books. They enter the buying process not knowing enough to make a sound buying decision – either because they have an incomplete understanding of the solution or because they have not fully defined their problems, needs, and issues. It is your job to teach the customer what he doesn't know.

Consultative salespeople create value by raising their customers' awareness of potential problems; adding insights, and developing unique, innovative solutions. Since you are an expert, you are much more likely to anticipate likely problems than your customers are, so you need to help them see the implications of their actions down the road and guide them through a maze of alternatives. You need to manage their insecurities and coach them through the process, so they will make a good decision. However, you need to be careful not to create resentment as you lead customers through their learning processes. As much as we all want to prevent problems from occurring in theory, no one likes being told about what could go wrong.

Customers tend to resent being told all the ways that they might fail, so you need to indirectly build their awareness of the issues and their anxiety about the potential negative impact of their problems . You do this by asking them the right questions. As we discussed in Chapter 3: Build Value, the way you build customers'

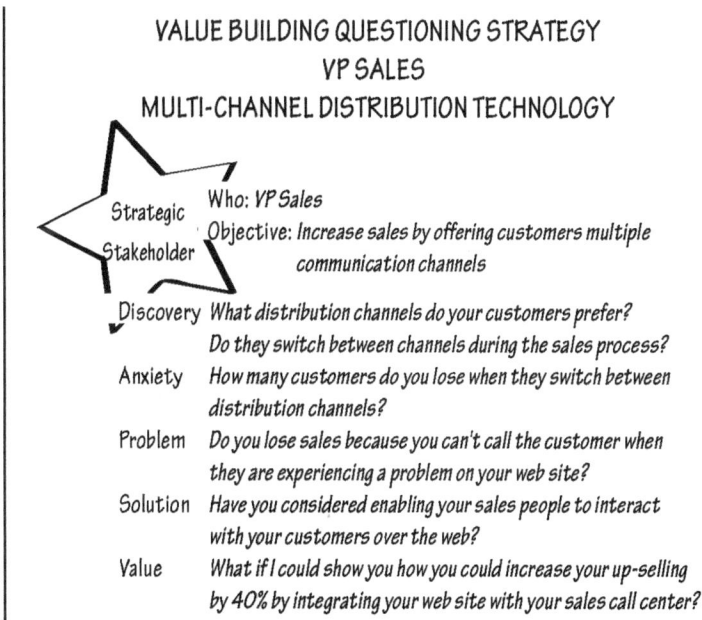

VALUE BUILDING QUESTIONING STRATEGY
VP SALES
MULTI-CHANNEL DISTRIBUTION TECHNOLOGY

Strategic Stakeholder

Who: *VP Sales*
Objective: *Increase sales by offering customers multiple communication channels*

Discovery — *What distribution channels do your customers prefer? Do they switch between channels during the sales process?*

Anxiety — *How many customers do you lose when they switch between distribution channels?*

Problem — *Do you lose sales because you can't call the customer when they are experiencing a problem on your web site?*

Solution — *Have you considered enabling your sales people to interact with your customers over the web?*

Value — *What if I could show you how you could increase your up-selling by 40% by integrating your web site with your sales call center?*

concerns about their problems so they appreciate the value of your solutions is by asking them Value Building Questioning Strategies.

If you don't play this role, someone else will. The greater the customers' fear about the decision, the more likely they are to exert control over the process. For example, they might hire a consulting or engineering firm or set up very narrow guidelines to manage their evaluation process. The more control the customer exerts, the more difficult it will be for you to build value, and the longer it will take to close the sale.

To sell business solutions, the customer must believe that you can anticipate and solve their problems. You build their trust by raising issues and then skillfully facilitating a positive resolution. The more times you do this, the more credibility you will build.

Build the customer's urgency to buy.

Each sale's momentum is unique. Some sales are quick and painless; others are so slow that you give up trying. As a salesperson, you can't control how fast your customers will make their decision, but you can influence it. You build urgency by raising the buying committee's emotional investment in the decision.

Business solutions sales cycles tend to be long and frustrating. More often than not, the sale gets bogged down in a myriad of real and perceived issues that the customer wants to resolve before they buy a solution. It may seems much easier to keep the sale simple and just sell products, especially in light of your quarterly quota. However, the value – e.g. what the customer will pay a premium for – is not in the product; it is in the solution. Customers are willing to pay you a lot of money because you are going to help them succeed. Boxes don't help them succeed; solutions do.

The challenge is not selling technology solutions, but figuring out how to sell them fast enough so you can meet your quota, and your company can build momentum in the marketplace. There are several ways to build urgency in a sale.

■ **Sell directly to the decision-maker.** No one questions the wisdom of selling high and early. Linking the value of your solution to the successful implementation of your customer's strategy motivates them to buy quickly. This is easier to do in early adoption sales, but works equally as well in early majority sales as long as you are selling directly to the decision-maker. You can capture the attention of the decision-maker by discussing strategic issues, solving significant problems, and opening up new opportunities. Once the decision-maker understands the value of your solution and how she will personally benefit from it, she takes action. Fast.

■ **Tailor the value proposition to each major stakeholder.** Showing each stakeholder how your solution supports his role in the overall strategic plan motivates him to support your decision. Most people are concerned about their little piece of the pie. The accountant is under pressure to close the books; the production manager wants to get the product out the door, and the salesperson wants to get the order. This limited point of view tends to focus them on the problems that get in their way. However, when you show them how they fit into the big picture, their perspective changes. They see the strategic impact of their tactical problems and the new opportunities that will come from solving them.

■ **Never underestimate the power of politics.** Apply your sales methodology in the account to sort out the leaders from the followers. Then use the political energy that runs rampant in the organization to build support for your solution. After all, your proposal makes them look good to their boss, so build sales momentum by enlisting people to vote for you, and communicating their preference to everyone on the decision-making team.

■ **Capture and channel market energy to drive the sale.** In Chapter 2: Harness Market Energy we discussed how the market is a source of dynamic energy that opens up new opportunities and changes the business environment. Constantly reminding the customer about how quickly the market is evolving is a great way to speed up the decision-making process. Since you have linked your solution to their business success, they can't afford to do nothing. Use the relentless pace of market evolution, the customer's competitors' strategies, and technological innovation to scare the customer into action. They can't afford to become obsolete.

BUILD URGENCY

Ask Your Customer:

? How quickly is the market evolving to the new technology paradigm?

? Have you noticed that your customers are asking you for the new solution?

? Are any of your direct competitors investing in new technology-enabled business strategies?

? What will be the impact of the new solution's benefits on next year's revenues? Operating costs? Market share?

Every time you solve a problem that reduces the customer's sense of risk, you build his confidence. Every time you build value, you create excitement. Every time you link his decision to the success of their bosses' boss, you inspire visions of success. Every time you show him how the market is moving relentlessly forward, you scare him. All of these emotions create energy to drive the sales forward, so use them to build momentum in your accounts.

WHAT YOU NEED TO KNOW TO SELL SOLUTIONS

Most high tech companies use a sales methodology that helps them manage the sales process consistently across the organization. Sales methodologies are useful because they provide a common framework within which sales teams can organize and implement their sales strategy. Most sales methodologies explain how the complex, multi-disciplinary technology decisions are made. They identify the key roles in the decision-making process and the type of issues the salesperson is likely to uncover. They also outline different kinds of sales strategies to provide roadmaps for strategic account planning.

Unfortunately, most sales methodologies are generic. Although they provide a common framework, it is still up to you to figure out whom to call; what stakeholders will care about, and how the technology solution builds value. This generally is not a problem when experienced salespeople are selling solutions with which they are familiar. However, when a sales team has to sell a new solution, their lack of product and market knowledge inhibits their ability to sell productively.

INFORMATION ➤ PERFORMANCE

The Business Application ➤ Figure out who will be impacted by the buying decision.

Decision-making Criteria ➤ Adapt your style to the customer's decision-making process.

Stakeholders ➤ Apply your strategic account planning process to selling the new solution.

Tailored Value Selling Strategies ➤ Build value with all your stakeholders.

Implementation Problems ➤ Sell consultatively to build confidence in your solution.

Selling Issues ➤ Build momentum in the account, and close the deal.

Success can be accelerated and sales productivity improved, by integrating the new solution's product and market knowledge with the company sales methodology. Figure out the range of business applications, the buying process, job titles for the key stakeholders, and customer needs and concerns. Then creatively treat the information so it is easy to apply to the sales process by writing questioning strategies, targeted prospecting campaigns, etc. This produces positive sales results much faster than expecting salespeople to figure it out by themselves.

Information required to sell solutions.

■ **The business application** – How business strategies that use the technology are implemented; how strategic business goals translate into economic, operational and technological objectives, and what functions are involved in the implementation, **so you can figure out who will be impacted by the buying decision and include them your discovery process.**

■ **Decision-making criteria** – How organizations tend to make these kinds of purchases, applying the urgency vs. commitment trade-off; how the solution appeals to different decision-making styles; technology adoption preferences for the solution; assessment of solutions performance against typical buying criteria, and ROI expectations and strategies, **so you can adapt your selling style to the customer's decision-making process.**

■ **Stakeholders** – Who are the decision-makers, stakeholders and gatekeepers; the role of the technical experts in the decision-making process; what functional titles to look for when identifying stakeholders; key stakeholders' compelling reasons to buy; and stakeholder anxieties and hot buttons, **so you can apply your strategic account planning process to selling the new solution.**

■ **Tailored value selling strategies** – Value propositions and value building questioning strategies by stakeholder, **so you can build value with all of the stakeholders, solidify your competitive position and increase your control over the account.**

■ **Implementation problems** – Typical problems associated with the solution; why they occur; preventative actions, and why your solution is superior in preventing the problems, **so you can sell consultatively and build the customer's confidence in your solution.**

■ **Selling issues** – Why sales stall; typical conflicts between functions; strategies to manage conflict positively, and how to build urgency for the solution, so **you can build momentum in the account and close the deal.**

SELL SOLUTIONS PROCESS SUMMARY

What	How	Information Required
1. Map the Buying Process Define the buying process and figure out to whom you need to sell.	1.1 Define the scope of the buying decision	How organizations make these kinds of purchases How business strategies that use the technology are implemented
	1.2 Identify decision-making style	How the technology solution appeals to different decision- making styles The urgency / commitment tradeoff
	1.3 Identify decision-making process	Technology adoption preferences for the solution Assessment of the solution's performance against buying criteria
	1.4 Identify decision-making roles and responsibilities	Job titles for decision-makers, stakeholders and gatekeepers The role of the CIO in the decision-making process Functional titles of key stakeholders
2. Personalize Solution Tailor your value proposition so everyone can see how they will benefit.	2.1 Map the solution's impact	How business strategies that use the technology are implemented How strategic business goals translate into economic, operational, and technological objectives supported by the solution ROI expectations
	2.2 Tailor the value proposition	Functional stakeholders' compelling reasons to buy Value propositions by stakeholder
3. Build Momentum Solve problems and build urgency to close	3.1 Solve problems.	Stakeholder anxieties &hot buttons Typical problems associated with the solution; why they occur Why your solution is superior in preventing problems Value build questioning strategies by stakeholder
	3.2 Build urgency	Why sales stall Typical conflicts between functions Sales strategies to manage conflict positively

HOW SELLING SOLUTIONS HELPS YOU SELL BETTER

■ **Focus prospecting faster**. Solutions selling accelerates your **prospecting** because it gets you up to speed quickly on how the technology enables new business strategies. Solutions-specific information about potential business applications and typical customer problems help you find customers likely to benefit from the technology. It also helps you figure out whom in the organization to approach and how to capture their attention with a compelling, personalized value proposition.

■ **Qualify the business need**. A clear understanding of how the solution works and its potential business benefits helps you **qualify** accounts more quickly and accurately. Information about decision-making roles and responsibilities; key needs and issues, and compelling reasons to buy helps you figure out who can help you qualify the customer's urgency, budget and needs. Solution-specific information dramatically accelerates the launch of a new solution because it enables salespeople to apply their qualification skills before they have built up enough experience with the new solution to be able to do it on their own.

■ **Ask the right questions**. Solutions knowledge is critical to a productive **discovery** process. Stakeholder-specific Value Building Questioning Strategies help you to quickly focus sales conversations on what the customer cares about. One of the primary goals of the discovery process is to educate customers by asking them the right questions at the right time. Questions that focus on the specific business needs and concerns of various stakeholders can dramatically improve the quality and effectiveness of the needs assessment process.

■ **Focus the proposal**. Business solutions expertise ensures that you **propose** the solution within the context of the decision-maker's most compelling needs. Tailoring the value proposition to the specific needs and issues of the people on the buying committee builds support for your alternative with the people who count. Also, your understanding of the solution's positive impact on the business results helps you build an accurate and compelling ROI justification.

■ **Negotiate success**. When **closing,** business solutions expertise helps you negotiate better because you know who is making the decision, what they are trying to accomplish, and the strategic benefits of the successful implementation. You are more likely to be able to negotiate better terms, secure greater commitment and justify your asking price if you can show them how your solution will help them deliver strategic results.

SELLING SOLUTIONS THROUGHOUT THE SALE

★ Use solutions expertise to capture the customer's attention.

★ Use solutions to help you qualify the customer's urgency, budget, and needs.

★ Use solutions-specific, personalized questioning strategies to educate the customer.

★ Propose the solution within the context of the buying committee's most compelling needs.

★ Negotiate better terms, more commitment, and justify your asking price.

TAKE ACTION

■ **Figure out who cares and why.** Create a solution that helps you organize how the core strategy breaks down into specific functional objectives. Then figure out who is responsible for achieving each objective and why they care about the technology purchasing decision.

WHO CARES AND WHY WORKSHEET

1. Refer to your Market Energy Map to identify the business strategies your technology enables.
2. Identify which stakeholders care about these strategies.
3. Explain why they care.

■ **Map your strategy to get to the decision-maker.** Each stakeholder has a different role to play in accomplishing the business strategy. Although your technology solution enables the entire strategy, it impacts each department differently. Figure out your strategy for getting to the decision-maker as efficiently as possible. Identify the key members of the buying committee, and associate their objectives with the strategic objectives of the decision-maker. Then write for each player personalized value propositions that you can use to capture their attention.

SOLUTIONS MAP WORKSHEET

Account _____

Solution Value _____

Proposition _____

Decision Maker
Who: _____
Why: _____
Value: _____

Strategic Stakeholder
Who: _____
Why: _____
Value: _____

Economic Stakeholder
Who: _____
Why: _____
Value: _____

Coach
Who: _____
Why: _____
Value: _____

Coach
Who: _____
Why: _____
Value: _____

Operational Stakeholder
Who: _____
Why: _____
Value: _____

Technical Stakeholder
Who: _____
Why: _____
Value: _____

Coach
Who: _____
Why: _____
Value: _____

Gatekeeper
Who: _____
Why: _____
Value: _____

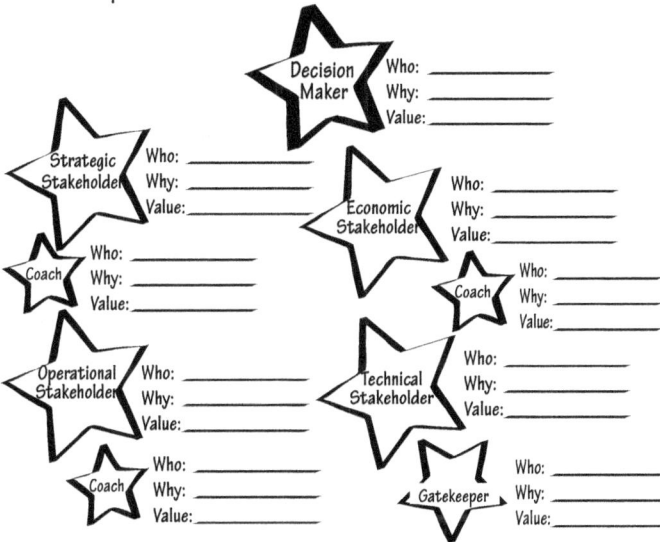

Strategies to Get to the Decision Maker

Traditional _____

Normal _____

Fastest _____

Best _____

1. Identify the key players involved in the decision-making process.
2. Identify why they care about the technology buying decision.
3. Identify value drivers for each stakeholder.

■ **Customize your sales methodology to the new solution.** Selling a new solution requires a steep learning curve because you have to integrate several different knowledge areas into your personal selling style. Customized questioning strategies and sales tools that integrate product knowledge and business expertise with the sales process help you get up to speed faster.

■ **Document issues and solutions.** As you try to sell different accounts, document the problems challenging your customers and how your solution resolves them. Each customer is different, but eventually you will start seeing trends. Share these thoughts with your peers, and you will see the commonalties even sooner.

■ **Write a personalized value proposition for each stakeholder.** Write a simple statement that clearly shows how your solution links the success of the tactical project to the overall business strategy.

PERSONALIZED VALUE PROPOSITION WORKSHEET

Who _____

What _____

Results _____

_____

How _____

_____

Why _____

1. Identify whom you are addressing.
2. Describe what the project is.
3. Describe how the results of the project support the business strategy.
4. Describe how your solution uniquely enables the desired results.
5. Describe why this benefits him or her.

■ **Develop questioning strategies by stakeholder.** Once you know how to appeal to each stakeholder, write a Value Building Questioning Strategy so it builds their anxiety and appreciation for your solution. Remember, you are the expert, not them, so you're your questioning skills to lead them through their learning process.

VALUE BUILDING QUESTIONING STRATEGY WORKSHEET

DM Role   Who: _____

_____ Objective: _____

Discovery _____

Anxiety _____

Problem _____

Solution _____

Value _____

1. Identify the stakeholder and their role in the decision-making process.
2. Describe what specific objectives they need to accomplish to contribute to the success of the business strategy.
3. Write 2-3 open questions asking the customer to describe their business strategy and the results they expect it to achieve.
4. Write 2-3 questions that raise the customer's awareness about what will happen if they don't achieve these results.
5. Write questions to help the customer analyze their problems/needs. What do they need to implement the strategy successfully?
6. Write several questions that help you introduce the relative functionality of your technology solutions that satisfies the need or salves the problem. - What if I could show you...
7. Write several questions that help the customer visualize the value created by the benefits of your solution.

■ **Build references.** References are critical when you are selling business solutions. Remember you are pitching people who have a completely different agenda than you do. They will want proof that you will be able to do what you are promising. The qualities of a good reference evolve as the market evolves. The early adopter wants proof that you are flexible, innovative and will work around the clock until her project is successful. Early majority buyers are more cautious and want proof that your solution works, can be implemented quickly, and delivers results.

■ **Share war stories.** Salespeople learn by synthesis. Sharing war stories is often more productive than giving them a process to follow. Post wins. Explain losses. Send out awards for the most embarrassing story. It is how salespeople learn.

CONCLUSIONS

■ **Walk a mile in the customer's shoes.** The solution is how customers use your technology to accomplish a goal that is important to them. The solutions selling process helps you better understand the customer's decision-making process, needs and issues so you can position your solution within the context of what is important to them.

■ **Find the buying decision in the big picture.** The benefit of selling your technology solution within the context of the customer's business strategy is that it makes the buying decision part of a larger, more important initiative.

■ **Apply technology adoption theory to adapt your selling style.** The stage of market evolution influences how decisions are made; who makes them; decision-making styles; the relative importance of risk vs. reward, and the competitive environment.

■ **Find the decision-maker.** The person responsible for the business results is the ultimate decision-maker. He probably is not a technologist. There is a good chance that you will never meet the decision-maker face-to-face.

■ **Teach and you will learn.** Solutions selling is basically a process for managing the customer's learning process, with special attention paid to how the decision will be made. It is your job to teach the right people what they need to know so they can confidently make a decision to buy your solution.

■ **Organizations don't make decisions, people do.** When you personalize the solution's benefits, you encourage stakeholders to support the decision by helping them understand 'What's in it for me?'

■ **Build momentum.** As people get closer to making decisions, they become more concerned with the risks, which slows down the process. Use outside sources of energy – market, competitive, political – to keep the sale moving forward.

■ **Trust minimizes the customer's sense of risk.** Selling consultatively means that you help your customers solve problems. You build customer awareness of their issues and their anxiety about the potential negative impact of the problems by asking them the right questions.

Chapter 5

Compete Strategically

Use Competitive Energy to Build Value

COMPETE STRATEGICALLY

What   Build competitive advantage by differentiating your solution.

Why   Competitive differentiation builds the customer's perception of the value of your solution.

How   1. Analyze the competitive landscape, so you can find opportunities where you will have a competitive advantage.

              2. Create differentiation, so you enhance the customer's perception of value around the unique benefits of your solution.

              3. Build competitive advantage, so you win the deal.

So What?   Competitive differentiation builds customers' perceptions of the unique value contribution of your solution, which motivates them to make the buying decision and increases their commitment to implementing the technology solution successfully.

WHAT IS A COMPETITIVE STRATEGY?

A competitive strategy builds the customer's perception that your solution is the best alternative to choose.

In a technology sale, competition can come from other company's products or services that offer similar technology – *Oracle's CRM solution verses Seibel's CRM solution*; internal alternatives for accomplishing the same objectives – *creating a CRM solution from scratch*; or even non technology-enabled strategies that accomplish the same business objectives – *a direct mail campaign, lower prices, etc.*

To build a competitive strategy you add the dynamics of competitive activity to what you already know about the customer, your solution, and the market. You already know what your customer needs; how your solution can help them; who is making the buying decision, and what is motivating their decision-making process. What you don't know is who else is trying to convince the customer that their solution is better than yours.

Competition improves your sales performance because it focuses you on the customers most likely to buy your solution; challenges you to consciously shape your customer's perceptions, and motivates you to build sales momentum in the account.

WHY IS COMPETING STRATEGICALLY IMPORTANT?

Competitive positioning helps you build your customer's perception of value. By analyzing the competitive landscape, you will be able to better anticipate which competitors you are most likely to find in your accounts. The threat of competition forces you to focus your efforts on the customers where you are most likely to win. It also crystallizes your unique differentiation, so you focus your customer's attention on the issues where you can contribute the greatest value.

- **Build credibility.** A good competitive strategy builds your credibility. The biggest benefit of competition is that it helps the customer make a better decision. Most people have to consider several alternatives before they are confident enough to make a decision. It is human nature. In this chapter you will learn how to help customers understand how your solution compares to other alternatives in a way that builds your credibility. If you do your job well, the customer will make a good decision.

- **Build value.** Effective competitive positioning builds the customer's perception of the value of your solution. You build value by showing how your solution enables their business strategy. If your solution is unique, you increase its value even more. Furthermore, if you can prove that other choices don't deliver the same results, your solution becomes the only choice. In this chapter you will learn how to differentiate your solutions the customer believes it is their only viable alternative.

■ **Ask better questions**. Competitive analysis focuses you on the unique benefits that only your solution can offer. This clarity focuses your questioning strategies around the issues vital to your customer's success. It also helps you write competitive 'landmine' questions, which are a clever way to undermine your competition and build the value of your solution at the same time.

■ **Sell consultatively**. Learn how to use competitive activity to build a consultative relationship with your customer. When you lay competitive traps, you raise the customer's consciousness about potential problems. Problems are good because they give you an opportunity to show the customer how your solution can solve them. When competitive traps are laid for you, the customer will ask you a lot of questions. As long as you expect them, questions are good because they give you an opportunity to explain how your solution works and its benefits.

■ **Build sales momentum**. A competitive sale is supercharged with energy. You have many more people investing resources, time, and ideas into the decision-making process than in a non-competitive situation. It is hard for a sale to get stalled when there are several aggressive salespeople doing whatever they can to motivate the customer to make a decision.   Learn how to use this energy – yours and your competitors' – to build momentum.

WHY COMPETE STRATEGICALLY?

★ Help the customer make the best decision.

★ Increase the relative value contribution of your solution.

★ Use competitive comparison to increase the customer's perception of value of your solution.

★ Use competitive energy to build sales momentum.

HOW TO DEVELOP A COMPETITIVE STRATEGY

Effective salespeople apply their competitive intelligence throughout the entire sales process. First you use your knowledge of the competitive marketplace to find opportunities where you have an inherent competitive advantage. Next you analyze your and your competitors' relative strengths within the context of the customer's needs and issues so you have a realistic assessment of your competitive power. You differentiate your solution by proving to the customer that it produces unique, superior results. Finally, you need to recognize when the competition is winning and what to do to turn the game around.

COMPETE STRATEGICALLY PROCESS

1. Analyze Competitive Landscape

   ➤ Determine areas of competitive advantage.

2. Create Differentiation

   ➤ Build customer desire around unique competitive advantages.

3. Build Competitive Advantage

   ➤ Neutralize your competitors' influence and build your credibility as a trusted advisor.

STEP 1: Analyze the Competitive Landscape

Competitive analysis helps you find 'sweet spots' of opportunity. When considering how to find new customers or sell new solutions to existing customers, competitive analysis helps you evaluate how well your solution satisfies their needs. It also helps you anticipate which potential competitors you will encounter and how well you will be able to sell against them.

Competitive advantage is always relative. In any given situation one solution does a better job. As you move from account to account, the situation changes, and so does relative competitive advantage. Because of this relativity, one solution cannot claim to be always be superior to another.

Find the source of competitive advantage.

The core of competitive advantage lies in what the customer values. As markets mature, the definition of value evolves, and, consequently, the essence of competitive advantage evolves along with it. What makes a solution irresistible to the early adopter is often a red flag to an early majority buyer. Increasingly competitive advantage is built through the completeness of your solution instead of technological innovation. This changing perception of value dramatically impacts the competitive environment as the market evolves.

COMPETITIVE STRENGTHS & WEAKNESSES

+

Turn Key Solution
Global support
Superior performance
Ease of use

Pragmatic, Reliable, Evolution

—

Obsolescence
Lack of differentiation
Impact on legacy systems

Fast time to market
Innovative solutions
Technical superiority
Innovation & Radical Change

Limited implementation options
Proprietary technology
Limited development & support

In the early market, technological innovation creates competitive advantage. Early adopters value innovation because it enables them to create new business strategies. The source of competitive advantage is found in what the new technology enables that has not been possible to do before. The inherent limitations that come along with innovation – proprietary technology and a limited supply of people who can apply the technology to build specific applications– are competitive disadvantages. However in the early market is possible to overcome these disadvantages because the visionary business executive doesn't perceive them as negative. However as the market evolves, these disadvantages become barriers to growth. As the market matures, sources of competitive advantage focus more on the ability to implement the technology solution – performance, reliability, ease of use, global reach, etc. – rather than on the technology at the core of the solution. Likewise competitive disadvantage is based on an inability to support large implementations. *For example, integrating with legacy systems becomes a huge issue in the minds of the pragmatic, early majority buyer. If you are not offering a turn-key solution or don't have access to a large pool of system integrators, then you will not be able to compete effectively against the larger competitors who do. Even if your technology performs better, you won't win the deal.*

As a salesperson you must analyze every selling situation to determine your potential to develop competitive advantage and win the business. This is a two-step process. First, you apply your understanding of what drives value to help identify your and your competitors' sweet spots. Then you evaluate your and your competitors' solutions in light of your customer's needs and issues to determine relative strengths and weaknesses.

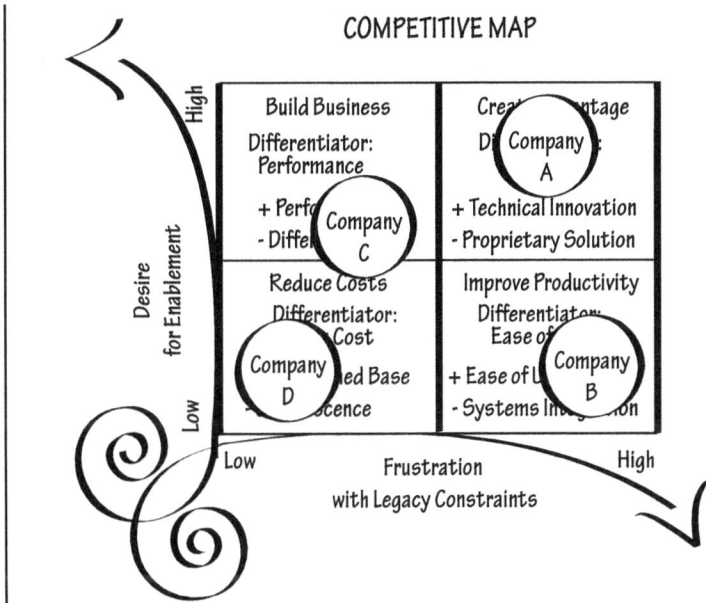

At the core of this process is a Competitive Map, which is a model of the competitive marketplace. It evaluates each vendor's competitive strengths and weaknesses and positions them within the context of what drives value in each market segment.

To build a Competitive Map, first refer to your Value Drivers worksheet to identify the value drivers in each market segment. Remember value is defined as how the technology enables the customer's strategies.

VALUE DRIVERS

	Build Business	**Create Advantage**
High	Performance Reliability Scalability	Unique Capabilities Fast Implementation Flexibility
Low	**Reduce Costs** Consolidation Strategic Sourcing Outsoucing	**Improve Productivity** Ease of Use Reduces Complexity Uses Standards

Desire for Enablement (vertical axis)

Low — Frustration with Legacy Constraints — High

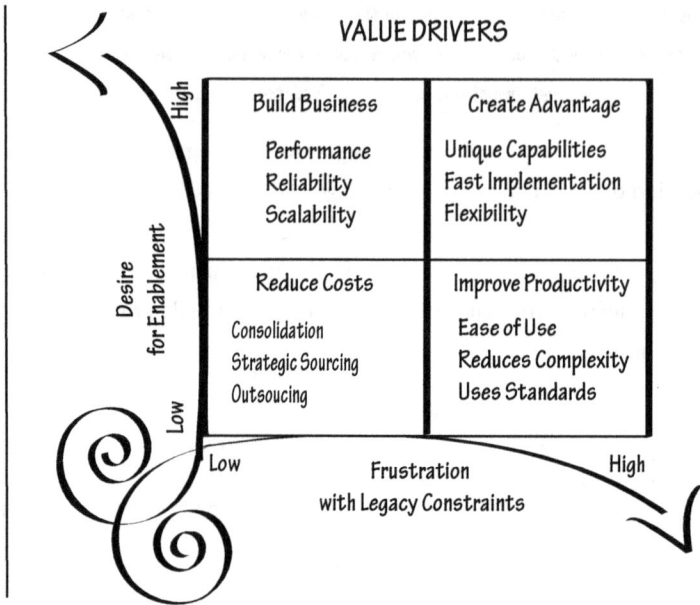

Then apply your understanding of the technology to determine what aspects of the solution build value in each market segment. This analysis tells you what factors build competitive advantage. These are competitive strengths. Then consider what aspects of the solution get in the way of building the desired value. This tells you strategic competitive weaknesses.

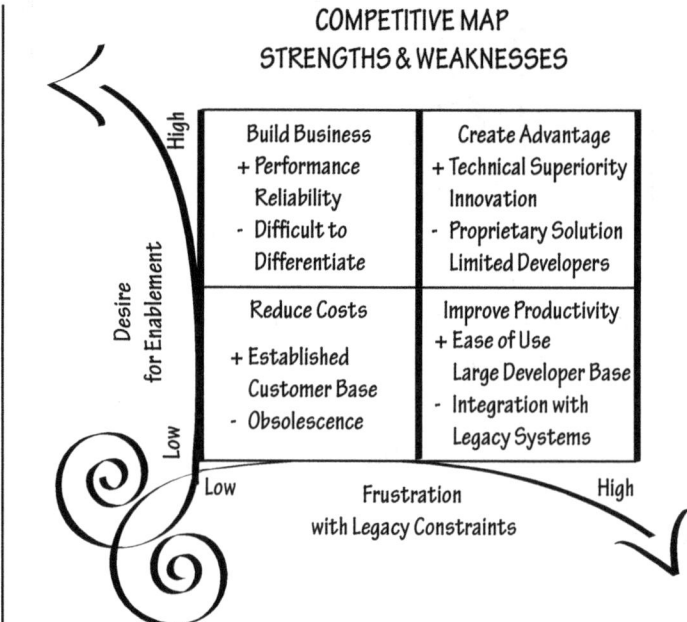

COMPETITIVE MAP
STRENGTHS & WEAKNESSES

	Build Business	**Create Advantage**
High	+ Performance Reliability - Difficult to Differentiate	+ Technical Superiority Innovation - Proprietary Solution Limited Developers
Low	**Reduce Costs** + Established Customer Base - Obsolescence	**Improve Productivity** + Ease of Use Large Developer Base - Integration with Legacy Systems

Desire for Enablement (vertical axis)

Low — Frustration with Legacy Constraints — High

Find your sweet spot.

Next, review each of your competitors' value propositions to determine where their positioning places them in the market. You will find that each competitor has a quadrant where they do the best job at building value. This is their sweet spot.

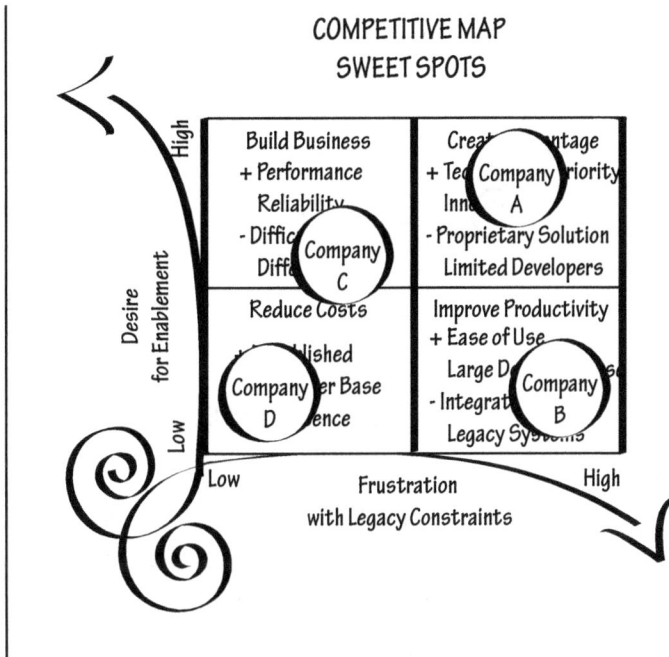

COMPETITIVE MAP
SWEET SPOTS

Understanding where your sweet spot is relative to your competitors helps you in two ways:

- First it helps you figure out where you are most likely to win a competitive contest. By comparing your Account Planning Worksheet to your Competitive Map, you can clearly see which accounts fall into your sweet spot.

- Secondly, it helps you anticipate which competitors you will encounter in which accounts. Expect to compete in any accounts found in your competitors' sweet spots. Since their value proposition targets what these customer's value, they are likely to already be there.

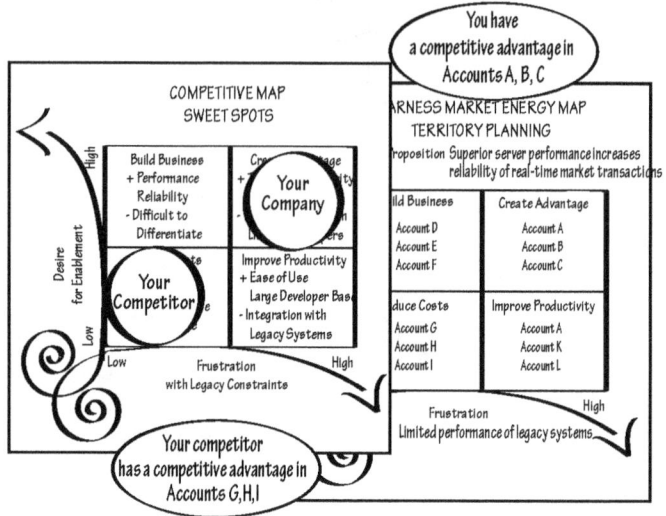

COMPETITIVE ANALYSIS
USING YOUR SWEET SPOT TO FIND OPPORTUNITIES

ANALYZE COMPETITIVE LANDSCAPE

Ask Yourself:

?   What drives value in each market segment? What creates competitive strengths or weaknesses by market segment? How will these strengths and weaknesses change as the market evolves?

?   How does each competitive solution create value by market segment? What are each competitive solutions' strengths and weaknesses in each market segment? Where is the sweet spot for each competitive solution?

?   How aligned is your company story and solution track record with the technology adoption needs in each quadrant?

Drill down to the facts with a comparative analysis.

The next level of competitive analysis is to compare the key features of each competitive solution. Drilling down from the high-level value propositions to specific functionality helps you identify the facts that you can use to prove that your solution delivers superior results.

Facts build competitive credibility. The purpose of most competitive tactics is to undermine your credibility by creating confusion in the customer's mind. If you tell them one thing and your competitor tells them a conflicting story, they know that someone is not being honest. Unfortunately, they don't always know enough about the situation to know who is lying, so they suspect everyone. When a customer thinks you are lying, your credibility erodes. Facts are the only way you can clear up the customer's confusion. If you can prove you are right with relevant facts, the customer will know that you are telling the truth. This builds your credibility, so you need to have a good supply of objective facts upon which you can build your competitive strategy.

To generate the competitive facts, refer to your Value Map. Identify the technology needs and problems generated by your customer's business strategy. Then write down how your and your competitors' solutions satisfies these needs and the resulting benefits. Be as objective as possible during this analysis. Distorting the facts to make you feel better about your solution won't do you any good when you are in the heat of the competitive battle. They will just cause you to make untrue claims, which erode your credibility even more.

COMPARATIVE ANALYSIS
ALTERNATIVE PRINTING TECHNOLOGIES

Strategy *Use color to increase effectiveness of promotion flyers*
Need/Problem *Low cost, short run, high quality color printing*

	Feature	Benefit	Strength	Weakness
Competitor A: Laser	Lower cost per page	Cheaper in the long run	Can run more promotions and wider distribution	Higher up-front cost to buy equipment
Competitor B: Ink jet	Low cost equipment	Lower up-front investment	Cheaper to try out new promotions	Higher cost per page

Let's say you want to sell a store a color printer. A comparative analysis would help you see which printing technology, laser vs. ink jet, would be the best choice.

Through this analysis you will find that, even in a competitor's sweet spot, there are specific customer needs that they can't satisfy as well as you can. Even better is when there are problems you can solve and the competitor can't. These discrepancies are where you want to focus your competitive strategy.

Solving problems is an especially powerful way to build competitive advantage. By shaping the customer's perception that the problem must be solved to ensure the successful implementation of the solution, you can make what may be a small technical point into an emotional competitive issue. Emotional problems are great ones to solve because their resolution releases a lot of positive energy into the sales process.

Look for weaknesses where the competitive solution can't satisfy the customers' needs or solve their problems because of a technological limitation. These are significant weaknesses because they are facts that cannot be altered through competitive tactics. *The higher cost per page of inkjet technology is a fact.* It is inherent in the technology.

ANALYZE COMPETITIVE STRENGTHS AND WEAKNESSES

Ask Yourself:

? What drives value in the account?

? What are the key technology needs that need to be satisfied? How does each competitive solution satisfy these needs? Which competitive solution satisfies it best? Why? How can this competitive strength be proven?

? What are the key problems that need to be solved? Who cares about this problem? How does each competitive solution solve these problems? Which competitive solution solves it best? Why? How can you build the emotional impact around solving the problem?

STEP 2: Create Differentiation

Differentiation is when your customer can easily describe what is unique about your solution and why these unique attributes make it the best choice. **The most powerful competitive advantage is when your solution uniquely satisfies the customer's compelling reason to buy.** Unfortunately, you rarely find yourself in this situation. From the customer's point of view, most technology solutions appear to be pretty similar. They don't understand the subtle differences in the technology or the impact these differences will have on their success. Your job is to help them understand and care about these differences. It is not an easy job, especially as the market matures.

As technology markets mature, they consolidate. In the early market there are lots of little companies who all have slightly different, proprietary approaches to implementing the technology. This variety of choice delights early adopters because they want to build strategic advantage enabled by unique applications of the technology. Lots of choices enable them to creatively apply the technology to building innovative business strategies. As the market matures, however, increasingly pragmatic buyers pressure the market to standardize on several viable alternatives.

Customers prefer technical standards because they make solutions easier to develop and cheaper to maintain. Technology companies like proprietary solutions because they enable them to build differentiation and, consequently, value. The conflict of 'standards-based' verses proprietary solutions generates a tremendous amount of competitive activity, which in turn generates market energy.

MARKET CONSOLIDATION

As these conflicts resolve themselves, the energy is released into the market place, which speeds technology adoption and market evolution. During this time a market leader who sets defacto standards for the technology, emerges. Once leadership is established all other competitors need to refocus their message. When you are fighting for initial position, you try to differentiate what is really unique about your solution. Once there is an established leader, all the customer wants to know is in how compatible your solution is with the market leader's solution.

However, since early and late majority buyers are rational decision-makers they want a few competitive alternatives to survive, so no one vendor has a monopoly. Therefore, along with the market leader, the market awards several other companies enough business to fuel their growth, too. This ensures customers will always have several alternatives from which to choose. It also means that every sale will be a competitive one.

Why you?

As the market consolidates, it becomes increasingly difficult for you to differentiate your solution. The purpose of standardization is to eliminate complexity by making different alternatives work together. However to do so the unique benefits of the proprietary functionality are eliminated. As the market matures and competition intensifies, it gets harder and harder to carve out a unique, differentiated market position.

To identify competitive differentiators, review your comparative analysis to find how each competitive solution uniquely builds value. Ask yourself why these solutions are unique – What do they enable that the other alternatives cannot? *The new Volvo's are the only cars equipped with side impact air bags.* Then determine the benefits the customer can expect from this unique solution. *In a car crash your children sitting in the back seat will be better protected than if they were in any other car.* If possible, quantify these benefits, so you have a very clear understanding of the potential value of the differentiation. *Since side impact air bags reduce injuries by 57%, your car insurance goes down.*

This analysis is the core information upon which you will build your competitive strategy. As you build your competitive positioning strategies consider the "whole solution." The best product doesn't always win. Sometimes the security of a well-established company beats the innovative technology of a start-up.

What differentiates technology solutions evolves as the market matures. Early in the market, innovation is often a key competitive differentiator. As the market matures, superior performance and ease of use become more important differentiators.

Once again you will find that the competitive differentiators change by market segment. In some market segments, you will be able to build your competitive differentiation, and, consequently, the value of your solution because your solution does a better job of enabling the kinds of business strategies that these customers want to implement. Of course, the same is true for your competitors.

COMPETITIVE DIFFERENTIATORS

	Performance	Innovation
	Low Cost	Ease of Use

High ← Desire for Enablement → Low

Low — Frustration with Legacy Constraints — High

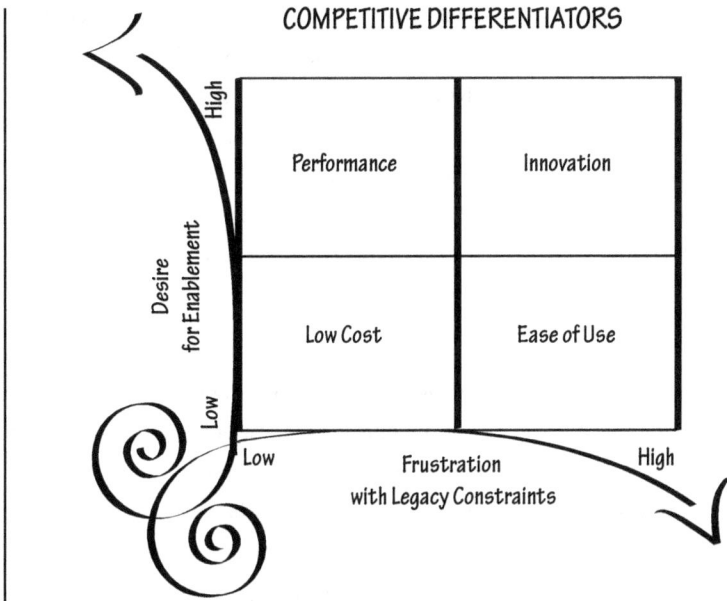

Build a competitive differentiation strategy.

You can only win points over the competition when you can offer something that your competitor can't, so build your competitive positioning strategies around the areas of competitive differentiation. In areas where your competitor has an advantage, you must plan how you can minimize the customer's perception of value around this need. Conversely, in areas where you have an advantage you need to figure out how you can make it one of the compelling issues driving the buying decisions. You do this by figuring out how to increase the emotional energy around the differentiator.

BUILDING THE EMOTIONAL SALE
SERVER TECHNOLOGY

For example, let's say your server's transaction processing performance is superior to your competitors. To build value around this need, you might call on the VP of Sales since she has bottom-line responsibility for the company's sales that the server tracks and records. Once you explain to this executive the importance of processing performance in ensuring that all the sales are recorded during usage peaks, you will probably have a passionate supporter of your solution. Although transaction performance and reliability may only be one of the many criteria in the RFP, by selling the value of this functionality to a senior business executive you have greatly heightened the emotional significance of this need.

You need to build competitive differentiation in every account early in the sales cycle. Most competitive battles are won during the discovery phase. When you are conducting a needs analysis, you have much greater liberty in asking questions than later in the sales process. Customers expect you to raise issues and quantify the impact of problems. It is part of the consultative selling process. However, they don't necessarily expect you to be building competitive advantage. They don't know enough about the alternatives yet to recognize the competitive traps you are setting. Use this short-lived innocence to build your advantage while you can.

Value Building Questioning Strategies help you to build competitive advantage. To build the competitive value of your solution, first raise the customer's pain around needs that can only be satisfied by your unique competitive advantage by asking problem **analysis** and **anxiety** questions. Analysis questions focus the customer on what is causing their problems – *'Do you understand how insurance companies take a car's safety features into account when calculating insurance rates?'* Anxiety questions quantify the impact of the problems – *'How important is it that your children riding in the back seat will be safer in an accident?'*

Then you set up the competition by asking 'competitive landmine questions,' which encourage the customer to ask the competition questions about how their solution solves the problem – *'Have you asked the dealers of the other cars you are considering about their back seat safety features?'*

IDENTIFY COMPETITIVE DIFFERENTIATION

Ask Yourself:

? Why is each solution unique? What does it enable that competitive alternatives cannot? What are the benefits of this capability?

? How does it improve the customer's ability to accomplish his business strategy? How do the benefits of this differentiator link to the ability of the customer to deliver strategic results? What are alternative ways to accomplish the same thing?

? What problems does the customer have without this capability? What are the negative impacts of these problems? Who cares about these problems?

Effective competitors are masters at the subtle art of suggestion. They use non-confrontational suggestions to lay competitive landmines and defuse competitive traps. They win by shaping customer's buying motivations and building the value of their unique solution. Really effective competitive players are rarely involved in head-to-head comparisons, because the other players never make it to the short list. They are so good at differentiating their unique value proposition that the customer believes there is only one choice.

STEP 3: Build Competitive Advantage

A good rule of thumb is to spend no more than 20% of your time on competitive issues. If you spend more than that, your energy gets directed away from the customer and is wasted in nonproductive competitive contests. Using this guideline forces you to focus your competitive activities on only the most compelling issues.

Thanks to your competitive analysis, you should be able to anticipate the key issues early in the sales cycle. Consider them as you create your sales strategy, so you build competitive advantage throughout the sales cycle.

The pecking order influences behavior.

If you represent the market leader, you can use competitive comparisons as a way to demonstrate the superiority of your solution. As the market leader you are probably well established in the most important accounts. This relationship helps you to set up the rules of the competitive game to your advantage. Thanks to your dominant position, you can get away with using proactive competitive tactics to build your competitive advantage – *writing the decision criteria to favor your solution's functionality in the RFP; gaining direct access to the decision-maker, so you can pitch your proposal over lunch instead of in a formal presentation, or suggesting how to set up the benchmarking pilot so your solution wins.*

As the market leader you have a lot of competitive power. However, over time most market leader sales teams tend to grow arrogant, which is the source of their competitive weakness. After a few years of consistently exceeding quotas and making lots of commissions, the market leader sales force gets lazy.

This is when other competitors have a unique opportunity to increase their market share through competitive selling. Because they are the underdog, they are always selling against the market leader, and after a while they become very good at it. They become experts in how to win business away from the market leader and develop all sorts of clever ways to undermine the market leader's credibility. Since they have little to lose, they take risks that the market leader's sales force would not dream of – *such as showing up at the decision-maker's office with pizza and making him an offer he can't refuse or raising show stopping issues in middle of the closing presentation, etc.* They will do whatever they can to stall the sale, so they have time to build their competitive advantage and undermine the market leader's account control.

COMPETITIVE CONFLICT
CREATES ENERGY

If you have the competitive advantage in an account, you will want to close the deal as quickly as possible. If you are in second place, you want to stall the sale so you have time to undermine the credibility of the competitive leader and build your competitive advantage. The conflict between one competitor trying to hurry the sale and the other one trying to stall it creates competitive energy. This is energy you can use to your advantage to improve your position. Conflict causes confusion, which sets up new opportunities for you to solve problems and build the customer's sense of value.

Lay competitive traps.

Strike first. There is a psychological advantage to saying something first. Whether you are convincing your customer that she cannot live without your exclusive benefits or trying to neutralize your competitor's strengths, it is to your advantage to bring the competitive issue up first. *Have you considered how much color printing would improve the response rate of your weekly promotional flyers?*

It is much easier to help someone to make up her mind than to try to change it. If you are the one to help the customer think through the issues, then you are going to be the one they trust with their concerns. In the process, you can have a lot of influence.

Use your competitive analysis and differentiators to determine the specific customer problems to focus on. *For short-run, full color printing, laser printing technology is faster, color fast and less expensive than ink jet printing.* Write a questioning strategy that builds the customer's pain around the problem. Set competitive traps by asking the customer to carefully consider how each alternative solves the problem. *Have you compared the output of the laser printer to the dot matrix printer?* Then explain exactly how your solution will solve the problem, why it is better than the alternative solutions and the benefits the customer will reap. Offer very specific benefits. Reinforce your claims with facts. *Did you know that the per page cost of inkjet printing is four times more expensive than with laser printing?* Use this opportunity to reinforce the value of your solution by showing how solving the problem will increase the likelihood that the customer's business strategy will be successful. *Since it is so much cheaper to print copies, you can afford to print more promotional flyers each week, which will in turn increase your sales.* Quantify the value contribution. It will build the customer's belief in the superiority of your solution.

Prove your competitive claims.

Sometimes the only way you can do this is to encourage a competitive comparison. If you just come out and tell customers that your solution is the only one that can deliver a certain capability, they either won't believe you or they won't perceive it as very important. However, if you can get them to talk to your competitor about whether their solution can deliver a certain benefit and it can't, but they admit the capability is important, then you increase the customer's perception of the value of your solution.

Competitive comparisons reinforce your image as the caring consultant. Not only are you helping the customer solve his problem, but also you are encouraging him to consider competitive alternatives. By demonstrating to the customer that you are not afraid of the competition, you reinforce the perception that you are working in the customer's best interest when you invite comparison. You appear strong and confident, which builds your credibility with the customer.

SET COMPETITIVE TRAPS
COLOR LASER PRINTING TECHNOLOGY

Differentiation *Lower cost, Better quality*

Discovery	*Have you considered how much color printing would improve the response rate of your promotional flyers?*
Anxiety	*Are your competitors using color in their weekly promotional flyers?*
Problem	*Four color looks great, but isn't it expensive to print?*
Solution	*The HP Laser enables you to print full color promos for about 1/4 cent per page. Would you like to see a sample?*
Advantage	*Did you know that laser printing is color fast? Have you seen an ink jet printed page when it gets wet?*
Value	*Would you I print more flyers if it cost less to do so? Would a higher quality flyer attract more customers?*
Quantify Value	*If you doubled the effectiveness of your promotions, how much would your business increase?*
Invite Comparison	*Why don't you compare the costs of laser and inkjet flyers? Why don't you leave this inkjet sample out in the rain?*

Fight back.

Just as you set traps for your customer, your customer will set traps for you. Suddenly the customer will ask you a question that you don't expect. Most likely it is a 'landmine question" planted by your competition. *So, is it true that color laser printers cost four times more than color ink jet printers?* To maintain your credibility you will need to respond immediately and use this question as an opportunity to build competitive advantage.

In these situations you have to quickly recognize the customer's attitude, figure out what is causing it, and react appropriately. In competitive situations customers generally demonstrate three kinds of negative attitudes. They either:

■ Don't know the facts about what you are offering.
■ Don't care about what you are offering, because they don't perceive a need for it.
■ Don't believe what you are saying, because you lack credibility.

Sometimes customers are just confused about your product or its benefits. Either they don't understand what you are saying, or they haven't got a clear handle on the facts. They may be confused because you are using technical jargon they don't understand, or they may have heard the same idea from a competitor who used different terminology, In this case you need to use simple language and good communication skills to clear up the misunderstanding. *Actually, our new color laser printer is very reasonably priced at $700.*

Other times the customer understands what you are saying but is confused because your information conflicts with something else that he has heard. This can happen if a competitor or another person has given the customer false or misleading information about your product. In this situation, you need to present the facts and offer proof to clear up the misunderstanding. *You need to consider the total cost of printing your color flyers. This means you add the initial cost of the printer to your operating expenses – the cost per page. When you do you will find that it is three times more expensive to use ink jet technology. Once you have fully depreciated your capital investment in the equipment, using inkjet technology is five times more expensive than laser technology.*

When customers are indifferent to what you are offering, they just don't care about what you have to say. This happens because they don't feel any pain. They are satisfied with the status quo and don't see any reason to "rock the boat." Indifference may be caused by a loyalty to a competitive company or a commitment to a legacy system. Personal needs, like fear of change or a desire for control, can also fuel an indifferent attitude. The way to handle indifferent customers is to increase awareness of their need for your solution. Use anxiety questions to heighten their pain around the problems that your solution can solve. *Have you tested the pull rates of color verses black and white printed promotional flyers? Did you know that the store down the street has just started printing their weekly flyers in color?*

The most difficult attitude to deal with is when customers don't believe what you are saying. Maybe a competitor has told them something that makes them doubt your claim, or the news media has criticized your product. If customers hear inconsistent messages, they think you are lying, and your credibility goes right down the drain. This is why your competition is always trying to confuse the customer with misinformation about your solution. Even if what they say about you isn't true, it still creates doubt in the customer's mind, which erodes your competitive advantage.

No matter what the cause, it is difficult to deal with someone who thinks you are lying. In these situations you need to offer proof. *Let me print next week's flyer for you in color, so you can see how much more powerful a color promotion can be.* Benchmarking demonstrates that you can deliver on your promises. Reference and site visits are invaluable to helping you overcome a customer's skepticism.

INFORMATION TO LAY AND DIFFUSE COMPETITIVE TRAPS

- ☑ Real world examples of traps set by competitors
- ☑ Facts to use to diffuse common traps
- ☑ Facts that quantify the value of key benefits
- ☑ Competitive press releases
- ☑ Benchmarking trials
- ☑ References
- ☑ Frequently Asked Questions (FAQ's)

WHAT YOU NEED TO KNOW TO COMPETE

Many salespeople are afraid to compete because they lack the information they need to build effective positioning strategies. Corporate competitive intelligence tends to either be too vague to be useful or too technical to easily apply to customer's business needs. Furthermore, competitors are constantly changing their strategy, so competitive intelligence can become obsolete overnight.

Very often competitive intelligence is done by product engineering or marketing people who focus on the technology's features and functionality. Although this kind of information is important, it is only one piece of the puzzle. Salespeople need a much broader view of the competition if they are going to be able to anticipate their behavior and come up with strategies to trip them up.

It is pretty easy to do competitive analysis for your solution because you have complete information. However, amassing the same amount of reliable information about competitive solutions is another story. Most companies have competitive specialists who gather, analyze, and disseminate information about the competitive marketplace. Unfortunately, these staff specialists don't have the practical expertise that you do, so you will need to verify their information with your customers, partners, and peers.

INFORMATION ➤ PERFORMANCE

Company Profile ➤ Assess your competitors' market power.

Key Messages ➤ Learn your competitors' sales pitch.

Customer Lists ➤ Understand who likes which competitor.

Target Markets ➤ Find your competitors' sweet spot.

Sales Strategies ➤ Learn to think like your competitors do.

Fulfillment Capabilities ➤ Undermine your competitors' promise to deliver.

Technology Assessment ➤ Assess your competitor's technology.

Product Profiles ➤ Determine competitive strengths and weaknesses.

Point-by-point Comparison ➤ Find areas of differentiation.

Information required to compete strategically

- **Company profile** – Company revenues, growth rates, channel relationships, ownership, capitalization, location, and key executives, **so you can assess the competitor's market reputation, reach, and resources.**

- **Key messages** – A summary of company story, market positioning, and strategic vision, **so you understand what the competitor is pitching to the customer and can determine how they will use market energy to drive their sales process.**

- **Target markets** – Strategic market segments, market share by segments, and strengths and weaknesses by market segment, **so you can anticipate competitive activity and better evaluate your chances of winning a deal in a dominated market segment.**

- **Customer lists** – Key accounts, references, key wins and losses, and replacements of competitive solutions, **so you better understand the kinds of companies that buy the competitor's solution and can figure out why the competitor wins or loses deals.**

- **Sales strategies** – Sales methodology, key positioning strategies, selling style, key partnerships, alternative distribution channels, and war stories of key wins and losses, **so you can understand how your competitors think and take preemptive action against them to diffuse the effectiveness of their strategies.**

- **Fulfillment capabilities** – Location and capacity of major production and fulfillment resources, implementation consulting resources and partnerships, etc. **so you can**

COMPETE STRATEGICALLY PROCESS SUMMARY

What	How	Information Required
1. Analyze Competitive Landscape Determine areas of competitive advantage.	1.1 Determine what builds competitive advantage	Value Drivers Competitive strengths & weaknesses
	1.2 Find your and your competitors' sweet spots	Competitors' strategic messaging, company story, target markets, customer lists Company profiles Strategic market segments, market share by segments, and strengths and weaknesses by market segment Evaluation of core technology, innovation track record, innovation style, and technical direction
	1.3 Do a comparative analysis	Description of key functionality, how it satisfies customer needs, how it resolves customer problems, and relative benefits Description of current product, future products, quality assessment, key strengths and weaknesses
2. Create Differentiation Build customer desire around unique competitive advantages.	2.1 Identify key differentiation	Identification of unique differentiators and explanation of how they build competitive advantage
	2.2 Build a competitive differentiation strategy.	Win/loss analysis Analysis of competitive replacements Competitors' sales strategies and tactics Analysis of competitors' fulfillment capabilities
3. Build Competitive Advantage Neutralize your competitor's influence and build your credibility as a trusted advisor.	3.1 Lay competitive traps	Competitive advantages Competitive questioning strategies Guidelines for inviting competitive comparison
	3.2 Compete in real time	Competitors' performance records Proof sources for your solutions Examples of competitive traps by competitor and how to handle them Win/loss analysis of recent deals Competitive pricing information

anticipate implementation issues and lay competitive traps to undermine the customer's confidence in their ability to deliver what they are promising.

- **Technology assessment** – Evaluation of core technology, innovation track record, innovation style, performance records, proof sources, and technical direction, **so you can assess competitors' technical credibility.**

- **Product profiles** – Description of current product, future products, quality assessment, key strengths and weaknesses, and cost of product, so **you can do a comparative analysis and determine relative strengths and weaknesses of the products and services that make up their solution.**

- **Point-by-point comparisons**– Description of key functionality, how it satisfies customer needs, how it resolves customer problems and relative benefits, **so you will be able to determine areas of competitive advantage around which to develop customer pain.**

- **Pricing** – Published price schedule, discounting policies, bundling, and promotions, **so you can price competitively and judge how much value you need to build to win the deal.**

You are only as good as the information you have.

Companies jealously guard their competitive intelligence. It is a valuable asset, so it is hard to get accurate, competitive information. Although a wealth of competitive information can be found in marketing literature, web sites, etc., most of the really important information is well protected. Furthermore, the competitive environment changes constantly, so all information needs to be regularly updated.

There are two great sources of competitive intelligence that are often under utilized – your customers and other salespeople. By asking your customer the right kinds of questions, they will often unknowingly tell you about your competition. Another great source is other salespeople, so figure out how to create a competitive intelligence network among your peers.

HOW COMPETITIVE POSITIONING HELPS YOU SELL BETTER

- **Find your sweet spot.** A Competitive Map focuses your **prospecting** efforts on your company's 'sweet spot.' Since it clearly shows where your strengths are and what kinds of prospects are most likely to be implementing business strategies that your solution enables, it helps you find high potential opportunities where you already have an inherent competitive advantage.

■ **Qualify harder.** Competitive strategy improves your ability to **qualify** an account. Using a Competitive Map to evaluate potential selling opportunities dramatically improves your ability to qualify accounts. Each quadrant provides you with information that helps you determine your potential competitive advantage. It also helps you evaluate how close the account is to your "sweet spot." The better you qualify accounts, the more likely they are to close.

■ **Use discovery to build competitive advantage.** **Discovery** is when your competitive knowledge and positioning skills are best put to use. In the discovery process you uncover customers' needs and encourage them to discuss the issues that must be resolved before they can make their buying decision. This is the perfect time to heighten the customer perceptions of pain in areas where you have a competitive advantage. *If the customer thinks that the car has to be blue and you sell the only blue car in town...* It is also the most effective time to lay competitive traps and diffuse any traps the competition may have been set for you. In the discovery stage needs are still emerging, and no one has become too emotionally invested in a specific solution. It is a good time to clear up misunderstandings or to demonstrate to the customer why a certain feature or function is not as important as the competitor has made them think

■ **Prove your superiority.** If you use specific information about competitive strengths, weaknesses and differentiators when you **build** your solution, you will better showcase the superiority of your solution. The perfect time to handle all of the tactical competitive issues is when you demo your solution. This is also when you use competitive comparison to force the customer to resolve competitive issues. By highlighting competitive differences around key issues, you force customers to discuss them and figure out what they want to do.

■ **Use unique value to build differentiation.** As you **propose** your solution, reinforce your competitive advantage by emphasizing why your alternative is the best one. By this point in the buying process, everyone knows who is competing against whom and the relative advantages and drawbacks of each competitive offering. In the proposal you handle the strategic competitive issues by reinforcing the value of your solution and its unique ability to enable the customer's business strategy. You also address the decision-maker's competitive concerns, which are more likely to be about strategic and organizational issues – technological vision, financial stability, implementation capability – than the specific features and functions outlined in the RFP.

■ **To the winner go the spoils.** As you **close**, it is likely you will be competing head-to-head with one or two alternative solutions. This requires applying all your competitive knowledge and skills in front of the customer. It is very important that your competitive information is current and accurate. If you are in doubt about a competitive detail, don't mention it. Competitive information changes constantly. If you use out-of-date information, it ruins your credibility, not your competitor's.

COMPETE STRATEGICALLY THROUGHOUT THE SALE

★ Target prospects whose strategy puts them in your competitive sweet spot.

★ Use competitive intelligence to qualify accounts.

★ Lay competitive traps and build pain around differentiators during discovery.

★ Prove your superiority by demonstrating the unique benefits in your solution.

★ Use your unique differentiators to build value in the proposal.

★ Leverage your competitive intelligence network to polish your close.

TAKE ACTION

■ **Create a competitive intelligence network.** Competitive intelligence is constantly evolving. Clever competitors are constantly changing their strategy and tactics. Unpredictable behavior makes it much harder to set them up. You need to have real-time access to accurate and timely information. Setting up an easy-to-use resource of competitive intelligence is critical to giving salespeople what they need to fight on the front lines.

■ **Collect proof sources.** Facts build competitive credibility. Once a competitor has sown the seeds of doubt in your customer's mind, the only way you can recover your credibility is to prove that your solution delivers on your promises. A ready supply of proof sources – references, testimonials, articles, test results, etc. – are critical to your ability to respond quickly and credibly to your customer's concerns.

■ **Practice competing in real time.** You never know when the competition will strike, so make a habit of practicing how to handle and lay competitive traps. Use your

competitive map to create a set of competitive traps and then practice setting them
with your peers. At the same time have them ask you embarrassing questions, so
you be ready to handle them when the customer 'innocently' asks you a trap that
has been laid by your competitor.

■ **Develop a Competitive Map.** Building a Competitive Map is a time-intensive project.
There is a lot of information to be gathered and significant analysis required to
make sure it accurately reflects the reality of the competitive marketplace. It is
worth the effort. However, it is unproductive to have each salesperson build his or
her own version. Commission a cross-functional team of market analysts, product
engineers, account executives, and sales engineers to build a generic version. Then
run field workshops so each sales team can customize the Competitive Map to
reflect what is happening in their territory.

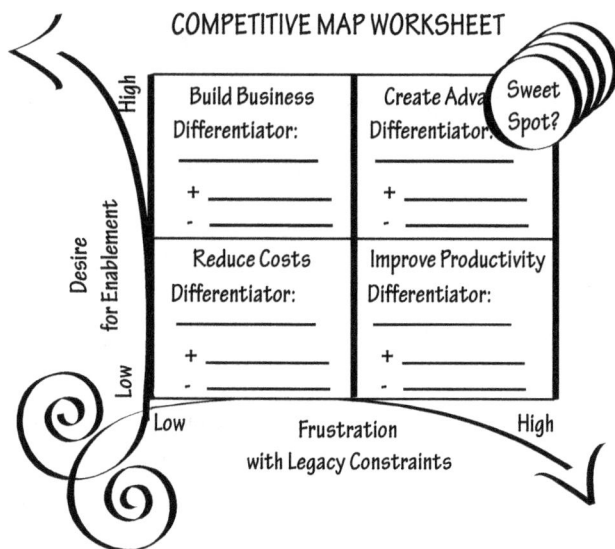

COMPETITIVE MAP WORKSHEET

Build Business Differentiator:

_____

+ _____
- _____

Create Advantage Differentiator: Sweet Spot?

_____

+ _____
- _____

Reduce Costs Differentiator:

_____

+ _____
- _____

Improve Productivity Differentiator:

_____

+ _____
- _____

Desire for Enablement — High / Low

Frustration with Legacy Constraints — Low / High

1. Refer to your Market Energy Map.
2. For each business strategy, describe the functionality
   that builds the greatest value. These are the core
   differentiators for each market segment.
3. Identify competitive strengths and weaknesses for each
   market segment. What do customers in these sectors
   perceive as providing value or creating risk?
4. Review each competitor's value proposition and locate
   their sweet spot on the Competitive Map.

■ **Write killer kits.** Killer kits are comparative analyses of each competitive solution. They include a point-by-point comparison of how each solution builds value, satisfies needs and solves problems. They also explain which alternative is the best choice and why. Killer Kits discuss points of competitive differentiation and provide facts and proof sources to support your differentiation building strategies. They are vital to being able to compete effectively. Without this kind of competitive intelligence you are fighting in the dark.

COMPARATIVE ANALYSIS WORKSHEET

Strategy _____

Need/Problem _____

	Feature	Benefit	Strength	Weakness
Competitor A:				
Competitor B:				

1. Refer to your Value Map.
2. Identify the customer's business strategy.
3. List key technology needs and problems generated by the strategy.
4. Compare how the each competitor's technology solution satisfies the needs or solves the problem. Write feature/benefit statements for each solution.
5. Then consider how they customer would perceive each feature/benefit statement based on their strategic motivation. Write down what the customer perceives as the strengths and weaknesses inherent in each feature/benefit statement.

■ **Commission a Competitive Challenge.** In Chapter 8: Discover Solutions, you will learn about Competitive Challenges, computer-based simulations that challenge you to compete for business against your most feared competitors. These simulations are great ways to build your competitive prowess and confidence. To experience a Competitive Challenge, visit www.sellresults.com.

■ **Develop competitive traps**. The best competitive traps are the ones that are laid without the customer being aware of what you are doing. Competitive traps should be integrated into Value Building Questioning Strategies so they both build pain and plant the seeds of doubt at the same time. Writing these kinds of questions requires an intimate knowledge of customer needs, the solution's value proposition and your and your competitor's differentiators.

SET COMPETITIVE TRAPS WORKSHEET

Differentiation _____

Discovery _____
Anxiety _____
Problem _____
Solution _____
Advantage _____
Value _____
Quantify _____
Value
Invite _____
Comparison

1. Identify your differentiation - How does your solution uniquely build value for the customer?
2. Write 2-3 open questions asking the customer to describe their business strategy and the results they expect it to achieve.
3. Write questions to help the customer articulate the specific problems that your solution can do better than any competitor's solution.
4. Write 2-3 questions that raise the customer's anxiety about what will happen if they don't solve these problems.
5. Write several questions that help you introduce how the relative functionality of your technology solution solves the problem. - What if I could show you...
6. Write follow up questions that helps the customer see the advantage of this particular aspect of your solution.
7. Write several questions that help the customer visualize the value created by the benefits of this solution.
8. Write questions that help the customer quantify the value of the solution.
9. Write questions that help the customer to compare your solution to your customer.

CONCLUSIONS

- **Serve your customers.** The greatest benefit of competition is that it helps your customer make a better decision.

- **Hone your skills.** Competing improves your sales performance because it focuses you on the customers most likely to buy, challenges you to shape their perceptions and motivates you to build sales momentum in the account.

- **Channel competitive energy.** A competitive sale is supercharged with energy. You have many more people investing resources, time and ideas into the decision-making process than in a non-competitive situation.

- **Technology markets consolidate as they mature.** You must win the early strategic deals to show the market that you are a serious contender. As soon as the market begins to consolidate, references become critical to building the credibility required for wide scale market adoption. Early majority buyers won't buy your solution until they can see proof that it has worked for someone else.

- **Standardization intensifies competition.** Customers prefer standards because it make solutions easier to develop and cheaper to maintain. Proprietary solutions enables technology companies to build differentiation, and consequently, value. The conflict of 'standards-based' verses proprietary solutions generates market energy.

- **See the big picture.** Many salespeople are afraid to compete because they lack the information they need to build effective positioning strategies. Salespeople need a broad view of the competition if they are going to be able to anticipate their behavior and come up with strategies to trip them up.

- **Consistency builds credibility.** Clear consistent messaging is the only way you can build credibility with your customer and in the marketplace. If your customers hear inconsistent messages they think you are lying, which is why your competition is always trying to confuse the customer with misinformation about your solution.

- **Momentum builds competitive advantage.** If you have the competitive advantage in an account you will want to close the deal as quickly as possible. If you are in second place you want to stall the sale so you have time to undermine the credibility of the competitive leader and build your competitive advantage.

- **Build differentiation.** You only win points over the competition when you offer something that your competitor can't, so build your competitive positioning strategies around the areas of unique differentiation.

Section Two

How To Do It

Salespeople don't get paid to think. They get paid to execute, so let's 'net it out.' What do sales superstars do differently?

Exceptional technology salespeople pay more attention to what is happening in the market than the rest of us. They are often the first people to see the business applications of the new technology. They prospect more efficiently and strategically. They have a lower prospect-to-close ratio because they find the best opportunities, approach line executives with compelling value propositions, and then use whatever power they can borrow to get to the decision-maker as quickly as possible. They qualify harder. If they can't build value, negotiate customer resources to develop the solution, or don't have a competitive advantage, they don't pursue the deal. They only invest their precious sales resources in the accounts where they really believe they can win.

Superstars spend more time in discovery. Once they decide to develop an account, they go all out. They outsell the competition because they pay more attention to how quickly the customer is learning. They involve the customer in the solutions building process. They solve problems. They demonstrate every day that they really care about the customer's success, and because they do, the customer trusts them. They get the inside scoop, so they know when to turn up the heat and close the deal. Sales superstars act decisively and confidently. They strike first. They play hard. In this section of **Sell Results**: *What Every Technology Salesperson Needs to Know,* you can learn to do what they do.

- ■ **Learn how to find high potential opportunities and build your competitive advantage from the first moment of contact with the customer.** A full pipeline of high potential accounts ensures you make your quota. By finding and cultivating only the best opportunities, you will sell more deals; increase your personal productivity, and improve the profitability of your business. Approaching a business executive with a compelling business proposition enables you to build credibility and cultivate a powerful, internal coach. In Chapter 6: Prospect for Energy, you will learn how to attract the attention of the right person and use him to help you penetrate the account.

- ■ **Learn how to be an expert qualifier.** Good qualification skills ensure that you will invest your limited sales resources and energy in the deals that are most likely to close. When qualifying an account, you evaluate whether the prospect is likely to buy, who will make the decision, and how difficult it will be to bring the account to closure. By making tough calls at this stage of the sales process, you greatly increase the odds that you will invest your energy in only the best opportunities.

■ **Learn how to define the unique solution that enables the customer's success.** The value of a technology is what it enables, which is different in each account. By collaborating with the customer to create a tailored application of your technology, you are ensuring that the solution will work, the customer is committed to its successful implementation and expected results will be realized. In Chapter 8: Discover Solutions, you will learn how to use the discovery process to build the customer's commitment to your solution and eliminate competitors in the account.

■ **Learn how to create an offer and orchestrate a series of events that sell your solution to the customer.** Buying an enabling technology is a complex process that requires building consensus among a wide variety of constituents and the resolution of many cross-functional issues. In Chapter 9: Propose Value you will learn how to break the buying decision down into a series of smaller decisions you can use to build organizational commitment to your solution, so you end up with a better educated and more confident customer.

■ **Learn how to close the deal so it delivers results.** During the closing negotiations it is easy to lose sight of the what it will take for the deal to result in an implementation that delivers the results everyone expects. By closing effectively, you ensure that your solution will live up to the promises you have made both to the customer and your management. In Chapter 10: Close Fast you will learn how to survive the stressful negotiating experience with your profit, reputation, and sense of humor intact.

Who's on first?

Have you ever noticed how hard it is to find the information you need when you need it? In general, you don't get the support you need to learn as fast as you need to. Most high tech training is 'death by foil'– lots of technical information put together by either engineering or product marketing that doesn't relate to the customers' needs and issues. Marketing tends to put out vague, high-level value propositions that have little practical application. Furthermore, sales information is often out of date and hard to find. By the time the training and marketing departments have written the sales training programs, the information is already old news. Since the opportunity cost of pulling salespeople out of the field is so high, sales information is often disseminated in incredibly complex web sites, where it is almost impossible to find anything. Since creating and maintaining 'sales ready' information is hard to do, most companies don't do it. They create information that is 'good enough.' But is it?

In this section of this book, you will find guidelines that make the information gathered in Section One useful. Each chapter explains how to apply information about the market, value proposition, solutions, and competition to execute a key step in the sales process, so you can use it on the job, today. NOW!

Each chapter is organized into sections that support the sales process:

- The first few pages summarize what happens in this step of the sales cycle— **'What is...'** defines the process and **'Why is understanding ... important'** helps you understand why mastery is critical to successful selling.

- Next comes the **'How to...'** section. This section explains what you need to do, why you need to do it, and how to do it. It shows you what information you need to use to move the sale forward.

- The **'What you need to know...'** section links back to the specific strategic thought processes that are discussed in Section One. If you decided to jump directly to Section Two, then it will tell you what information you need and why. (Who knows? It might inspire you to read Section One if you skipped.)

- The **'Competencies'** section summarizes all this information into a list of abilities you need to develop if you want to become an exceptional salesperson. This is your job description. If you can do all the things on the list, then guess what? You are a sales superstar!

- **'Take Action'** presents ideas designed to package strategic selling information into 'sales ready' tools. These ideas have all been field tested! They work. Salespeople love them. Use them to improve your performance. If you want to see examples of these tools, visit our website: **www.sellresults.com.**

- The **'Conclusions'** section summarizes the key points into a few pages. Hopefully, these are pages you will turn to often in the future as you integrate the ideas and techniques into your daily sales behavior.

Chapter 6

Prospect for Energy

Find the Executive Who Cares

PROSPECT FOR ENERGY

What — Find high potential opportunities, and enter accounts in a way that builds strategic advantage.

Why — Approaching an executive who cares with a compelling business proposition enables you to build credibility and cultivate a powerful, internal coach.

How —
1. Find high potential accounts, so you will be in the right place at the right time.

2. Tailor your value proposition, so you can capture the prospect's attention.

3. Develop a solution selling strategy, so you get to the decision-maker faster.

So What? — A full pipeline of high potential accounts ensures you make your quota. By finding and cultivating only the best opportunities, you will sell more deals, increase your personal productivity, and improve the profitability of your business.

WHAT IS PROSPECTING?

Prospecting is the process of finding and attracting the attention of potential customers for your technology solution.

Good prospecting ensures that you will be in the right place at the right time with a compelling value proposition. This helps you harness market energy and use it to motivate the prospect to buy. A prospecting process improves your sales productivity through better allocation of sales resources, strategic account entry, and improved timing.

To prospect effectively you apply information about the market, your technology's value proposition, and solutions selling to the process of finding opportunities and approaching accounts in a way that builds strategic advantage. To do so, you must find prospects when they are ready to buy; figure out why they need your solution; identify the optimum people to approach; capture their interest, and build enough credibility so they facilitate your penetration of the account.

Prospecting is the step in the sales cycle that has the greatest potential to improve with the right information. If you don't know what kinds of companies could benefit from your technology solution, you will waste a lot of time and energy trying to pitch your solution to people who don't care. If you don't know which business executive to call on, you will probably find yourself stuck in the IT or engineering department. However, if you have access to accurate and insightful information about the market, the solution, and its value proposition, you can dramatically improve the productivity of your sales prospecting efforts.

WHY IS PROSPECTING IMPORTANT?

Sales is a numbers game. In every business there is a prospect-to-close ratio that defines the number of prospects you need to ensure you close enough deals to make your quota. Many different factors affect your prospect-to-close ratio, including market share, product quality, brand equity, customer loyalty, market momentum, pricing, etc.

The lower your prospect-to-close ratio is, the better. If you have a high prospect-to-close ratio, you have to sell to many accounts at the same time. Since selling technology solutions is a consultative sale, working many deals at once is exhausting, if not impossible. You just don't have the time, energy, and resources to work more than a few deals, so you need to get better at finding the prospects where you have a high probability of closing. The lower your prospect-to-close ratio, the less hard you will have to work to make your number.

Fewer, better quality prospects is a much easier way to make a living. There are lots of ways to lower your prospect-to-close ratio – selling value, calling higher in the organization, competing aggressively, lowering your price, etc. However, the best way to do it is to do a better job at prospecting, which sets the stage for the entire sale. Effective prospectors not only find accounts that need their solution, they know who to approach to optimize their strategic positioning in the account. The art of prospecting is not just finding opportunities but knowing how to strategically develop them from the start.

- **Increase sales.** Developing a prospecting pipeline is the best insurance that you will make your quota. In this chapter you will learn how to build a market development plan that aligns your pipeline with the market's technology adoption lifecycle. This plan enables you to harness market energy and use it to fuel your prospecting efforts. This also increases the probability that you will knock on the customer's door early in their buying cycle, which increases your chances of winning the deal.

- **Build credibility.** Effective prospecting is the result of insightful market analysis and perceptive problem solving. In this chapter you will learn how to approach new accounts with a pitch that shows that you understand the prospect's business and have ideas about how to help them, so you immediately establish your credibility.

- **Close deals faster.** A good prospector enters a new account in a way that optimizes his/her strategic positioning. Learn how to introduce yourself as a problem solver to high-level executives, so you can quickly build rapport with people who can become powerful coaches. Business executives are in a hurry to solve their problems and produce strategic results. Staff IT managers and engineers are not. By strategically entering the account, you gain quicker access to the decision-maker and close deals faster.

- **Deliver consistent results.** Every sales manager's dream is a sales team that delivers consistent sales results in a steady upward trend. The only way you can fulfill this dream is by aligning your prospecting efforts with the market's evolution. Effective prospectors balance their pipeline so they have a steady stream of quick wins and big hits. Prospecting techniques described in this chapter will help you improve the predictability of your forecast and ensure that you will deliver consistent results.

WHY PROSPECT?

★ Harness market energy.

★ Build credibility faster.

★ Find a powerful coach.

★ Get to the decision-maker faster.

★ Deliver consistent results.

★ Increase sales productivity.

HOW TO PROSPECT FOR ENERGY

To prospect effectively, you apply market, value building, and solution selling expertise to build a pipeline that harnesses market energy. You use your market perspective to analyze the market and find high potential accounts. You also apply your understanding of the market's evolution to build a market development strategy that keeps you one step ahead of the competition.

Once you find an account, you apply your solutions selling expertise to find the most politically powerful point of entry. By applying your value building skills, you will be able to capture the attention of key stakeholders. With this executive support you will create an account penetration strategy that facilitates your qualification process and gets you to the decision-maker as quickly as possible.

PROSPECTING PROCESS

1. Find high potential accounts.

   ➤ Analyze market to find market energy.

2. Tailor your value proposition.

   ➤ Personalize your pitch, and make it to the right person.

3. Develop an account penetration strategy.

   ➤ Strategize to solve problems and qualify need.

STEP 1: Find High Potential Accounts

A high potential prospect is a company who needs your solution NOW! Ideal prospects have these following characteristics:

- A company whose business strategy can be significantly enhanced by your technology – e.g. your technology can help them implement their strategy faster, cheaper, or better.
- An executive who has a problem that you can solve with your technology in a way that accelerates the desired results of their strategy.
- A technology adoption profile that is consistent with the current stage of market evolution.

To fill your sales pipeline you need to find a steady stream of ideal prospects. The only way you will be able to do this is by developing a market perspective, which helps you be in the right place at the right time. When prospecting, this means finding early adopter prospects in the early stages of market development and a steady stream of early majority prospects as the market develops.

Analyze the market.

Technology markets develop slowly at first and then grow fast and furiously as the technology is adopted by increasingly conservative buyers. When you prospect, you can improve your success rate by targeting accounts based on the current stage of market adoption.

In Chapter 2: Harness Market Energy you learned how to use Market Energy Maps to better understand emerging markets. A Market Energy Map focuses your prospecting by identifying high potential market segments and predicting which segments are likely to buy first. It also tells you why prospects need your technology and the market trends driving prospects to adopt the new technology. You can use this information to focus your search for new opportunities and to optimize your timing when approaching new prospects.

If it is early in the market, you should be looking for early adopters. Found in the upper right quadrant of your Market Map, early adopters have a high desire for enablement and are very frustrated by legacy constraints. These are companies who are in a hurry to buy. They know that their competitive advantage depends on being first to market, so they are motivated to make quick decisions and implement

MARKET ENERGY MAP

Technology Value Proposition

Early Adopter Profile

Build Business Adoption Motivators Business Strategies	**Create Advantage** Adoption Motivators Business Strategies
Reduce Costs Adoption Motivators Business Strategies	**Improve Productivity** Adoption Motivators Business Strategies

Desire for Enablement

High

Low

Low

High

Frustration with Legacy Constraints

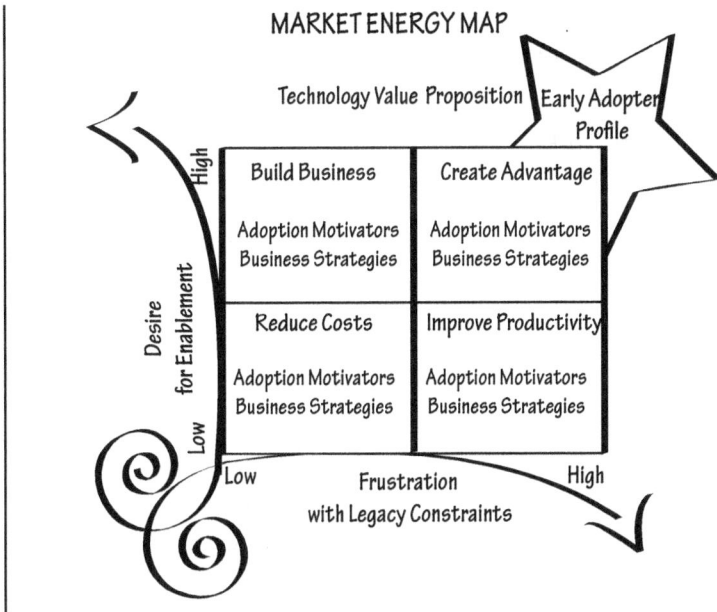

your solution as fast as possible. Early adopters fuel your growth, so the more you can find, the better.

Once you have creamed the market of potential early adopters, you need to identify and approach early majority customers. Your Market Energy Map can help you find early majority prospects very early in their buying cycle, which is the ideal time to approach them. Due to their consensus-building decision-making style, early majority sales cycles tend to be long and complex. Adapting your selling style to their buying preferences is frustrating, especially if you are in the process of selling early

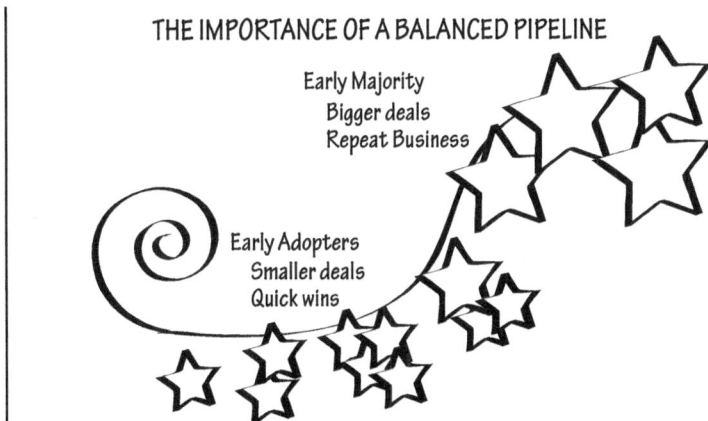

THE IMPORTANCE OF A BALANCED PIPELINE

Early Majority
Bigger deals
Repeat Business

Early Adopters
Smaller deals
Quick wins

adopters who make quick decisions. However, you need a balance of early majority
deals in your pipeline to ensure your long-term success. Early Majority buyers have
bigger budgets and are more loyal to the vendors they choose. Ideally your pipeline
will have a healthy mix of early adopters who are giving you smaller deals and early
majority buyers who will give your big wins at a slower pace.

Broaden your reach.

As you analyze the market, don't limit your search to a single Market Energy
Map. Build a series of maps combining different market trends, so you have several
market segments to explore. Look for the most powerful market drivers, as they are
the ones that are causing the greatest change in behavior and consequently the biggest
opportunities – *Internet trading, the aging of the baby boomers, outsourcing production, etc.* Market
trends create energy you can use to develop accounts. If you know what is causing
the market to change, then you can channel this energy towards prospects in order
to galvanize them into action.

Evaluate each market segment for its readiness for market adoption.
Technology adoption theory explains how prospects' compelling reasons to buy
evolve from a visionary desire to build competitive advantage to a more pragmatic
need for improved productivity. Use your Market Energy Map to identify ways that
your technology solution enables emerging strategies that build competitive advantage.
This information helps you identify potential early adopters.

Timing is a critical success factor in selling technology. Forecasting the
market's tipping point helps you anticipate when market demand will accelerate.
Building your market development strategy around when you expect the market to

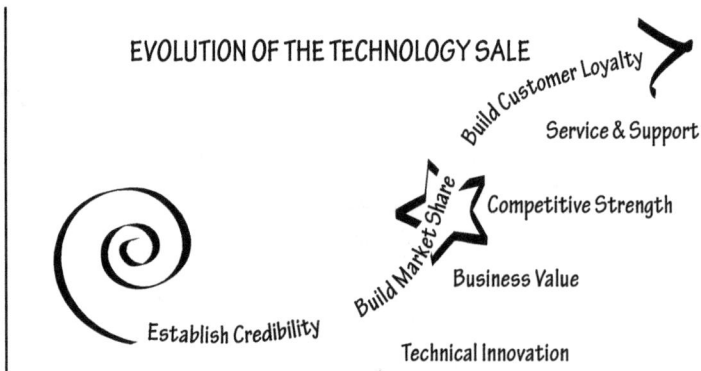

EVOLUTION OF THE TECHNOLOGY SALE

Build Customer Loyalty
Service & Support
Build Market Share
Competitive Strength
Business Value
Establish Credibility
Technical Innovation

tip optimizes your prospecting investment. If you can earn enough market credibility in the early market, you will be considered one of the primary competitors when the tipping point occurs, and you will reap the rewards of the tremendous buying frenzy driven by mass adoption.

Build a prospecting plan.

A prospecting plan guides your prospecting activities. It is the insurance policy that guarantees you will achieve your sales quota. It tells you how many prospects you need to cultivate the optimum balance between early adopters and early majority prospects and the timeline for developing your territory.

First, you need to figure out how many new prospects you need every quarter to achieve your quota. Divide your quarterly quota by the average account size. This will give you the number of new accounts you need to close per quarter. Next, use your company's prospect-to-close ratio to determine how many prospects you need to generate.

HOW MANY PROSPECTS DO YOU NEED?

$$\frac{Quarterly\ Quota}{Averge\ Size\ of\ Account} \times \frac{Prospect\text{-}to\text{-}Close}{Ratio} = \frac{\#\ of\ New\ Prospects}{/Quarter}$$

$$\frac{\$500,000}{\$25,000} \times 10 = 200$$

Once you know how many new prospects you need, you want to figure out the optimum mix of accounts, so you can align your prospecting activities with the market's evolution.

The perfect balance of early adopters and early majority prospects helps you build market momentum. Early adopters close faster, but they are usually smaller deals that use up a greater percentage of your pre-and post-sale resources. Early majority accounts have longer sales cycles, but result in larger, repeat business deals.

To figure out the optimum balance you calculate the relative percentage of early adopter to early majority prospects required to make your quota as the market evolves. Early in the technology adoption lifecycle, you need a higher percentage of smaller early adopter accounts. Later in the technology adoption lifecycle, you need to focus on fewer, larger, early majority sales. So, you need to generate more prospects early in the life of your solution than later.

BUILDING A PROSPECTING PLAN

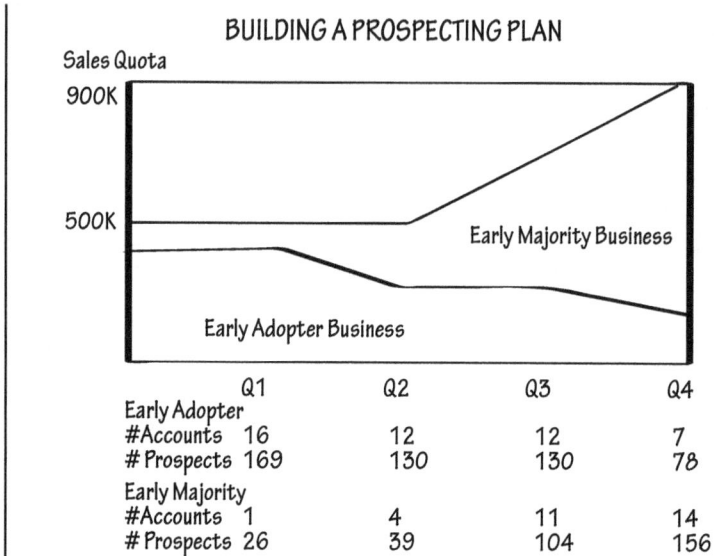

	Q1	Q2	Q3	Q4
Early Adopter				
#Accounts	16	12	12	7
# Prospects	169	130	130	78
Early Majority				
#Accounts	1	4	11	14
# Prospects	26	39	104	156

For example, let's say you are selling a new technology solution into a rapidly developing market. Your annual quota is $2.65 million. You expect that the market will tip late in the third quarter, so your quarterly quota grows from $500K in Q1 to 900K in Q4. Your average size account is $25K for early adopters and $50K for early majority accounts. Your prospect-to-close ratio averages 10:1.

To calculate the optimum mix of prospects, multiply the number of new prospects you need to make your quota by the percentage of them you expect to have an early adopter profile. So in Q1, when you expect 80% of your business to be early adopters, you need to find 169 early adopter prospects. However, since you expect that you will need early majority accounts as early as Q2, you also need to find 26 early majority prospects.

When is the right time to knock on the prospect's door? Once you have determined the optimum mix of prospects you need to figure out the optimal timing of your prospecting efforts. You need to build momentum into your prospecting so you have a constant supply of new prospects ready to buy as the market matures. By working backward from your forecast of the tipping point, you can estimate deadlines for prospecting each market segment. Early adoption represents the first 10% of the market adopting the new technology. It spans the time period between the launch of the new solution and when the early adopters' projects have been successfully implemented. The next stage of adoption, the early majority, takes about the same amount of time, yet market adoption grows from 10% to 90%. About half way through this period is the tipping point. To reap the benefits of this buying frenzy, you need to be actively selling early majority prospects while your early adopters are implementing their solutions.

FORECAST ADOPTION TIME LINE

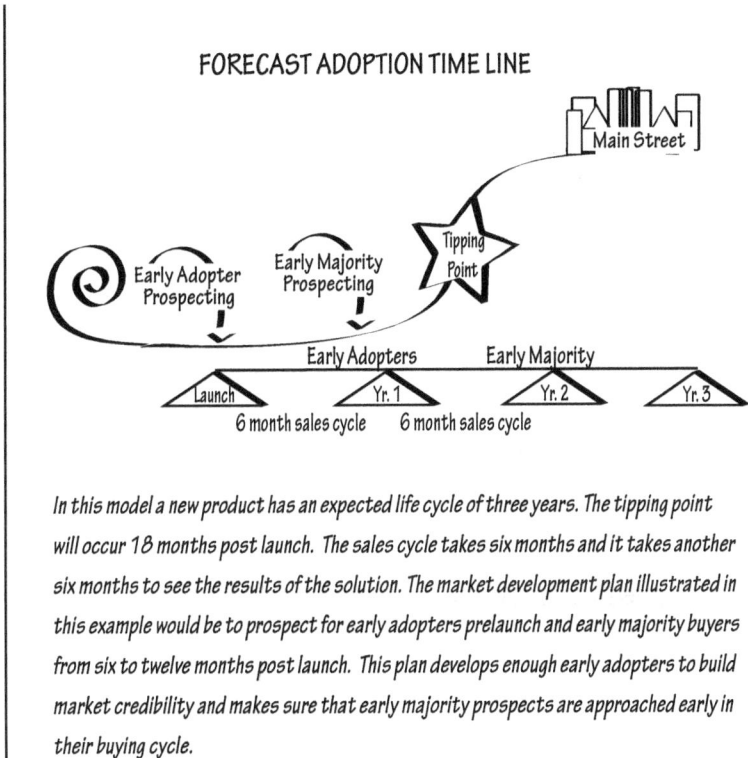

In this model a new product has an expected life cycle of three years. The tipping point will occur 18 months post launch. The sales cycle takes six months and it takes another six months to see the results of the solution. The market development plan illustrated in this example would be to prospect for early adopters prelaunch and early majority buyers from six to twelve months post launch. This plan develops enough early adopters to build market credibility and makes sure that early majority prospects are approached early in their buying cycle.

To forecast when you need to start prospecting by market segment you:

1. Estimate how long it will take from the market launch to when your early adopters have successfully implemented their first projects successfully.

2. Project the same amount of time into the future, and divide by two. This should give you a rough estimate of when market growth will begin to accelerate.

3. Subtract the length of the sales cycle to come up with a deadline for your early majority prospecting efforts. You need to approach all of your early majority prospects by that time so you are well positioned when the market begins to "tip."

STEP 2: Tailor Your Pitch

Once you identify high potential prospects, you need to figure out how to tailor your pitch so you capture their attention and jump-start the sale. Use your Value Map to determine how your technology builds value by enabling key business strategies.

VALUE MAP

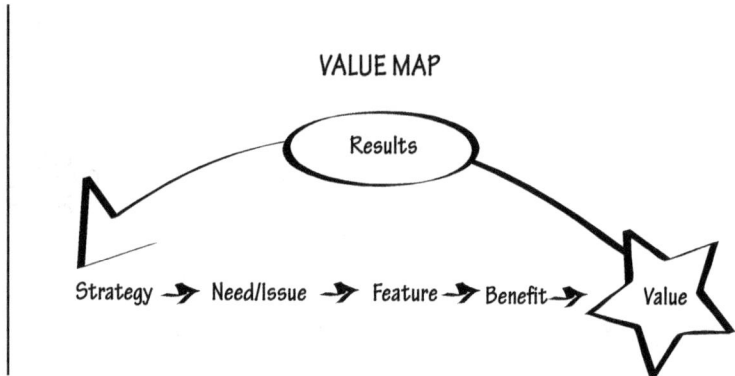

Then dig deeper to uncover typical problems organizations encounter when trying to implement these strategies. Refer to your Solutions Map to identify business executives who would be most concerned about these problems. The combination of this information provides you with a list of target executives and their potential hot buttons, and an understanding of how your solution solves their problems.

Find the optimum point of entry.

Once you know how many potential prospects you need, figure out why they might want to buy your solution. Your Value Map helps you understand the customer's compelling reason to buy and how the technology supports the customer's business strategy. A Value Map explains how companies are responding to market change. It documents the business strategies prospects are implementing to capitalize on new opportunities being caused by the changing market – *In order to accelerate the time-to-market of technologically complex products, companies must cost effectively increase their computing power, so they are migrating to GRID computing infrastructures.* It also helps you understand how these business strategies create technology needs, and more importantly, problems. *The development of technologically complex products, such as genetic engineering solutions, requires enormous computing power, which is expensive.* A list of how your technology solution solves problems is the most valuable information you can have to drive your prospecting.

Solving a problem is a great way to introduce yourself into an account because it facilitates entry at the executive level. It helps you capture the attention of the people who count. By solving problems that are linked to the prospect's business strategy, you establish credibility as someone who can help executives think through strategic issues. By starting the account relationship with the right conversation, you are positioning yourself as a business consultant who wants to help them, not a technology vendor who just wants to sell them some 'boxes.'

STRATEGIC ENTRY INTO AN ACCOUNT

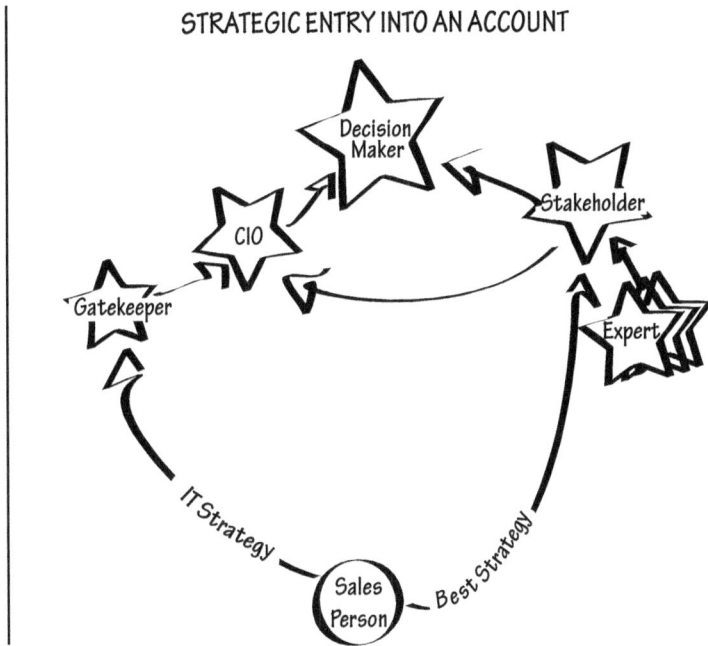

Problems also enable you to circumvent the gatekeepers that have been put into place to restrict your access to the decision-maker. It is always to your advantage to have coaches with bottom-line responsibility and authority. They are much more powerful than the staff members of the decision-making team. You can always get to the IT or Engineering departments through a coach who is a business executive, but you can't always get to the economic decision-maker through your technical contacts.

What problem should your solve? Ideally you solve a problem that optimizes your positive exposure in the account. When you solve a prospect's problem, you are giving him something of value, and in return you want something of value – **a coach**. Therefore, you want to solve the problem of a business executive who will be most likely to support your sales efforts. The ideal coach is someone who is high enough in the organization to make things happen; can provide access to the decision-maker, and has a business problem that your technology solves.

To find the business executive who has a problem you can solve, you need to consult your Solutions Map, which tells you who cares about your technology solution and why they do. A Solutions Map tells you who owns the results of the business strategy and the roles of the various stakeholders in implementing the business strategy.

The optimum point of entry into an account is a line executive who has a problem that your technology can solve. *The Chief Scientist has just won a research grant to study genetic mapping.* Ideally you want to enter the account one level below the decision-maker. You don't want to enter the account directly at the level of the decision-maker, because although you want to meet him early in the sales process, you don't know enough to have a meaningful discussion with him on the first call.

SOLUTIONS MAP
GRID COMPUTING TECHNOLOGY

Account — Genetech Engineering Solutions
Technology Value Proposition — Grid Computing offers a flexible and scalable architecture that efficiently aggregates and allocate heterogeneous computing resources. This augmented computing power improves productivity, increases computational power, and speeds time-to-market.

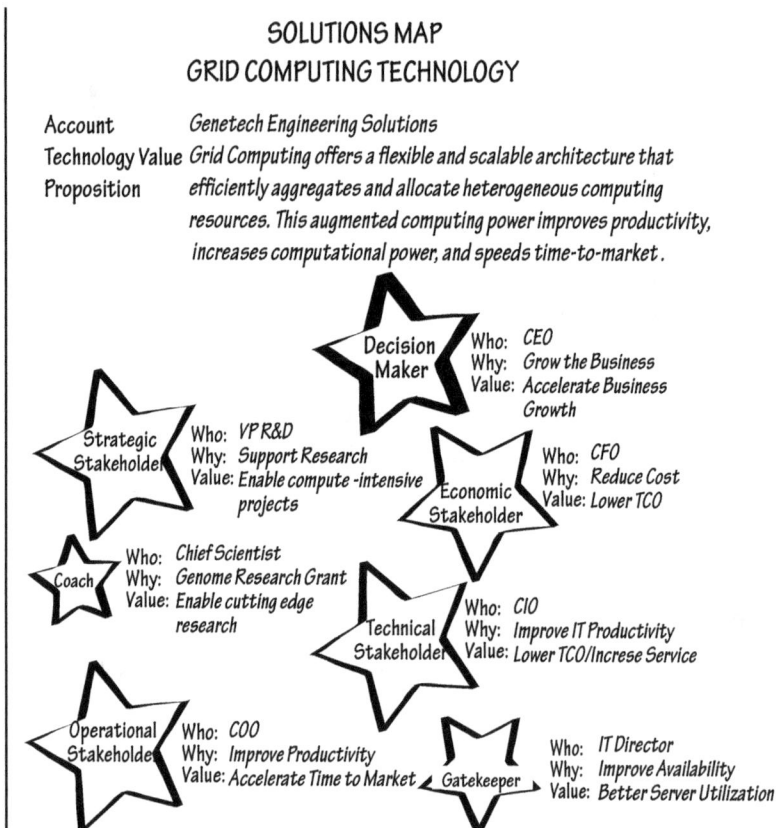

Decision Maker — Who: CEO; Why: Grow the Business; Value: Accelerate Business Growth

Strategic Stakeholder — Who: VP R&D; Why: Support Research; Value: Enable compute-intensive projects

Economic Stakeholder — Who: CFO; Why: Reduce Cost; Value: Lower TCO

Coach — Who: Chief Scientist; Why: Genome Research Grant; Value: Enable cutting edge research

Technical Stakeholder — Who: CIO; Why: Improve IT Productivity; Value: Lower TCO/Increse Service

Operational Stakeholder — Who: COO; Why: Improve Productivity; Value: Accelerate Time to Market

Gatekeeper — Who: IT Director; Why: Improve Availability; Value: Better Server Utilization

To find an ideal coach, consider the executives responsible for the major projects that deliver the business strategy's results – *the VP of R&D or the Chief Scientist.* These executives own a big part of the solution, yet are close enough to the action to be acutely aware of the problems. It has to be an executive who personally feels the pain caused by the problem, but high enough in the organization that he has the power to do something about it.

Once you know the title of your ideal coach, your next step is to research the company to confirm his commitment to the business strategy and to identify contacts who are probably experiencing the pain of problems you can solve. If you are mining an existing account, this is not really hard to do – you can probably just ask your friends in the account the right questions, and they will tell you who owns the problem. If this is a new account, seek out this information through secondary research, partner sales teams, etc. By confirming the problem before you approach the account, you are greatly improving your chances for success.

Personalize the value proposition.

Now that you have the name of who to approach, why he needs your solution, and a clear idea of the immediate problem you can solve, you need to figure out how to approach him in a way that captures his interest. Write a value proposition that identifies the problem; explains how the problem negatively impacts the successful implementation of the business strategy, and how your solution can solve it. Then embellish the value proposition by explaining how market trends are exacerbating the problem. This will heighten the prospect's anxiety about the problem, which will make him more likely to talk to you. You can further refine your value proposition

---

PERSONALIZED VALUE PROPOSITION
GRID COMPUTING TECHNOLOGY

Who	*VP R&D*
What	*By migrating to a grid computing infrastructure,*
Results	*You will be able to complete the research for your new grant twice as fast with your current number of servers.*
How	*Grid computing enables you to accelerate and complete complex, compute-intensive projects by consolidating workload management, providing capacity for high-demand applications, and reducing cycle times.*
Why	*So that you are first to market with the new products based on this important research.*

by paying attention to the prospect's technology adoption profile.

Use your value proposition to attract the attention of your target prospect. Choose the best medium to get his/her attention – email, voicemail, proposal letter – and propose the value proposition as a rhetorical questions. *What happens if your R&D group cannot do adequate research due to limited computational resources?*

Ask him to commit to a 10-minute phone conversation so you can explain how you can solve his problem. *Would it be worth 10 minutes of your valuable time to learn how a grid computing infrastructure makes it easier to transparently deploy massive amounts of new computational cycles quickly and provides your researchers with seamless access to more computational power as they need it?*

Then develop a Value Building Questioning Strategy that you can use to lead the prospect through a phone conversation that will earn you the right to make a sales call. Value Building Questioning Strategies are designed to build the prospect's awareness of the urgency and impact of problems and confidence in your ability to solve them.

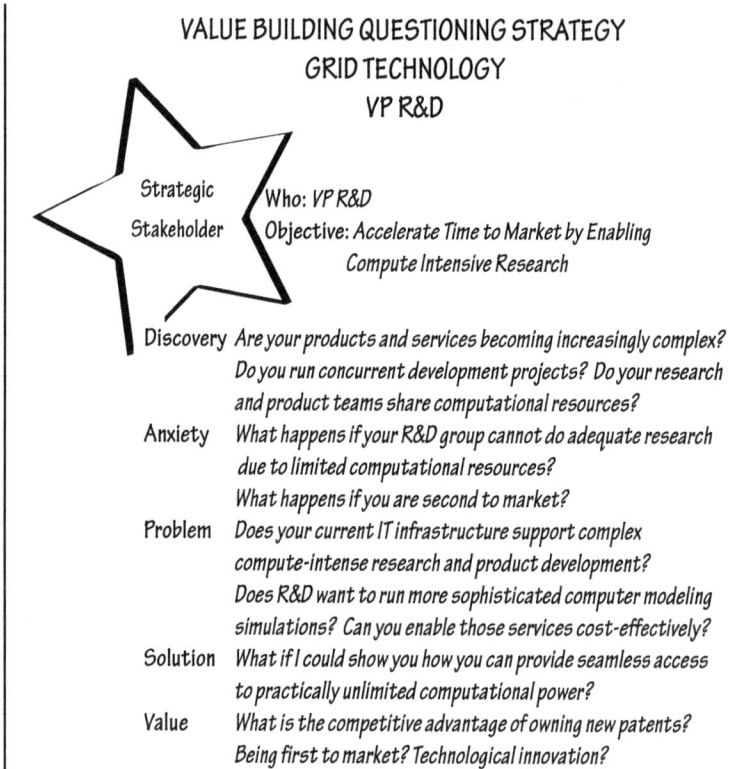

VALUE BUILDING QUESTIONING STRATEGY
GRID TECHNOLOGY
VP R&D

Strategic
Stakeholder

Who: *VP R&D*
Objective: *Accelerate Time to Market by Enabling Compute Intensive Research*

Discovery *Are your products and services becoming increasingly complex? Do you run concurrent development projects? Do your research and product teams share computational resources?*

Anxiety *What happens if your R&D group cannot do adequate research due to limited computational resources? What happens if you are second to market?*

Problem *Does your current IT infrastructure support complex compute-intense research and product development? Does R&D want to run more sophisticated computer modeling simulations? Can you enable those services cost-effectively?*

Solution *What if I could show you how you can provide seamless access to practically unlimited computational power?*

Value *What is the competitive advantage of owning new patents? Being first to market? Technological innovation?*

STEP 3: Develop a Solutions Selling Strategy

The goal of your prospecting efforts is to fill your pipeline with lots of high potential prospects. You can only evaluate if they need your project by talking to the right people. A solutions selling strategy helps you get to those people as efficiently and quickly as possible.

Approach contact with a personalized value proposition.

Use the Value Building Questioning Strategy to manage your initial phone call with the prospect. The purpose of this phone call is to capture the attention of the prospect and to get him to commit to an initial sales call. You do this by keeping the conversation focused on the prospect's problem, not your solution.

Build your credibility with the executive by demonstrating your understanding of the problem. Also, emphasize the benefits of solving the problem and how a quick and timely resolution increases the probability that his business strategy will succeed. Keep the conversation focused on the business, not the technology.

Close the phone call by first asking a few anxiety questions to help raise the prospect's sense of pain about the problem, and then suggest a face-to-face meeting where you can discuss the matter further. If you have done a good job demonstrating your understanding of the prospect's business, he will most likely commit to a meeting. Congratulations, you have made your first close!

Focus the conversation on value from the start.

The purpose of the prospecting sales call is to confirm your potential coach's problem and to convince him that you can solve the problem if he introduces you to the right people in the account. Do your homework before the first meeting. Use your Value Map to create a tailored presentation about how your technology supports the prospect's business strategy. Tailor a white paper to focus on the key issues around the solution, and show how it enables the business strategy. Focus the first sales call discussion on the executive's business and the potential value contribution of your solution.

This business-focused strategy should win the prospect's confidence. Your goal is to become a key member of his team as quickly as possible. Position yourself as someone who can help him navigate the shoals of technology discussions and decisions.

If your contact is a line executive, it is likely that he doesn't understand the problem from a technical perspective. You can offer him the technical expertise required to intelligently discuss the issues with the IT or engineering groups. This helps you become the business executive's ally. In most companies, executives don't really trust the technical departments because they have conflicting agendas, so the odds are good that the business executive will be happy to have you work with technical folks to solve his problem. Propose that you represent his interests in preliminary discussions with the IT department.

Once you convince the executive that you understand the issues and are sincerely committed to solving the problem, it is likely that he will share important information – the company business strategy, the political infrastructure, who the economic decision-maker is, technical issues and contacts, etc. – with you. You can use this information to build an account penetration plan.

Collaborate with the customer to build a plan to explore the issues and solve the problem. By positioning account qualification activities as a way for you to help the executive solve his problem, you can use his position power to schedule your qualifying sales calls. Don't leave the office without a plan and the prospect's promise to open the door for you with the people you need to talk with to qualify the account. Congratulations again; this is your second close!

WHAT YOU NEED TO KNOW TO PROSPECT

■ **A Market Perspective** helps you prospect more effectively because it builds your understanding of how market drivers interact to create change. Change creates problems, which in turn create opportunities for your new technology.

To prospect effectively, you need solutions-specific information about market segmentation, spending patterns, economic and technical drivers, and technology adoption forecasts by industry. It is also important to know about factors that may trigger a fast market change, such as the regulatory environment, demographic changes, or political events.

Salespeople need access to Market Energy Maps that demonstrate how market trends are creating high potential segments and how the buyer's motivations for adoption change by segment. Profiles of early adopters help you spot opportunities early. A market forecast of the technology adoption lifecycle and,

PROSPECTING COMPETENCIES

★ Understand the market, its size and growth, buying segmentation, supplier segmentation, spending patterns, and economic and technical trends driving technology adoption.

★ Understand the emerging strategies the technology enables, early adopter profiles, why they are adopting, and the results of early trials of the new technology.

★ Understand economic, technological, or regulatory environment and the impact of changes, such as new legislation, on existing accounts and new accounts.

★ Know who to call on, their compelling reasons to buy, and typical concerns and problems of the key stakeholders.

★ Be able to articulate the fundamental value proposition of the technology solution.

★ Be able to apply the technology's value proposition to a wide variety of business strategies.

★ Be able to forecast the market tipping point.

★ Be able to build a prospect plan that builds market momentum and technology adoption.

most importantly, the tipping point are also critical to optimizing the prospecting process and ensuring accurate forecasts.

■ **Value Building Strategies** help you better understand why prospects need your solution and how your technology enables emerging business strategies. Companies respond to market change by adopting emerging strategies and they need to buy technology to do it. Understanding how your solution enables these business strategies helps you find prospects that are likely to be early adopters.

A Value Map helps you anticipate customer needs and identify potential problems. It also helps you tailor your value proposition into a focused and compelling pitch, which breaks through market noise, captures the prospect's attention, and earns you the right to call on the prospect. Selling value opens doors.

- **Solutions Selling knowledge** helps you figure out who to call on and which value proposition will be most appealing. Use a Solutions Map to create an approach strategy that optimizes your initial positioning. This information will help you figure out who in the organization to approach and how to capture their attention with a compelling, personalized value proposition.

PROSPECT FOR ENERGY PROCESS SUMMARY

What	How	Information Required
1. Find High Potential Accounts Analyze market to find market energy	1.1 Analyze the market	Market Trends Emerging business strategies enabled by technology Strategic motivations for technology adoption Technology adoption curve and forecast of the tipping point
	1.2 Build a prospecting plan	Annual quota Estimated prospect-to-close ratio Estimated sales cycle Profile of early adopters
2. Tailor Your Value Proposition Tailor your pitch to attract the attention of the right person	2.1 Find the optimum point of account entry	Value propositions for each emerging business strategy Decision-making process for technology solution Solutions Map - Who cares and why Typical problems and issues caused by legacy technology or market evolution
	2.2 Personalize your value proposition	Technology Value Proposition How your solutions saves typical problems and issues Value Map
3. Develop a Solutions Selling Strategy Neutralize your competitor's influence and build your credibility as a trusted advisor.	3.1 Approach contact	Value Building Questioning Strategies by Stakeholder
	3.2 Strategize collaboratively	Solutions Map

TAKE ACTION

Prospecting is part of any good sales methodology. However, without the right information, even the best prospectors waste time and energy. To accelerate your time to market with a new solution, you need to create prospecting tools that specifically integrate the solutions-specific market, value, and business solutions knowledge with sales tools that facilitate the prospecting process. See examples of these sales tools at www.sellresults.com.

- **Prospecting Tool Kit.** The launch of every new solution should include a prospecting tool-kit that helps you quickly integrate the new solution into your selling conversations. The Prospecting Tool Kit uses the information in the solutions-specific Market Energy Maps, Value Maps and Solution Maps. Prospecting Tool Kits include an overview presentation that summarizes the key information about the market evolution, technology's value proposition, customer problems, and interested executive stakeholders. It should also include key metrics – such as average size of account, prospect-to-close ratios, etc. – to facilitate the development of a market penetration plan. The more practical a Prospecting Tool Kit is, the better. Salespeople learn by experience, so the best way to accelerate their learning about how to sell a new technology solution is to get them in front of prospects as quickly as possible. Ideally the Prospecting Tool Kit integrates the new solutions-specific information with the sales methodology that your company already uses – call planning, forecasts, CRM software, etc.

- **Value White Papers.** Targeted white papers that clearly explain how your technology solution enables business strategies are great tools for capturing a prospect's interest. A good white paper applies the technology's value proposition to emerging business strategies, and explains how the solution builds value, solves problems and accelerates success. Although technology companies often commission white papers, they are usually too focused on the technological aspects of the solution to be very useful to a business executive. Ask your marketing group to write a series of short (3-4 pages max!) White papers that focus on the Value Building Strategies that are described in chapter 3. The most useful white paper is one that explains the relationship between market trends, emerging business strategies, and potential problems in simple, business language. Even more useful is a template of value building arguments that the salesperson can use to easily create a custom white papers addressing the specific problems of a target prospect.

- **A Prospecting Challenge** simulates real prospecting situations and challenges you to uncover quality opportunities quickly. Prospecting games use the information found in Solutions Maps and Value Maps to simulate early calls with potential prospects. A Prospecting Challenge helps you learn about potential applications and which business executives will be most likely to respond positively to your pitch. Prospecting games are fun to play. They can be developed as group activities or as web-based simulations. Salespeople love them because they are an easy way to prepare for prospecting calls in a simulated environment. They can also be used as an organizational assessment on the sales force's understanding of how to prospect for the new solution.

- **An Elevator Pitch Exercise** challenges your ability to tailor a value proposition to a specific company or person. In an Elevator Pitch Exercise you have to articulate a two-sentence value proposition and tailor it to the needs of specific business executives. Elevator pitch exercises are a great way to internalize value building and solutions selling information. If you are able to articulate your technology solution's value proposition in the time it takes to ride in an elevator, then you are ready to call prospects on the phone. Having to 'net out' your solution's value in a variety of simulated situations helps ensure that your message is consistent and credible.

- **Stakeholder Value Building Questioning Strategies** help you develop compelling business conversations with your target executive stakeholders. Value Building Questioning Strategies provide you with the questions you need to ask prospects to develop their awareness of the potential problems they will encounter as they implement their business strategy. Good questions also help you raise their anxiety, and consequently urgency, about problems, which motivate them to solve them. Value Building Questioning Strategies also help you position your solution as a way to resolve their problems, which builds your credibility and encourages the prospect to enlist you as part of their problem solving team.

CONCLUSIONS

- **Prospect strategically.** To prospect effectively, you apply information about the market, your technology's value proposition, and solutions selling to the process of finding opportunities and approaching the account in a way that builds strategic advantage.

- **Improve your sales productivity.** Prospecting is often the most unproductive step of the sales cycle. Prospecting is the step in the sales cycle that has the greatest potential to improve with access to high quality information about the market, the business solutions sale, and the technology's value proposition.

- **Work smarter, not harder.** A prospect-to-close ratio defines the number of prospects you need to generate to close enough deals to make your quota. The lower your prospect-to-close ratio is, the better.

- **Deliver consistent results.** Targeting accounts by aligning them with the current stage of market development can improve your success rate. Ideally your pipeline mixes early adopters, who provide small, quick wins, and early majority buyers who will give you big wins at a slower pace.

- **Harness market energy.** Good prospecting ensures that you will be in the right place at the right time with a compelling value proposition. This helps you harness market energy and use it to capture the attention of the executive.

- **Call high.** Solving a problem is a great way to introduce yourself into an account. Problems enable you to enter the account at the executive level with a discussion about the customer's business strategy. Solve a problem that optimizes your positive exposure in the account. Problems enable you to circumvent the gatekeepers that have been put into place to restrict your access to the decision-maker.

- **Find a coach who cares.** The ideal coach is someone who is high enough in the organization to make things happen; can provide access to the decision-maker, and has a business problem that your technology solves. To find an ideal coach, consider the executives responsible for the strategic initiatives that deliver high-priority, business results.

- **Borrow and use power.** The purpose of the prospecting sales call is to confirm your potential coach's problem and to convince him that you can solve it if he introduces you to the right people in the account. By positioning account qualification activities as a way for you to help the executive solve his problem, you can use his position power to get the sale moving and to meet with the people who count.

Chapter 7

Qualify Potential

Focus on the Best Opportunities

QUALIFY POTENTIAL

What	Determine the likelihood of closing an opportunity profitably, productively and quickly
Why	Good qualification skills ensure that you will invest your limited sales resources and energy in the deals that are most likely to close.
How	1. Qualify your potential value contribution, so you are sure that it is an appropriate application for your technology and the prospect is serious about making a buying decision.
	2. Map the solutions sale, so you focus your sales efforts on the people who count.
	3. Decide whether to commit resources, so you increase your chances of closing a profitable deal and optimize your sales productivity
So What?	When qualifying an account, you evaluate whether the prospect is likely to buy, who will make the decision, and how difficult it will be to bring the account to closure. By making tough calls at this stage of the sales process, you greatly increase the odds that you will invest your energy in only the best opportunities.

WHAT IS QUALIFYING?

Qualifying an account is when you and your sales team evaluate the likelihood of developing a profitable account relationship by closing a specific deal and deciding whether to dedicate sales resources required to winning the business.

Qualifying accounts to find the best opportunities is the key to sales productivity. A complex sale eats up a lot of sales resources, so you need to selective about the ones you choose to develop. By using the qualification process to confirm the prospect's commitment to finding a technology solution and enlisting their support in your selling activities, you are greatly increasing the chances that you will successfully and productively close business.

To qualify an account, you determine if the prospect has a need for the solution; the money to pay for it, and the urgency to buy it. To do so, you must understand the political landscape of the account; what is compelling the prospect to buy, and the value your solution will create for the prospect's business. You also need to understand the current technological environment in the account, entrenched competitors and other factors that might impact the sales process and the probability of closure.

Ideally every account would be a win-win deal that benefits both the prospect and the vendor. For customers to benefit your solution must enable them to accomplish their business strategies better, faster, or cheaper. For your company to benefit you need to qualify an account from several perspectives – how likely the deal is to close; how profitable the deal will be, and the strategic importance of the account to your company's success.

WHY IS QUALIFYING IMPORTANT?

Sales is a limited resource game. The sales team only has so much time and energy to close a predetermined amount of business. The more productively you allocate your time and resources, the more likely you are to make your quota. The qualifying process helps you figure out where to use your precious selling resources.

Effective account qualification shortens the sales cycle by eliminating prospects that are likely to end the buying process in a non-decision. According to a sales productivity study conducted by Value Vision Associates, one-third of all sales cycles ends up with the customer not making a decision at all. "No single selling skill can have as much influence on increasing your close rate and improving the productivity of your selling resources as better prospect qualification. The biggest mistake both junior and senior salespeople continue to make is in investing their time and company's resources in prospects that are never going to buy."[1]

Assuming that you are participating in sales that never close, you are eroding by 33% your chances of achieving your quota. This is like taking every third day off to play golf! Improving your ability to qualify a prospect's commitment to making a timely and intelligent buying decision will result in improved sales productivity and greatly increases the probability of making your quota.

WHY QUALIFY?

★ Use your sales resources wisely.

★ Close deals faster.

★ Score early wins by choosing prospects carefully.

★ Find out who counts early.

■ **More productive sales team.** Good qualifiers can make an extraordinary difference in overall sales productivity and a company's profitability. Often they can cut out days of unproductive sales calls by asking the prospect's executive team about their business strategy. Learn how to combine value building and solutions selling techniques to dramatically improve your ability to accurately and quickly qualify an account.

■ **Shorter sales cycles.** When you qualify, you confirm up-front the prospect's buying cycle. Learn how to set mutual expectations about working together to make the best decision. Then use these expectations to keep the sale moving forward. It will help you drive a faster, more efficient decision-making process.

■ **Faster time to market.** When you are launching a new solution, building credibility in the early stages of market adoption is critical to your long-term success. Learn

---

[1] Sappington, Lloyd. *Prospect Qualification: Increasing Sales Productivity.* Value Vision Associates. 2002

how to identify early and quick wins, so you can build the track record you need to ride the energy wave caused by wide scale adoption of the new technology.

- ■ **Gain higher level commitment.** In the qualification process, apply solutions selling techniques so you can identify the key players on the decision-making team. This helps you focus your precious sales resources on the people who count, resulting in more wins because it focuses you on the business issues and facilitates your access to the decision-maker.

HOW TO QUALIFY POTENTIAL

The qualifying process optimizes your sales productivity, so you make your quota. To qualify effectively you use information about how your technology solution improves the value of the prospect's business strategy. Then you to verify the prospect's needs and commitment to implementing a solution. You also apply your knowledge of solutions selling to mapping the sale so you can identify the key players and test whether you will have the access to them need to sell the solution successfully. As part of the qualification process you balance your estimate of the probability of successfully closing the business against the opportunity cost of investing your sales time and resources in other deals.

Good qualification skills help you find the best opportunities. They also help you engage your technical and expert sales resources early in the sales cycle. By using their expert advice, you can gracefully avoid poor deals and enlist the enthusiastic support of key sales resources for good ones.

QUALIFYING PROCESS

1. Qualify the Potential Value Contribution.

    ➤ Verify the prospect's commitment to making a decision.

2. Map the Solutions Sale.

    ➤ Test your access to the key players making the decision.

3. Decide Whether to Commit Resources.

    ➤ Increase your chances of closing a profitable deal.

STEP 1: Qualify Your Potential Value Contribution

When qualifying an account the most important question to ask is whether or not your solution will build the value of your prospect's business. Value is always contextual. What creates value in one situation does not necessarily create value in another, so the primary purpose of your qualification sales calls is to determine the potential value contribution of your solution for a specific account.

Assess your value contribution.

To determine value you must know the prospect's compelling reason to buy. If you cannot find a direct and significant link between your technology solution and the decision-maker's compelling reason to buy, then it is unlikely that you will be able to build enough value around your solution or create enough urgency to drive the sale to a successful and timely conclusion.

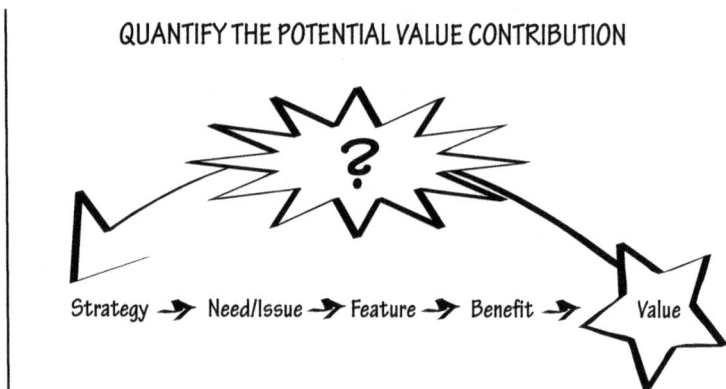

QUANTIFY THE POTENTIAL VALUE CONTRIBUTION

Strategy → Need/Issue → Feature → Benefit → Value

To uncover the prospect's needs, you need to learn as much as you can about her business strategies and how they translate into technology needs and problems. Core technologies usually support a wide range of solutions. When qualifying an account, you need to narrow the scope of what you could do down to the specific applications the prospect needs to implement her business strategy. The more specifically you can define the prospect's needs, the better you will be able to estimate the potential value of your solution.

There are several levels of qualification – sales, technical, and expert. Most account executives are generalists and don't have the technical expertise or business experience to thoroughly assess the prospect's application. In most high tech deals, a team of people qualify an important account – an account manager, a technical expert and a business applications expert. First the account manager identifies business reason compelling the customer to buy the technology and if the company has the funds to buy it. Then a technical person evaluates whether the technology solution can actually deliver the results the customer wants. Once the account manager and sales engineer have qualified the account, many companies bring in a business expert – a sales manager, product marketing executive, business development consultant, etc. – to further qualify the opportunity. Usually these people are very experienced in applying the technology. A good qualifier can often evaluate the potential for closure in a short telephone conversation with the prospect's decision-maker.

QUALIFYING THE PIPELINE

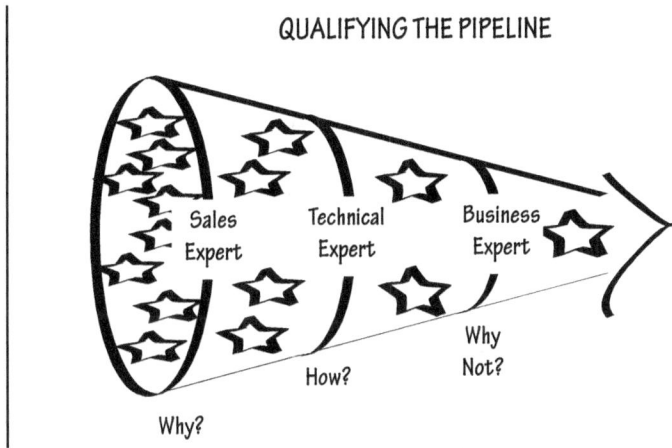

Sales Expert

Technical Expert

Business Expert

Why?

How?

Why Not?

Once you have confirmed the prospect's need and the appropriateness of your solution, you need to assess the potential value of the solution from the prospect's perspective. Although this may seem to be a straightforward process, it rarely is.

Value is always subjective. It is not easy to predict how much value you will be able to build over the course of the sales cycle, especially since you don't yet know the stakeholders' needs and concerns. However, the best indicator that you will be able to build value successfully is if you can clearly differentiate your solution. If your solution can deliver unique results, then you have a greater chance that you will both win the deal and justify a premium price.

Refer to your Competitive Map to identify the unique differentiators of your solution. Then see if they can be applied to the current sales situation. Once again, you may need to enlist the help of your technology and business experts to help you assess the potential value of your solution's benefits for this specific account. However, if your solution is unique, you will be able to build competitive advantage and the customer's perception of value, both positive indicators of your ability to win the deal.

COMPETITIVE MAP

Quantify the prospect's perception of value.

As part of the process of quantifying your potential value contribution, you need to test the prospect's pricing sensitivities by proposing logical ROI scenarios and confirming whether the current budget is realistic. Although there will be many opportunities during the sales cycle to expand the budget by selling across the organization, you need to have the confidence that there is already some kind of financial commitment to the acquisition and that the prospect has realistic expectations for the total cost of the project.

As discussed in Chapter 3, value is dependent on many different factors – market adoption, stage of the sales cycle, decision-making role, etc. Early in the buying cycle, the customer is focused on the opportunity, so it is a good time to evaluate the potential value contribution of your solution. Run a trial ROI justification to determine the financial potential of the benefits. Then use these figures to test the customer's pricing expectations. Determine if the potential value contribution justifies the price in the prospect's mind.

You can also use this discussion to confirm whether the budget has been approved for the project. If the budget has not been approved, then you need to question how serious the prospect is about buying. If the budget has been approved, then you want to find out who has the authority over the budget.

QUALIFY VALUE

Ask Yourself:

?   Does the prospect have a compelling reason to buy?

?   What is the prospect's business strategy? How does the strategy translate into specific needs and problems? How does your solution satisfy her needs and solve her problems?

?   Can you deliver a unique value proposition? Can you drive up the value of your solution? Can you quantify the value contribution? Will the value contribution justify your pricing?

?   Does the prospect have the budget? Is the budget approved? Who owns the budget?

STEP 2: Map the Solutions Sale

Now that you have confirmed the basics – there is need you can satisfy and the prospect has the money to pay for it – you need to understand the buying process and confirm her commitment to making a decision within a realistic time frame.

Most likely your company uses a sales methodology to identify and document your strategic account planning. Any methodology works fine as long as it identifies the key steps of the buying cycle; closing criteria for each step to move the process forward; the roles and responsibilities of the key players, and an estimation of the sales resources required to satisfy the process.

Define the decision.

How quickly and profitably you can sell a deal depends largely on the prospects' buying preferences, so when qualifying an account, you need to understand how the prospect wants to manage the buying process and who will be involved in making the decision.

A buying process is designed to help the prospect slowly winnow down a field of potential options to the best choice. Each company's formal buying process is slightly different. Add the vagaries introduced by informal politics and competitive tactics, and you will find that each sale is unique.

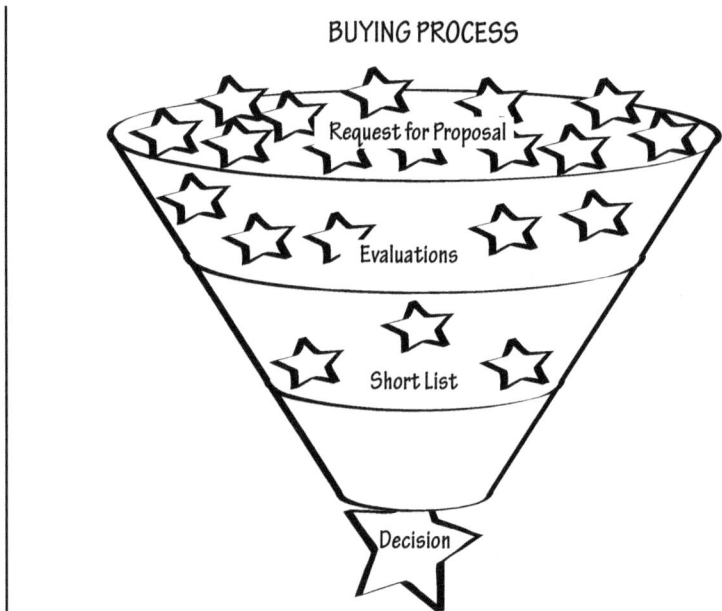

BUYING PROCESS

Request for Proposal

Evaluations

Short List

Decision

The first and most important question to answer is, "Where is the decision to purchase a technology solution in the prospect's decision-making chain?" As discussed in Chapter 4: Sell Solutions, the primary benefit of selling your solution within the context of the customer's business strategy is that it makes the technology buying decision part of a more important, strategic business process. Therefore, one of things you want to do early in the sales cycle is to confirm the business decisions that have preceded the current buying decision. If the strategic decisions have been made, then the decision to buy your solution becomes the next step in getting the job done. If, however, the prospect has not yet committed to the business strategy your solution enables, then most likely the sales cycle will be long and might not ever materialize into a sale.

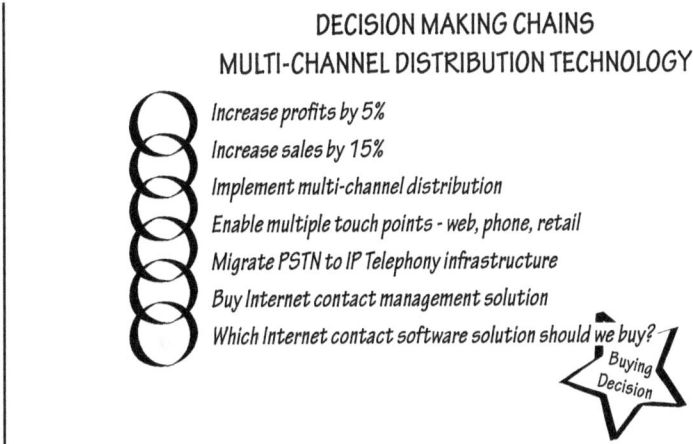

DECISION MAKING CHAINS
MULTI-CHANNEL DISTRIBUTION TECHNOLOGY

Increase profits by 5%
Increase sales by 15%
Implement multi-channel distribution
Enable multiple touch points - web, phone, retail
Migrate PSTN to IP Telephony infrastructure
Buy Internet contact management solution
Which Internet contact software solution should we buy?
Buying Decision

Discussing the decision-making chain with your prospect gives you an opportunity to confirm your understanding of the company's business strategy and its expected results. This important information helps you determine your solution's potential value contribution. Also important is whether you will be able use the company's commitment to achieving the strategy's results to increase their urgency to buy your solution.

By confirming what decisions have been made before the current one you will be able to identify all the executives who have a vested interest in the successful outcome of the solution, and find out whether they are on the formal decision-making team or not. This is very useful information because it enables you to sell your solution outside of what may be a narrowly defined decision-making team. Technology decisions, especially infrastructure purchases, are often perceived to be 'plumbing' by line executives, so they are delegated to the IT or Engineering departments. However, the only way you can sell value is by appealing to the business executive. Early identification of potential executive stakeholders enables you to call 'high and wide' from the start.

It is also important to find out the organizational ground rules for the buying decision. You need to determine the relative importance of building consensus among the decision-making team. If everyone has to agree on the decision, then the prospect will most likely make the safest decision possible. If you happen to be the market leader, this bodes in your favor. However, if you are offering a cutting edge solution, a consensus driven, decision-making process will take a long time and most likely not result in a sale. You might be better off trying to find an early adopter prospect who will be excited about the novelty of your solution and be happy to make a quick decision.

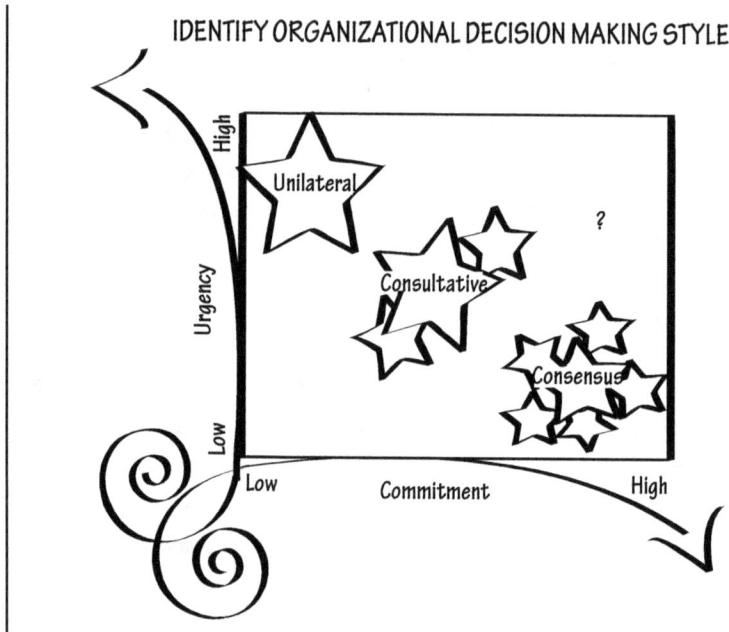

IDENTIFY ORGANIZATIONAL DECISION MAKING STYLE

Map the buying process.

To map the steps of the buying process, you need to list each sales event – RFP, executive presentations, short list qualifications, demos, comparison pilots, etc. – when it is scheduled to be completed, who will be involved in the event, and the criteria for completing it successfully. Make sure that the prospect assigns dates to each of the milestones of the decision-making process. This will give you some idea of the prospects expectations for the length of the sales cycle. (Of course these dates are likely to slip, so you probably want to multiply the sales cycle by a factor of two, but at least it gives you some idea of how long it will take to close the deal.)

While you are discussing the steps of the buying process, find out whether the prospect has already developed a Request for Proposal (RFP). If the RFP has been written before you enter the account, your chances of winning the deal are significantly reduced. Undoubtedly a competitor is already deeply entrenched in the account, and he has most likely influenced the RFP requirements in his favor.

BUYING PROCESS ACCOUNT PLANNING MAP

	Event	Responsibility	Outcome	Players	Date
1.					
2.					
3.					
4.					
5.					

Expected Length of the Sales Cycle = ?

Borrow the political clout of your coach. The best way to map the buying process is in a meeting that includes your coach and the gatekeeper who is managing the formal buying process. Use this meeting as an opportunity to confirm the roles and responsibilities of all of the key stakeholders. During this meeting stress the importance of confirming the prospect's commitment to finding the best solution, and use your coach to support your request to contact everyone on the decision-making team.

Although the gatekeeper will try to limit your access, you can use the political clout of your coach to gain the gatekeeper's approval of your initial sales activities. It is still very early in the game, and, if the gatekeeper makes too big of a fuss about limiting your access to the decision-making team, you can always choose not to pursue the deal. This is not in the gatekeeper's best interest because, at this point in the buying process, she wants to keep all of her options open. Feel free to play a little hardball in this meeting. It will help you assess how much freedom you will have during the sales process. If your hands are tied, then there is no point spending precious sales resources on an account where you probably will never be given a chance to sell.

Test your potential to negotiate.

There is a common misconception that you don't have to negotiate until it is time to close the deal. Throughout most of the sales process you work hard to convince customers that you are on their side. When you negotiate, you risk appearing adversarial, so it may seem counter intuitive to test your negotiating strength with a prospect early in the sale. However, as part of qualifying the account you need to assess whether the prospective account will be willing to work collaboratively with you, which means that they don't always get their way.

To successfully sell a technology solution, you need to be able to negotiate fairly throughout the sales process. For example, you will need to negotiate about who will attend demos and other key meetings, important decision criteria, and how many resources you will commit to help them build a solution. If you are too eager to give away valuable resources – *engineering consulting days, customer education seminars, face time with your executives and key technology gurus* – you are setting up a costly precedent for later in the sale. If you give things away too easily early in the sale, then it isn't unreasonable for the customer to expect the same behavior when it is time to negotiate the contract.

Establishing an early precedent that you expect 'fair trade' for the services you offer the prospective client – *if you schedule an executive demo, then the prospect will hold it off-site and ensure that the decision-maker shows up* – helps set expectations for later in the sales process. In the proposal phase you will take increasing control over the buying process. You won't be able to do so if you haven't already established credibility as a strong negotiator. In the closing phase the prospect's perception of your negotiating strength and power is critical to selling a profitable deal.

Test your ability to negotiate with the prospect in the qualification phase by asking for access to stakeholders. Then ask these executives to commit their resources to a needs assessment. If the prospect asks you for early concessions, make sure that you ask her for something in return. If she isn't willing to deal early when it is easy, she won't be willing to deal later, so test her flexibility and sense of fairness early in the sales process before you have invested too much of your time in the account.

Confirm commitment.

Next you want to confirm with the decision-maker and stakeholders their commitment to the strategic project that is driving the purchase of your solution. You also need to assess if you will be able to build enough rapport in the account, so they trust you. You need to test the waters to see how open they are to new ideas and how easily you can build credibility. The most effective way to do this is to engage each stakeholder in a business discussion about her needs and concerns.

Thanks to your Value Map, you have a pretty good idea of the kinds of problems various stakeholders have to deal with as they implement their business strategy. Use these problems as a way to engage each stakeholder in a short

MAP THE SOLUTION SALE

Ask Yourself:

?   What is the prospect's decision-making process? What is the level of consensus required for the decision?

?   Where is the decision in the prospect's decision-making chain? How does the decision relate to the prospect's business strategy? Can you use the business strategy to drive the prospect's urgency?

?   Who are the players in the decision-making team? What are their relative roles and responsibilities in the decision-making process? Do you have access to all of the key players?

?   Who is the decision-maker? What is the probability that you will be able to engage the decision-maker directly during the sales process? How early in the sales process can you meet the decision-maker? What is the technology adoption profile of the decision-maker?

?   Who is your coach? Can you develop multiple coaches? Will your coaches facilitate access to the decision-maker and other stakeholders? Do the stakeholders have problems you can solve to help build your credibility?

?   What are the steps of the buying cycle? Where is the prospect in the buying cycle right now? Is it too late to influence buying criteria (RFP?)

?   How flexible is the prospect? Will you have the negotiating power you need to sell productively?

phone conversation during which you present the problem, test a personalized value proposition, and confirm her commitment to the buying decision. Use your Stakeholder Value Building Questioning Strategies to help the various executives think through the issues surrounding the decision. Help them anticipate problems, and encourage them to share their concerns. Remember, the more problems you find early in the sales process, the better. Each problem is an opportunity for you to build credibility and the prospect's perception of value.

Present stakeholders with a tailored value proposition and ask them for permission to conduct discovery interviews with their team. If the stakeholders are willing to commit their resources to this next step, then there is a good chance they are serious about their role in the buying process. If they won't commit to a needs analysis, then you must determine if their reluctance stems from a lack of interest in your solution or in the buying process in general. In either case, this reaction should be a red flag for you as it portends a long sales cycle rife with political intrigue.

When you are confirming commitment is a good time to involve your qualifying expert – sales manager, business development expert, product marketing manager, etc. – in your sales process. Often you can connect executives over the phone under the guise of providing the prospect with access to a "world renown expert." Both sides get to ask each other tough questions under the guise of exploring the problem. Usually this results in improving your credibility with the prospect and in winning the approval of the qualifying expert to develop the account.

STEP 3: Decide Whether to Commit Resources

You may think that the most important task in the sales cycle is the close. It is not. The most important thing you do is to make a conscious decision whether or not to develop an account based on your qualification activities. The sales resources required to sell a complex, technical project are expense and precious. Don't waste them.

Assess risk factors.

Before you decide whether or not to commit developing the account, you need to look for any risk factors that could get in the way of successfully closing the deal, *such as an entrenched competitor, a corporate commitment to non-compatible technology standards, etc.* Although there is always the possibility that you might win in spite of these factors, they can seriously reduce your chances.

First you need to analyze the competitive environment. Use your Competitive Map to analyze the account within the context of the competitive landscape to evaluate how close it is to your "sweet spot." The closer it is, the better. This analysis helps you predict likely competitors. If the prospect's needs fall into the sweet spot of one of your major competitors, you can expect that you will be selling against them. You need to consider what the customer is looking for and if you will be able to build a unique competitive advantage.

Your Competitive Map will help you determine your relative strengths and weaknesses vis-à-vis any incumbent competitors. Ask your engineers and product experts to help you objectively analyze your competitive positioning. Then brainstorm with your sales team how you can build competitive advantage throughout the sales process.

Use your understanding of the prospect's buying process and technology adoption profile to assess how competitive the sales process will be. An analytic process led by early majority pragmatists will emphasize competitive comparisons. If you have a clear competitive advantage, this can work to your benefit. However if you don't, then maybe this is not a good opportunity to pursue.

At this stage it is easy to confirm if there are competitors in the account. Qualifying is a bit like dating. There are not a lot of expectations, and neither side has made a formal commitment to building the relationship, so you can get away with asking lots of questions about potentially embarrassing topics. Since no one has made much of a commitment it is easy to ask questions about preexisting technology platforms, which systems integrators or software packages they use and how much they like them. This information provides clues about whether there is already an incumbent competitor and the likelihood that the prospect will consider adopting your new technology.

You also want to ask about current technology standards and the company's openness to adopting new technologies. You can assess prospects' adoption readiness by evaluating how much they value your solution and its benefits. A prospect's technology adoption profile might be conservative, even though their business strategy requires an innovative technological approach. On the other hand an insular focus and commitment to legacy constraints might reduce their openness to adopting a new solution.

Your technical resources can help you predict the impact of your technology solution on the prospect's current and planned technological environment. *For example, if a company has stringent IT standards and you are selling an innovative solution requiring a nonstandard platform, you chances for success diminish substantially.* Offering an innovative, nonstandard solution is not necessarily a show-stopper. Many times the unique potential value of your solution can overcome rigid guidelines. However, you are better off recognizing this up-front and taking it into account as you forecast the probability of successfully closing the deal.

ASSESS RISK FACTORS

Ask Yourself:

?   What is the competitive environment? Are there entrenched competitors?

?   How close is the prospect to your sweet spot? Do you have a unique differentiation that the prospect values?

?   How easy will it be to build competitive advantage? Does your solution deliver greater value then the primary competitive solutions?

?   What competitive traps do you anticipate? How effectively will you be able to handle them?

?   What is the current technology environment? Do they have company standards? What is the company IT policy for adopting new standards? Can the incumbent standards accommodate the needs created by emerging business strategies?

Estimate sales resources required to close.

By the time you have gathered and evaluated all of this information, you will have a good idea of how likely you are to win the deal. However, you also need to use your judgment to determine how many sales resources it will take to close the deal. You need to consider the opportunity cost of investing in this prospect. Some deals stretch your sales resources. Long, complex sales with lots of competitive analysis and comparative trials require an incredible investment of your and your technical support team's time, so when you are qualifying an account you need to decide the relative payback of this resource investment.

This is always a difficult decision to make. Salespeople are motivated to close as many deals as possible. Sales management is motivated by the profit contribution of the sales team. This puts you at odds with your boss. In a perfect world, the final decision is made based on the strategic importance of the sale to your company's growth. In the early market, companies often choose to pursue deals that eat up tremendous amounts of technical support because they represent early, strategic wins that build market credibility. Later in the market evolution, companies want to close as many deals as easily as possible. Geoffrey Moore even suggests during the 'tornado' caused by rapid technology adoption, companies bill and ship and worry about the consequences of poor selling or implementation problems later.[3]

How long will it take to close this deal?

The final question you need to ask yourself when qualifying an account is "How long will it take to close?" You need to consider whether you will be able to build enough urgency so the sales cycle progresses smoothly and you close the deal quickly. The longer a sales cycle takes, the less likely it is to close.

Consider your energy sources for building urgency. How quickly is the market evolving, and will market momentum impact the prospect's window of opportunity? If the prospect's competitive advantage is based on being first to market, then you can use the energy created by market trends to drive the sale forward. You can also use competitive energy to accelerate the sales cycle. If you know your competitors well, you can probably predict what they will do to accelerate the sales process. Use competitive activities to energize your sales team to respond quickly to the prospect. Finally, if you have done a good job building alliances with the business executives, you will be able to use their position power and political clout to move the buying process along. *There is nothing like a phone call from the VP of Sales to light a fire under the technical review committee...* As you make your final qualification decisions, assess your ability to channel market, competitive, and political energy to accelerating the sales process and closing the deal.

Make Go/NoGo decision.

By now you are ready to predict how likely you will be to win the business. Through your qualification interviews you have determined if the prospect can buy (They have the money and commitment.) and should buy (Your solution creates value.) your solution. Now you have to take an educated guess about whether they **will** buy your solution.

There are many factors that can influence the eventual success of your sales efforts – *how long the buying process takes, availability of sales resources, competitive tactics, dramatic changes in the market, etc.* To qualify the account you need to anticipate all these factors and estimate the probability of their impact on the sale. Most sales methodologies provide complex formulas to help you forecast your business.

---

[2] Moore, Geoffrey. *Inside the Tornado,* HarperCollins. 1995

COMMIT RESOURCES

Ask Yourself:

? What is the potential for building urgency? Is there market energy? Competitive energy? Political energy?

? How fast is the market moving? Will market energy increase the prospect's urgency or pain level?

? How aware is the prospect of his problems? Can you build pain? How quickly can you do so?

? What could stall the sale? What can you do to move the sale forward if it gets stuck?

? What kinds of sales resources will it take to sell the prospect? Do you have access to these resources? Is this the best use of these resources? What is the opportunity cost of applying these resources to this account?

? How strategic is the sale to your company? What is the potential for repeat business? What is the potential to use this account as a reference to build your market credibility?

Generally, the qualifying process boils down to answering three simple, questions:

1. How sure are you that the customer will buy a solution at the price point you are selling?
2. Does your solution provide superior and unique value?
3. Do you have the sales resources you need to close the business?

As long as you can answer these three questions positively, it probably makes sense to develop the account. Support your decision by forecasting your probability of closing, the length of the sales cycle, and the amount of sales resources needed to close the deal. This helps you to estimate the potential profitability of the deal – both in terms of the current deal and the long-term potential of the account.

WHAT YOU NEED TO KNOW TO QUALIFY

■ **Value Building Strategies** help you better understand why a prospect might need your solution and how your technology enables emerging business strategies. Value

QUALIFYING COMPETENCIES

★ Understand the customer's business strategy, market positioning, and technological environment.

★ Understand the political landscape in an account – key players, decision-making process, and authorities, etc.

★ Understand at a high level the customer's compelling need for the technology and how it will enable emerging business strategies.

★ Be able to create demand by educating the prospect about the technology's value proposition and gain their commitment to exploring a solution.

★ Understand the technology adoption profile of the account, and be able to assess its readiness for adoption.

★ Confirm the available budget for a potential solution and the economic decision-maker's concerns and needs.

★ Be able to estimate the potential profitability of the account.

★ Be able to identify competitive differentiators, how they build unique value, and uncover incumbent competitors.

★ Be able to negotiate resource commitments to ensure a productive discovery process.

information also helps you quickly identify the customer's compelling reasons to buy. You use this information to verify the prospect's needs and problems and determine if you will be able to build enough value in the account to justify your price. Solutions-specific, Value Building Questioning Strategies help you anticipate the problems of the key stakeholders in the decision and to quickly build their perception of the value of your solution.

■ **Solutions Selling.** Knowing who to call on and how to tailor the value proposition accelerates your qualification efforts. When you do this during the qualification step of the sales cycle, you have an opportunity to test the prospect's commitment to the buying process by asking stakeholders to commit their resources to the

QUALIFY POTENTIAL PROCESS SUMMARY

What	How	Information Required
1. Quantify Your Potential Value Contribution Verify the prospect's commitment to making a positive decision	1.1 Assess your value contribution	Value Map Technical expertise to determine appropriateness of solution Compeittive map to define unique differentiation
	1.2 Quantify prospect's perception of value	Financial impact of adopting solution Financial impact of doing nothing Estimated total cost of implementation Size of budget allocated for project
2. Map Solutions Sale Test your access to the key players making the decision	2.1 Define the decision	Definition of the decision making chain Customer's decision making preferences and style
	2.2 Map the buying process	The customer's decision making process, key events and timeline Identify the decision maker and other key decision making roles and responsibilities
	2.3 Test your potential to negotiate	Assessment of customer's willingness to work collaboratively; actively participate in the learning process associated with making the decision, and negotiate fairly
	2.4 Confirm commitment	Value Map List of problems Stakeholder Value Building Questioning Strategies
3. Decide Whether to Commit Resources Assess your chances of closing a profitable deal	3.1 Assess risk factors	Competitive Map and Killer Kits Customer's openness to innovation and commitment to legacy standards
	3.2 Estimate sales resources required to close	Estimated amount of sales resources you will need to manage the sales process Cost per day of sales resources Potential profitability of deal
	3.3 Make go/nogo decison	Current sales forecast

discovery process. If they are willing to make this commitment, then they are serious about making a timely decision. Solutions-specific information about the decision-making process and who to involve in the buying process are critical for a quick and effective qualification process. Being able to anticipate the prospect's buying process so you only have to confirm it, helps you demonstrate your grasp of the buying issues early in the process. Also, if the prospect's buying process is very different from your company's experience in other accounts, you need to question the prospect as to why. You may find that they have not thought through the issues, or uncover some show stopping factors, like incumbent competitors or technology limitations.

■ **Technology Knowledge & Competitive Intelligence** It is important that you involve the technical members of the sales team in your account qualification activities so you can use their technology expertise to determine if the solution can be cost-effectively implemented in the account. A technical expert armed with competitive intelligence can also uncover incumbent competitors and identify if you need to bring in technology partners to broaden the solution or lower the risks of implementation. Using a Competitive Map to help you the determine unique differentiators you can use to build value is also very useful when you are qualifying. It also helps you identify how close the prospect's needs are to your sweet spot and the sources of competitive advantage, both good indicators of your ability to win the deal.

TAKE ACTION

During the qualifying stage, you are trying to do two things – figure out if the account can be developed profitability and productively and earn the right to move the sales process forward into the discovery stage. Although most technology sales teams know how to do this in theory, to do this with new content is very challenging. The following sales tools are designed to make it easier to apply your generic questioning and analytic skills so you can qualify opportunities faster and more efficiently. The faster an account is qualified, the sooner you can move on to the actual selling.

■ **A Qualifying Guide** provides you with an annotated checklist of buying criteria. The guide should include an overview of the buying roles and responsibilities of the key stakeholders – economic, operational, financial, and technological – likely to be involved in the decision-making process. It should list the various job titles, scope of responsibilities, key needs, typical concerns, and how they contribute to the successful implementation of the key business strategies. It should also include information that helps you verify an appropriate budget, confirm the buying cycle, schedule milestones, and assess any risk factors that could impact the sale. The guide should also provide strategic guidelines for estimating the potential profitability of the sale, opportunity costs of dedicated sales resources, and how to forecast the account.

■ **Solutions Selling Overview Presentation.** A short, succinct overview presentation of how to sell the solution is very useful. This presentation should link the information included in your Value Map to the information contained in the Solutions Map. It should include a overview of the business strategies that the technology enables and the results a business executive expects to see when the strategy is successfully implemented. Each business strategy should be described by the strategic, financial, operational, and technological objectives it generates and identifies the executives responsible for achieving these objectives. This information helps you identify the decision-makers and key stakeholders who are likely to be involved in the prospects' decision-making process. The presentation should also identify the each stakeholder's key problems, how the solution solves them, and delivers benefits that increase the prospect's sense of value. It is also very helpful to include success stories that illustrate how the technology solution has enabled similar business initiatives in other accounts. Salespeople learn through association, so including successful war stories is a great way to reinforce their understanding of the solution and help them spot similar opportunities when they come across them.

■ **A Technology and Solutions Overview Presentation** provides salespeople with an overview of what the solution is, how it works, and how it enables key business strategies. It should include a high level, graphic explanation of the fundamental technology and how these technologies are applied to create practical solutions for customers. It should include a summary of its key features and the benefits of these features within the context of implementing business solutions. It should also list the key differentiators of the solution, emphasizing how they provide unique value for the customer. It is important to remember that at this point of the sales process it is better to have a little bit of practical knowledge rather than a lot of profound technological expertise. If you need a thorough technological assessment of the situation to qualify the account, then bring in a sales engineer or product expert. Don't waste your time on verifying all of the technical requirements of the RFP until you are sure that the business executives are committed to buying a solution.

■ **ROI Value Calculator.** Since the primary goal of the qualification process is to determine the potential value contribution of your solution to the prospect's business, it is very helpful to have a sales tool to calculate the prospect's return on investment. During the qualification stage you do not need to do an in-depth ROI justification. You just need to be able to 'ball-park' what the solution will cost the customer to implement; how quickly the customer can expect a payback, and the scope of the financial benefits he can expect. The reason you want to estimate this early in the sales process is because it helps you evaluate whether the prospect's budget is appropriate to the scope of the project.

■ **Competitive Map.** Although you don't need in-depth competitive intelligence during the qualification stage of the sales cycle, it is helpful to be able to anticipate whether or not you will be able to build competitive advantage. A Competitive Map documents your and potential competitor's relative sweet spots and locates where the prospect's needs put them on the map. This helps you identify and verify any significant competitive issues. The Competitive Map is also useful in helping you assess if either you or a competitor has a unique value proposition that could swing the deal.

■ **A Value Challenge** is a simulation that teaches you how to quickly uncover stakeholders issues and tests your ability to apply Value Building Questioning Strategies to solutions-specific problems. In a Value Challenge game you apply your value building knowledge to uncovering potential problems; building anxiety about the impact of the problems; proposing a solution, and building the customer's perception of the value of your solution by selling its benefits. If you are successful in anticipating and addressing the prospect's hot buttons, you will win their approval to include their teams in your discovery process. You also must uncover potential show-stoppers. The goal of the simulation is to use your qualification skills and product knowledge to build the highest potential pipeline of accounts. Like the Prospecting Challenge described in the previous chapter, the Value Challenge is a solutions-specific simulation that is fun to play and builds confidence that you will be able to conduct account qualification sales calls successfully. It can also be used as a way to assess the entire sales team's mastery of new solutions-specific, product knowledge and its ability to qualify new accounts.

CONCLUSIONS

■ **Walk in the prospect's shoes.** The most important question to ask in qualifying an account is whether or not your solution will build the value of your prospect's business. To determine value, you will need to clarify the customer's business strategy and understand how this strategy will be implemented through tactical projects.

■ **Value, Time, Money...** To qualify an account, you determine if the prospect has a need for the solution, the money to pay for the solution, and the urgency to buy it.

■ **See the big picture.** You need to qualify an account from several perspectives – how likely the deal is to close; how profitable the deal will be, and its strategic importance of the account to your company's success.

■ **Three heads qualify better than one.** In most high tech deals, it takes a team of people to qualify the account – an account manager, technical expert, and a business expert.

■ **Why you?** One of your objectives in qualifying an account is to determine how unique your value proposition is for this account. If your solution can deliver unique results, then you have a greater chance that you will win the deal and justify a premium price.

■ **What is the process?** To qualify an account you need to understand how the prospect wants to manage the buying process and who the key players involved in making the decision are. It is important to find out the ground rules for the buying decision. You must also confirm the steps of the buying cycle and how far along the prospect is in developing decision criteria.

■ **Test the waters.** Use the qualification process as a way to present stakeholders with a tailored value proposition, and ask them for permission to conduct a discovery around their issues. If the stakeholders are willing to commit to this next step, then there is a good chance they are serious about the buying process.

■ **Will they trust you?** Part of the qualification process is also to figure out if you will be able to build enough rapport in the account, so they trust you. You need to test the waters to see how open they are to new ideas and how easily you can build credibility.

■ **Sales is a limited resource game.** A complex sale eats up a lot of sales resources, so you need to selective about the ones you choose to develop. The more productively you allocate your time and resources, the more likely you are to make your quota.

■ **What is the opportunity cost?** When making the Go/No Go decision, use your judgment to determine how many sales resources it will take to close the deal, and consider the opportunity cost of investing in this account.

■ **Where is the energy coming from?** Assess your ability to channel market, competitive, and political energy to accelerate the sales process and close the deal. Determine if you can create enough urgency in the account that the sales cycle progresses smoothly, and you will be able to close it as quickly as possible. The longer a sales cycle takes, the less likely it is to close.

■ **In a perfect world**, the final decision is made based on the strategic importance of the sale to your company's growth.

Chapter 8

Discover Solutions

Build Value and Sell Solutions

DISCOVER SOLUTIONS

What	Define a technology solution that enables the customer's business strategy.
Why	The value of a technology is what it enables, which is different in each account.
How	1. Discover needs and issues, so you can build a solution that works.
	2. Build value, so your solution clearly demonstrates the value it creates.
	3. Create momentum, so you build competitive advantage and close quickly.
So What?	By collaborating with the customer to create a tailored application of your technology, you ensure that the solution will work; the customer is committed to its successful implementation, and expected results will be realized.

WHAT IS DISCOVERY?

Discovery is the process of defining a customer's needs and tailoring your solution so it creates maximum value.

Discovery is the step of the sales process that turns an opportunity into a potential sale. You apply your product knowledge, business experience, competitive intelligence, and technology expertise to helping customers figure out what they really need.

During discovery you talk to everyone who will have a significant voice in the buying process. A thorough needs analysis ensures that you will make the short list. It also greatly increases your chances for winning the business. The discovery process helps you collect a vast amount of detailed information and boil it down to the most salient facts.

There is a downside to discovery, which is that it eats up your sales resources. Customers love getting something for free, and in the discovery process they are getting a lot of free consulting. Therefore, in the discovery process you need to continue to qualify to make sure that the investment you are making in the account will yield results.

Discovery is conducted through a series of conversations. During these conversations you educate the customer on how your solution enables his business strategy and why it is a superior choice. By leading them through the value building process, you help him understand how the business strategy translates into specific technology needs and how the benefits of your solutions satisfy these needs. Discovery helps you engage the customer in the solutions building process. As you identify the customer's compelling needs to buy, you will work with him to define the requirements for the solution. You also apply your consultative selling skills to help identify the issues that could slow or prohibit the sale and come up with a plan for resolving them. This collaborative problem solving builds your credibility and encourages the customer to trust you.

The discovery phase is the best time for you to build competitive advantage. You compete explicitly by setting competitive traps and minimizing customer misunderstanding caused by competitive traps set for you. You also compete implicitly by heightening the customer's perception of pain around the issues that require your unique differentiators to solve.

WHY IS DISCOVERY IMPORTANT?

Discovery is critical to any technology sales process. Because a technology sale is an intangible sale, the customer doesn't benefit from what the technology is, just what it enables. During discovery you work with the customer to apply your technology to the customer's business strategy, so you can define its value. By demonstrating your technological and business applications knowledge, you build your credibility in the account.

In the discovery process some very important things happen. You find out what the customer needs, and you lay the groundwork for building the customer's sense of value. You uncover the issues that might stall the sale. You assess the competitive situation and implement a strategy to build competitive advantage. You also uncover the political agendas and emotional factors driving the sale.

- **Build the customer's perception of value.** The discovery step of the sales cycle mirrors the customer's information gathering. From the buyers' perspective they are looking for new ways to implement their business strategy, so they are open to learning. When you educate customers on how their business strategy translates into technology needs and problems, you have a great opportunity to help shape the perceptions that will drive their comparative analysis and decision-making. Learn how to use the discovery process to walk the key stakeholders through the value building process.

- **Build competitive advantage.** Discovery is the phase of the sales cycle where you have the most freedom to compete. You can set competitive traps that build the customer's need for the differentiators that make your solution unique. By learning how to build your competitive advantage during the discovery process, you greatly increase your chances of winning the deal.

- **Build credibility, trust and rapport.** Discovery is the stage of the sales cycle where you can build trust and rapport through consultative selling. The more you educate customers during this phase, the more they will value your opinion. As you solve their problems, your credibility will increase. In this chapter you will learn how to apply value building strategies to build the customer's commitment to your solution.

- **Speed up the sales cycle.** During discovery you apply market and competitive energy to creating urgency and sales momentum. In this chapter you will learn how to uncover political agendas and cross-functional issues and use them to climb higher in the decision-making hierarchy.

■ **Increase your chances of winning the account.** Positioning during discovery sets up your proposal and close. During discovery you learn what you need to do to make it to the short list. You also collaborate with the customer in tailoring the solution, so they take ownership of it. Learn how to use the discovery process to create momentum towards a successful close.

WHY DISCOVER

★ Create unique differentiation by focusing customer pain.

★ Build broad-based commitment to your solution.

★ Build trust and rapport through collaborative problem solving.

★ Build advantage by setting competitive traps.

HOW TO DISCOVER VALUE

The goal of the discovery process is to create trust. Even though what you sell is delivered in lots of boxes, the results of your technology-enabled solution are always intangible. Customers won't buy intangibles unless they trust you.

To create trust you need to show customers that you care about them by asking insightful questions about their needs and problems. Then you show them that you listened carefully by building and demonstrating a solution tailored to their needs and concerns. This process creates value for the customers, which motivates them to make a decision. The more they trust you, the more likely they will be to decide quickly and to choose you over the competition.

DISCOVERY PROCESS

1. Discover Needs & Issues.

   ➤ Find out what really counts in the sale.

2. Build Value.

   ➤ Build a solution that produces results.

3. Create Momentum.

   ➤ Use competitive activity to build the customer's urgency.

STEP 1: Discover Needs & Issues

There is nothing worse that a know-it-all. Many technology salespeople make an arrogant impression because they assume that they know what the customer needs. Despite the fact that you may have sold hundreds of technology solutions, you don't know what new customers need, or more importantly want, until you ask them. Therefore, the first step of the discovery process is to ask customers what they want and why they think they need a technology-enabled solution.

Confirm needs.

As part of the qualification process, you have already confirmed the customer's compelling reason to buy your solution, which is to enable a core business strategy. You have also verified the decision-making process and players, so you start your discovery interviews knowing who to talk to and what the conversation should be about. This is a big advantage. However, you can't just sell the big picture. You need to drill down and uncover all the real and perceived needs that have to be satisfied before the customer will be able to make a buying decision.

With most technology sales, the process of uncovering needs is long and often tedious. *An ERP system can have thousands of functional and technological needs.* Furthermore, often customers don't know what they need, and it becomes your job to educate them. *The VP of Manufacturing couldn't care less whether the computer hardware has an open architecture until he learns that it will cut the implementation time of the ERP system in half.* You need to figure out a way to streamline your discovery interviews, so they are productive and build value.

A comprehensive needs analysis clarifies the customer's economic, operational, and technology needs. Economic considerations include the potential upside potential of the project – increased revenues, improved profits, increased productivity per employee, improved customer satisfaction ratings, etc. You also want to discuss negative financial impacts, such as write-offs due to obsolescence, cash flow concerns, risk factors impacting the projected ROI, etc. The more economic information you can gather about the projects, the more ammunition you will have when it comes to writing the financial justification for your proposal.

Operational considerations center around the impact of change on the current business processes and employee behavior. Most technology implementations fail because employees resist change and don't embrace the new technology-enabled business solutions. The opportunity cost of the new strategy is often not discussed, because it is a very threatening topic. By raising questions about change management needs, you are demonstrating that you care about the customer's success. You also have a chance to uncover all sorts of problems that need solving, which you can use to build your credibility in the account.

The discovery phase is the best time to uncover technology needs, too. You need to find out the customer's technology standards for computing, data management, telecommunications, networking, etc. More importantly, you must determine how flexible the company is about buying off the standards list and the process for doing so. In addition to defining the technology environment, you also need to understand how the technology budget is managed. Figuring out who pays for the new equipment purchases is critical to helping you figure out the power structure of the buying committee.

You also need to verify how each of the buying criteria documented in the RFP relates to the customer's business strategy. Lots of times RFP's are loaded up with obscure technical requirements that are not critical to the success of the strategy. As part of the discovery process you need to find out which requirements really count and why.

This is your chance to educate customers about why some of their requirements are irrelevant. This is especially important to do when your solution doesn't satisfy a particular requirement, and your competitor's solution does. Actually, a great competitive trick is to undermine the importance of nonessential requirements on the RFP. If you can do this without the competitor finding out about it and the competitor wastes the customer's time showing how well she can satisfy the requirement, it undermines the competitor's credibility because the customer no longer cares about the requirement.

Identify issues.

Another primary goal of discovery is to uncover issues that could slow or prohibit the sale and come up with a plan for resolving them. The earlier in sale you discover problems, the better. The more problems you can solve and issues you can resolve, the more credibility you build. When you solve customers' problems, you are showing them that you care and that you are capable of making things work. These are the essential ingredients to build the trust required for a positive decision.

Similar to uncovering needs, identifying problems requires that you apply your experience to the customer's situation. Often customers don't have a clue about what could go wrong. You are the expert, not them, so you are going to be better at anticipating problems before they happen or recognizing early symptoms.

You need to be careful as you do this because most people don't like to be told about problems ahead of time. People naturally ignore problems, so bringing them up as potential issues is often risky. However, if you can bring them up within the context of how the problems could get in the way of the successful implementation of the business strategy, then you are depersonalizing them. You are also setting the customer up for when you present your solution. If he has already recognized the problem could happen and your solution will prevent it, then you get credit for having solved the problem even though it didn't happen.

As the sale evolves, customers' issues evolve, also. Early in the sales process, customers focuses on their needs. As they get closer to making a decision they become more focused on risk. This is why you need to identify the issues early, but not necessarily address them until later in the buying process. However, if you have been able to plant the seeds of problems during discovery and then successfully address them during the proposal and closing stages, you can build the credibility you need to win the deal.

Discovery also helps you identify issues that slow down the buying cycle or prevent the sale altogether – *political turf battles, disappearing budgets, economic downturns, etc.* All of these issues can become sources of energy to drive the sale forward if they are identified early and you use them to your advantage – *A political war enables you to align yourself with the winner and build his credibility by accelerating results. A disappearing budget is a great excuse to go over the head of a gatekeeper or expand the sale across multiple departments. If you can show how your solution enables the customer to find opportunities in a downwardly spiraling market, you will be surprised at how quickly she may invest in it.*

STEP 2: Build Value

Once you have uncovered, documented, and verified what the customer needs, you need to build a solution that optimizes the technology's value contribution to the customer's business. In Chapter 3: Build Value, we discussed how to build value by translating the customer's business strategy into specific technology requirements and then showing how your solution satisfies those requirements in a way that enables the customer's business strategy. The more elegantly your solution does this, the more value you create, and the easier it is for the customer to appreciate it.

Create strategic value.

The fundamental goal of the discovery process is to figure out if your solution adds value to your customer's business. To do so, you need to understand what he is trying to accomplish – his business strategy – and how your technology can help. You need to understand what he is trying to do and then figure out whether your solution can help him do it better, faster, or cheaper. This is not an exercise in abstraction. You need to be specific. The more clearly you connect what your solution does to the realization of the customer's goals, the more value you will build and the more likely you are to win.

Strategies are implemented through a series of tactical projects, which have generate specific technology needs and operational problems. When you show customers how your solution supports their tactical projects by satisfying needs and solving problems, you build their confidence that your solution will deliver the value you are promising.

During the discovery process you need to drill deep and cast your net wide to uncover all the needs and issues that impact the business strategy. Most likely the

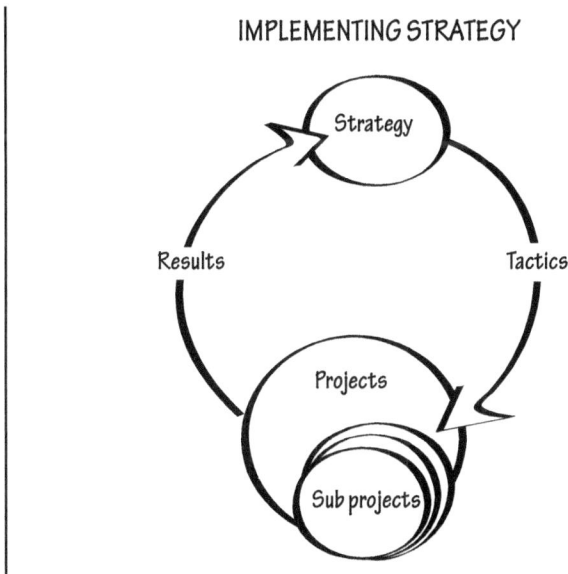

IMPLEMENTING STRATEGY

requirements listed in the RFP don't cover all the organizational issues that need to be addressed in the decision. As you drill down into the tactical initiatives, you find more and more people who will be impacted by the technology decision. These people might not get to vote directly in the decision, but they can influence it by communicating their concerns or preferences up the organizational chain.

To build a value chain you need to understand how the strategy will be implemented through tactical projects. The more specific information you can get about the projects, the better. At a minimum you need to know the project goals and projected time frame, who owns each of the projects, its performance expectations, and how they relate to the successful implementation of the business strategy. It is also useful to ask the customer to articulate what will happen if any of the projects fail, as it helps you understand his perceived fears and gives you clues about how to build the customer's anxiety, which helps you build urgency.

LINKING RESULTS TO STRATEGY PLANNING MAP
DREAM CABINS BUSINESS STRATEGY

Account: *Dream Cabins, Inc.*
Strategy: *Increase profits through mass-customization manufacturing*
Expected Results: *Double sales revenues and deliver 5% profit after tax*

	Project	Goal	Time Frame	Who Cares	Expected Results	Impact on Strategy
1.	Strategic sourcing	Increase options / Lower costs	6 months	Purchasing Director/ Architect	Lower COP by 20%	Enable greater customization
2.	Outsourcing kitchens	Improve quality & variety	12 months	VP Production Architect	Increase sales by 5%	Customers want more control over kitchen design

Make sure you define the entire solution as you build your value chain by clarifying how the new business strategy will impact the current organizational business processes. Ask the customer if she has involved the management of all the impacted departments in the decision. If she hasn't, ask for permission to contact the business managers to discuss the project with them. This will help you identify cross-functional issues that hopefully your technology-enabled solution can resolve.

It also broadens your base of support. The more business executives you can involve in the sale, the better. It helps you focus the sale on the business issues instead of technical comparisons. You are changing the playing field. It also provides you with ways to sell around the competition later in the sale if you need to.

Use value building questioning strategies.

Once you understand the business issues, you need to engage in a solutions building process the functional and technical managers responsible for implementing the various projects. The purpose of this process is to build a solution that clearly satisfies the needs and problems identified in the value chain.

The discovery process is a lot of work. It entails identifying needs, matching needs to features, explaining the benefits of the solution, and linking them to the solutions value. In a complicated solution, this process can take hundreds of hours of interviewing, analysis, and meetings.

It is also a process that can't be automatically delegated to a technician. The discovery process is where competitive battles are fought, and the customer's confidence is built. You need to use your best, most perceptive people to conduct your discovery interviews.

So how do you leverage your best people? The best way is to write Value Building Questioning Strategies that integrate business strategy, product knowledge, needs/feature/ benefit statements, and competitive positioning into questioning scripts. Although you will need to tailor each script to the specific concerns of the stakeholders you interview, having solutions-specific questioning strategies can significantly enhance your sales productivity. A good discovery script helps you focus on the right issues quickly. It is also designed to help you build the customer's pain and create anxiety before you propose a solution. This supports your efforts to create a sense of urgency, which motives your customer to take the appropriate actions required to move the sale forward.

Value Building Questioning Strategies also help you personalize the benefits of your solution. Benefits are much more powerful when a customer believes that your solution will help herself personally. Remember, companies don't buy solutions; people do. Answering the question of "What is in it for me?" for each of your stakeholders can help you figure out how to build emotional support for your solution.

However, you need to be subtle. Most people won't admit to making a multimillion dollar organizational decision because it helps them personally, so, if you are obvious about selling the personalized benefits, you will most likely turn the customer off. However, if you suggest the personal benefits as part of the value contribution of the solution, you are linking her personal benefits to the greater good of the company. This makes the customer look like a committed executive and at the same time drives home how she will benefit from the positive results of the solution.

Tailor solution.

Once you have a clear understanding of the value drivers in the account, you create a solution that specifically addresses the customer's needs. Most technology solutions can be applied to a wide range of needs. Your job is to narrow the focus of your solution so you can demonstrate to the customer how it satisfies the needs that they recognize as important.

Building the solution and figuring out the best way to demonstrate it to the customer's evaluation committee is a team effort. It requires the technical expertise of a technical expert to combine the appropriate functionality into a tailored solution; the account knowledge and competitive intelligence of the account executive to personalize the benefits and optimize the value proposition; and the practical experience of an implementation consultant to create a complete solution of products and services that ensure success.

As you build your solution, involve the relevant members of the buying committee as much as possible to visualize and create the solution. The more you involve them in the creation of the solution, the better they will understand it and the more committed they will be to it. By giving them choices to make, you build their ownership in the solution, a powerful motivation when it comes to making the buying decision. The more they own the solution, the more committed they will be to it.

This is important because you are rarely present during the technical decision. In most technology decisions, the short list competitors are asked to demo their solution to a subset of the buying committee. Each vendor makes a demo, and then the technical members of the buying committee select the best alternatives in a separate meeting and make a recommendation to the decision-maker. You are not at this meeting, so you need to be sure that at least a few members of the customer's decision-making team understand your solution well enough to explain how it works and its benefits. By involving some of them in the solutions building process, you are ensuring that this will happen.

Building the solution is a task that requires insight and discipline. There is always the temptation to add bells and whistles to your solution just because they are cool. Don't do it. The more focused your solution is on the customer's situation, the easier it will be for her to understand its value. As you build the solution, you need to make sure that every aspect directly builds its value contribution. Even if the standard solution comes with lots of other capabilities, don't include them in the solution you propose. Keep your solution focused on the customer's issues.

Solve problems.

Use the solution creation process as a way to raise issues and solve problems collaboratively with the customer. One way to discretely introduce potential problems is by positioning their resolution as part of the solutions building process. By offering the customer two alternatives and explaining how one solution resolves potential issues better than the other, you are in fact getting them to solve their problem before it happens. This helps them to minimize their risk, which becomes increasingly important as they advance through their buying process. You are also building commitment to your solution because it has already solved some problems, and they haven't even bought it yet. These are points that you can use to build competitive advantage and justify your price at the negotiating table.

The more problems you solve, the more trust you create. The goal of your discovery process is to build enough credibility, so you earn the right to make the 'short list' and pitch the decision-maker your value proposition.

STEP 3: Create Momentum

Throughout the discovery process your job is to constantly direct market, competitive, and political energy toward creating sales momentum. The longer a sale drags on, the higher the likelihood that it will end in a non-decision. It is to everyone's advantage to accelerate the process. The faster the decision, the faster the results.

Generate competitive energy.

Discovery is the time for you to apply all your competitive intelligence and positioning skills to building competitive advantage. If you are the market leader or incumbent supplier, you use the discovery process to set traps for competitors. If you are in second or third place, discovery is where you can narrow the gap.

Competition benefits customers, so it is your job to help them understand how your solution compares to other alternatives. The discovery phase of the buying cycle is the best time to do this because most competitive comparisons are about how your product works. In a comparative analysis each vendor will end up with some advantages and disadvantages. The evaluation doesn't determine who wins the deal, just who is considered in the final decision. You don't have to win the comparative analysis; you just have to come out of it on the 'short list.'

In most deals the competitive battle is usually won or lost during the discovery phase of the sales cycle. The reason you win is because you have convinced your customer that her most significant needs can only be satisfied by your solution. This means that you need to shape her perceptions about her needs and problems. The way you do that is by using your Value Building Questioning Strategies to build pain and anxiety around your unique differentiators. This helps you kill two birds with one stone. First of all, you are building competitive advantage. Secondly, you are using the customer's comparative analysis to increase her perception of value around your unique differentiators.

During discovery you want to set competitive traps that build points in your favor. The way you do this is by helping the customer explore all the options. Present a competitive advantage – a unique benefit that relieves an acknowledged pain – and then suggest the customer compare your solution to the competitions'. Of course when the customer asks the competitor about how his solution relieves the pain, his solution isn't as good, so you will win a point in your favor. This approach shows that you are not afraid of the competition and that you are working in the customer's best interest, which builds her confidence in your advice.

You want to handle as many competitive traps as possible during the discovery phase. The more competitive landmines that you defuse during the evaluation period, the fewer potential blow-ups you will have when you present your proposal. Competitive traps usually show up as strange or irrelevant questions. You will be having a great interview, and then all of a sudden the customer asks you a question that seems to come out of left field. You handle the trap by confirming your understanding of the question and then addressing the issue. If your solution doesn't deliver what the customer is looking for, be honest, but then make it your mission to try to minimize the pain around that particular requirement. If your solution does satisfy the need, then make sure the customer understands that it does and its benefits.

Like problems, competitive traps uncovered during discovery are good things because they help you understand your customer's anxieties better. If a competitor makes the effort to plant the seeds of doubt around a specific need or issue, then it is probably more important to the customer than you might have thought it was. Competitive traps also help you anticipate your competitor's strategy early enough in the sales process that you can do something about them. They are clues to understanding how the competition wants to structure the deal and the decision-making issues on which they will focus. This intelligence can help you change the playing field by minimizing the issues in the customer's mind or raising other issues where you have competitive advantage.

Another way to undermine the competition's credibility is to predict what he is going to do wrong. Sales superstars have a pretty good idea of how their competitors like to play the game and their tactics are not going to make everyone happy all the time. So use their negative behaviors to your advantage by predicting what they are going to do wrong and then showing the customer how you are going to do the job right. This builds your credibility enormously because it shows that you understand your competitors, and your warning helps the customer. Then you can come in and do the right thing, which just reinforces how much you care about the customer's success.

Remember, however, successful competitors change their sales tactics often just to confuse you. If you predict negative behavior and the competitor doesn't do what you have said his is going to do, then it undermines your credibility. Of course, the same principle holds true for you. If you change your selling tactics often, then you will confuse your competition.

Build urgency.

One of the problems of the evaluation phase is that it can drag on forever. The longer it takes, the more expensive it becomes, both for you and the customer, so it is in everyone's best interest to make it as quick and painless as possible.

Although customers may think that the purpose of the evaluation process is to choose the best alternative, it is not. The purpose of the evaluation is to learn enough about their needs, issues, and ways to enable their strategy that they are confident enough to make a decision.

Once you are past the very early stages of market development, any technology decision is going to require a group of people to evaluate more than one solution. This process eats up a lot of time– your, your competitors' and your customer's time – and, therefore, creates a lot of energy that you can use to create sales momentum.

The best way to channel this energy is not always obvious. It is like dancing. You need to be adjust your rhythm and movements to your customers', but not be afraid to lead when their energy starts to flag. The best way to lead the sale is to carefully match your sales resources with the key members of the decision-making team.

Figuring out who should conduct which discovery interviews is an art. Discovery interviews have a dual purpose – to help you understand your customer's needs and to help build your credibility with the customer. Discovery is your best opportunity to build friendships and trust, so don't waste this opportunity by sending the wrong people in to do the job. Try to match up players according to their technology adoption profiles – *visionary executives love to talk to inventors; pragmatists will appreciate a conference with a no-nonsense CFO.* By putting the right players together, you can foster a positive process and accelerate the close.

The speed of the discovery process is determined by how quickly the customer can learn. Customers are people, and some people learn faster than others because they are either smarter, more experienced, or trust their teachers more. To speed up the discovery process you need to find the smartest people in the buying organization and use them to accelerate the evaluation. The opinion leaders have earned their organizational credibility because they are smarter than the rest of us, so seek them out and pitch to them directly.

Match how aggressively you sell to the how the customer wants to make the buying decision. Determine the relative importance of consensus over urgency by asking the magic question: **'What is more important – a fast decision implemented quickly or a slower process that builds consensus and minimizes risk?'** Confirm the decision-making milestones, and relate them to the performance expectations for the business strategy. If they are not in alignment, help the customer understand the implications of the decision-making process on how quickly strategic results will be realized. Needless to say, this discussion is much more effective when conducted with the business executive than technical evaluators on the project team.

Never stop qualifying. As you coordinate the process, however, make sure that you continue to qualify the account. Sales resources are precious and expensive. *If you are going to fly your technology wizard out to meet with the customer's CIO, then make sure that the customer commits to an agenda focusing on the critical issues.* Use key sales resources to get higher in the organization. Ask for meetings with executives so you can solve their problems. Create energy or, better yet, use the energy of changing market dynamics, competitive activity, or political power struggles to move the sale forward.

Energy caused by the changing marketplace is another way to accelerate the discovery process because it builds the customer's anxiety. Use the information in your Market Energy Map to educate the evaluation team on why it is essential that they make the decision quickly. Most of the actual people on the evaluation team are probably not the business executives who will make the final decision. They are merely the approvers who do the due diligence required to make sure that the selected alternative will work. Educating them about the business issues and market drivers around the business strategy helps them make a better decision. It will also help them communicate better with their bosses. Because this makes them look good, they become more personally committed to your solution.

Finally, if you are done with your discovery and the evaluation committee seems to be bogged down, sell over their heads. Go directly to the decision-maker, and use your value proposition to motivate her to move the decision-making process forward. During discovery you will uncover all sorts of political energy that you can use to move the process along. If the decision-maker is the one who is slowing it down, then go to her peers, and use them to exert pressure to speed the process up.

Remember, as long as you are selling value that delivers measurable business results, time is on your side.

WHAT YOU NEED TO KNOW TO DISCOVER SOLUTIONS

In the discovery process you apply your knowledge about your solution's value, business applications, and technology so you can uncover the customer's compelling needs and issues. However, the art of discovery requires that you do not tell customers this information; you lead them through a questioning process that enables them to discover it for themselves. This means you have to be knowledgeable enough about your customers' business and your solution's capabilities that you are not afraid to ask probing and provocative questions. Building this level of comfort with new solutions is not easy. It requires that you have intelligent access to a wide range of information that accurately represents your solution and your company story.

- **Value Building Strategies** You can't conduct a discovery interview without a clear understanding of how your solution enables the customer's business strategies by satisfying technology and functional needs and solving operational problems. The purpose of the discovery process is to get customers to confirm that they need what you are selling and to acknowledge the benefits of your solution, which is the essence of your Value Map.

    Creating a clear and concise Value Map is the most important thing that your company can do to ensure your success. Once the content is developed and everyone agrees that it is accurate and clearly communicates the solutions value proposition, writing Value Building Questioning Strategies helps the sales team take the story to market quickly.

    Developing this information on your own is a time consuming and intellectually exhausting project. As a salesperson it isn't your job do build it. However, it is your job to deliver it, and you are the person whose income is directly dependent on the results. Therefore, insist that your marketing and technical team develop Value Maps for you.

- **Solutions Selling** Your Solutions Map also provides very useful information that helps you plan and implement a thorough discovery. You need to figure out who cares about your solution and why they do. This means that you need to be able to intelligently discuss the business and functional implications of buying the solution with a wide range of functional stakeholders.

    You can't be expected to know about how every business strategy is

DISCOVERY COMPETENCIES

★ Be able to translate the customer's business strategy into specific needs for the technology solution.

★ Be able to develop questioning strategies that uncover key business and technology needs and problems.

★ Be able to explain how the technology and the solution satisfy these needs and solve problems.

★ Be able to solve problems throughout the discovery process.

★ Be able to explain the technology concepts - basic architecture, elements, and functionality of the technology – in language executives understand.

★ Be able to explain (demo) how the technology works.

★ Be able to educate the customer on key factors to consider when implementing the technology.

★ Understand the competitive landscape – key competitors, market drivers, relative positioning, and buying characteristics.

★ Know the significant strengths, weaknesses and differentiators of key competitors.

★ Be able to uncover competitors in an account.

★ Be able to develop positioning strategies that build competitive advantage.

★ Be able to uncover competitive traps and resolve them throughout the discovery process.

★ Be able to set competitive traps against key competitors.

★ Be able to collaborate with appropriate members of the buying committee when building the solution.

implemented in every industry. You are expected, however, to be able to ask provocative questions, listen carefully to the customer and work with your sales team to develop a solution that satisfies their needs. If you have these skills and you can easily access specific information about how the solution works in various industries, across different functions, running in different technical environments, etc., you will be able to run a successful discovery in a wide range of accounts.

The information found in a Solutions Map coupled with Value Building Questioning Strategies that have been tailored to the specific concerns of various functional stakeholders and/or industries will provide you with the core knowledge you need to sell your solution successfully.

■ **Product and Technology Knowledge** Discovery is the first phase of the sales cycle where you need to demonstrate significant technical expertise to the customer. If you do not have technical support for the pre-sales process, you need to educate yourself about how your solution works and the technology that drives it.

Developing this expertise is rarely a problem in most technology companies for two reasons. The first is most of these companies have very knowledgeable sales engineers, who support the sale by conducting technology reviews and dealing with the issues around tailoring the solution. The second is that almost all sales training is written by product marketing or engineering people, who believe that the only really important information is product knowledge, so they do a good job of packaging and presenting it for the sales force.

■ **Competitive Intelligence** The competitive sale is basically won or lost in the discovery phase, so a clear understanding of your and your competitors' relative strengths and weaknesses is critical. You need easy access to accurate and current information about your competitors.

During discovery you need two types of competitive intelligence. The first is a clear understanding of your and your competitors' unique differentiators. – What can you, or they, do that no one else can do? This is important information because it helps you anticipate the issues that your competitors will emphasize with the customer. Like you, your competitors are trying to build the customer's perception of pain around the issues that only they can resolve. Your Competitive Map provides you with this information. Also, competitive killer kits that provide point-by-point comparisons about relative strengths and weaknesses can be very useful in helping your anticipate and build competitive differentiation.

The second type of competitive intelligence that you need is war stories describing how your competitors act in various selling situations. This kind of information is much more difficult to put together in a formal way. Generally it is undocumented because competitive analysts don't have the front-line experience to write about it, and even if they did, your corporate lawyers would go crazy if they saw the information written down. Competitive wisdom is usually shared over beers at sales meeting. This information is vital to developing a perspective that helps you anticipate competitive behavior.

DISCOVER SOLUTIONS PROCESS SUMMARY

What	How	Information Required
1. Discover Needs & Issues Find out what really counts in the sale	1.1 Confirm needs	List of economic, operational and technology needs Feature/Benefit analysis by key need RFP list of requirements Solutions Map - Who cares and Why
	1.2 Identify issues	List of typical problems Customer's organizational chart Competitive analysis
2. Build Value Build a solution that delivers results	2.1 Create strategic value	Value Map Explanation of how the business strategy will be implemented Expected results of all key projects required to implement the strategy Value Building Questioning Strategies
	2.2 Tailor solution	Technical expertise on how to apply the technology to create the solution
	2.3 Solve problems	Value Map
3. Create Momentum Use competitive activity to build the customer's urgency	3.1 Generate competitive energy	Competitive Map and Killer Kits Competitive traps Strategies for handing competitive traps and customer objections
	3.2 Build urgency	Solutions Map Running tally of cost of sales resources required to conduct discovery and build solutions

TAKE ACTION

The most useful training and sales tools to support discovery are ones that improve your ability to ask the right question at the right time. To do so you need an in-depth understanding of your solution's value and how the value proposition changes by function. You also need to be able to anticipate competitors' behavior and set and handle competitive traps. The following sales tools are designed to help you educate the customer about the value of your solution and to improve your competitive positioning.

- **A Value Selling Sales Wizard** is an easy-to-access database that helps you build value building sales strategies that focus on the customer's needs and issues. A Value Selling Sales Wizard organizes value building information – market drivers, business strategies, technology needs, implementation issues, solutions definitions, features and benefits, and value propositions – in a way that makes them easy to apply to accounts. The user interface is a diagnostic tool that helps you define the selling situation by choosing a business strategy, desired solution, or stakeholder needs. Then it generates appropriate value selling strategies based on how you have defined the account. Linking content-rich sales tools – Discovery Questioning Strategies, Value White Papers, Sales Presentations – to the content can enhance the practical utility of a Value Selling Sales Wizard. This enables you to strategize about the account and instantly create a set of sales tools that you can use to implement the strategy.

- **Value Building Questioning Strategies** integrate value building logic with solutions-specific information about the how your solution satisfies customers' needs, solves their problems, and enables their business strategies. They are also designed to raise customer awareness and pain around both the negative impact of not taking action and the positive benefits of choosing your solution, which helps build urgency. Effective questioning strategies include the subtle integration of competitive traps around your key differentiators, so you can build competitive advantage throughout the discovery phase. Writing scripts that help the salesperson educate the customer about your solution is the best way to leverage and accelerate your sales efforts.

- **The Big Deal** is a case study that simulates the discovery process. In The Big Deal a customer account is defined by a series of "interviews" across an organizational chart. The sales team has to choose who to interview and ask the right questions to uncover key information about the account. Salespeople like this approach to sales training because it challenges them to apply their product and sales knowledge within the context of how companies actually buy. The Big Deal can be implemented as a web-based game where individuals play against the computer or as a paper-and-pencil simulation completed by sales teams. The second alternative can be easily implemented in the field during regional sales meetings. This learning experience is especially effective when the simulation is followed by account planning reviews because it helps you apply what you have learned to actual accounts.

- **The Competitive Challenge** is a computer-based simulation that challenges you to sell against a competitive salesperson in account situations. The game is played on a game board that represents a variety of deals – in some you will have a competitive advantage and in others you don't. When you choose a customer, you are asked a question by the customer that is a competitive trap. You need to use your competitive knowledge to identify which competitor has laid the trap. If you correctly identify the competitor, you can lay a trap against him. If your trap works, then you have a chance to win the deal by identifying the customer's need that you can uniquely satisfy, and the competitors cannot satisfy. During the game the computer plays the part of the competitor, so you have the additional benefit of seeing how a competitive salesperson would handle the same situation by laying traps for you.

  The Competitive Challenge is a brilliant way to learn how to apply competitive intelligence and build competitive strategies. However, it is a difficult game to create. The content developer needs to have access to excellent, timely, competitive intelligence and honest win/loss analysis. She also must be able to write scenarios from the viewpoints of both competitors, which is hard to do. Creating a Competitive Challenge, however, is worth the effort. Salespeople love them. It is always the most highly rated activity in any web-based training initiative.

- **Competitive Killer Kits** organize competitive data so it is easy to analyze relative strengths and weakness. A killer kit identifies all of the information you need to do a competitive analysis, including company profiles, key market messages, target markets, customer lists, selling strategies, and a thorough assessment of the company's solutions. Killer kits are very useful when you are trying to anticipate or lay competitive traps. If they include accurate and timely data about the competitor they can be very useful as you develop your competitive tactics or if you have to address a specific competitive issue.

The problem with killer kits, however, is that the competitive information changes constantly, so it is more useful to post this information on a secure website than to actually print it. Also, killer kits make your legal department very nervous, so usually the most useful and insightful information doesn't get included for fear that the competitor will get his hands on it.

■ **Competitive Traps.** Like Value Building Questioning Strategies, writing competitive traps to build competitive advantage during discovery is very helpful. However, until you have had significant experience selling a solution against a competitor, it is hard to figure out what are going to be the hot buttons that drive the competitive battle. Inviting the right kind of competitive comparison is an excellent way to increase the customer's perception of the value of your solution. It also tends to energize the account and move the sales process forward. However, when salespeople are not familiar with the competitive environment, they are reluctant to invite competitive comparison because they don't want to risk it. By giving the sales team competitive landmines to plant that are sure to favorably showcase your solution, you can allay these fears and encourage them to take the risk of inviting competitive comparison.

CONCLUSIONS

■ **Create value.** Discovery is the process of defining a customer's needs and tailoring your solution so it creates maximum value. Its purpose is to define how your solution adds value to your customer's business.

■ **Build clear links.** The more clearly you can connect what your solution does to the realization of the customer's goals, the more value you will build and the more likely you are to win.

■ **Build trust.** The discovery process creates trust, which is essential in any sale. Customers won't buy intangibles unless they trust you. The more problems you solve, the more trust you create.

■ **Broaden your support.** During the discovery process you need to drill deep and cast your net wide to uncover all the needs and issues that impact the business strategy.

■ **Build ownership of the solution.** The discovery process helps you engage the customer in the solutions building process. Involving the buying team in visualizing and creating the solution encourages ownership and increases their commitment to your alternative.

- **Play your best players**. The discovery phase is the best time for you to build competitive advantage. The discovery process is where competitive battles are fought, and the customer's confidence is built. You need to use your best, most perceptive people to conduct your discovery interviews.

- **Do your homework**. A discovery script focus you on the right issues quickly.

- **Run at the customer's pace**. You need to match your selling style to he how the customer wants to make the buying decision by determining the relative importance of consensus over urgency.

- **Align your focus**. As the sale evolves, customers' issues evolves, also. Early in the sales process, customers focus on their needs. As they get closer to making a decision they become more focused on risk.

- **Facilitate the learning process**. The speed of the discovery process is determined by how quickly the customer can learn. Although customers may think that the purpose of the evaluation process is to choose the best alternative, it is not. The purpose of the evaluation is to learn enough about their needs, issues, and ways to enable their strategy that they are confident enough to make a decision.

Chapter 9

Propose Value

Take Control of the Account

PROPOSE VALUE

What	Create an offer, and orchestrate a series of events that sell your solution to the customer.
Why	Buying an enabling technology is a complex process that requires building consensus among a wide variety of constituents and the resolution of many cross functional issues.
How	1. Create an offer, so you can optimize the value of your solution. 2. Build sales momentum, so you can control the decision-making process. 3. Manage risk, so you can eliminate barriers to the sale.
So What?	By breaking the buying decision down into a series of smaller decisions, you can build organizational commitment to your solution, so, you end up with a better-educated and more confident customer.

WHAT IS PROPOSING?

Proposing is the process of making an offer and convincing the customer to choose your solution.

A proposal documents your offer. It states what the customer is trying to accomplish and how your solution will enable him to do it faster, better, or cheaper. It also tells the customer how much the solution will cost and the economic benefits of implementing your solution.

During the proposal process you create an offer that optimizes the value of your solution. You prove to the customer that your offer is the best choice technically, economically, and strategically. You schedule a series of events designed to build the prospect's confidence that your solution will deliver what you are promising. As you close each event, communicating what has been accomplished to the rest of the decision-making team, builds sales momentum. By working interactively with the prospect to solve problems, eliminate issues, and plan the implementation of the solution, you minimize the risks associated with the decision. Finally, you ask the decision-maker for the order.

When you propose an offer, you take control of the buying process. Your proposal documents why the customer should buy your solution. It solidifies promises made on both sides and crystallizes the issues around the decision. A good proposal encourages the customer to take action.

During the proposal phase of the sales cycle, the sale intensifies. The buyers become focused on everything that could go wrong. Competitors reach into their bags of dirty tricks. Politics run rampant. Your job is to take control of this emotionally charged environment and lead the customer through a rational decision-making process.

Throughout the proposal process, you lead your sales team, eliminate competitors, and apply your solutions selling skills to win over the prospect's decision-making team. It is an intense experience.

WHY IS PROPOSING IMPORTANT?

The sales cycle comes to a head when you propose your solution. At this point you know what the customer is trying to accomplish, his needs and issues and what will compel him to make a decision. Your proposal provides the customer with a way to actualize his intent.

As soon as the proposal is submitted, the risks of the decision become more important. Up until that point, the customer is very excited about the benefits. At the point of the proposal, when the cost and implementation plan is presented, the customer suddenly becomes very concerned about the risks associated with failure. This is why proposing the solution is more than just building a solution; figuring out what it will cost, and writing the proposal. It is about orchestrating a series of events designed to sell the proposal by building the customer's urgency to make his buying decision.

- **Accelerate the sales cycle.** In this chapter you will learn how to create momentum during the proposal phase. Presenting the proposal gives you a chance to schedule events that build excitement and motivate the prospect to make the decision. Each proposal event builds momentum toward the close.

- **Call higher.** In your proposal you are giving the customer something of value – your company's perception of his business strategy and recommendations of how to implement it. This is valuable information that captures the attention of the decision-maker and his key influencers. Presenting the proposal is a valid reason to schedule appointments with the people who count. Learn how to use the proposal as a way to get to the decision-maker.

- **Formalize promises.** Up until the proposal is submitted, everything is vague. Once you put your offer in writing, it gets an authority of its own. The proposal solidifies the decision, the issues, and the alternatives. The proposal not only documents your promise, but the promises and commitments that the prospect has made, too. Learn how to use the proposal to build commitment to the successful implementation of your solution.

- **Crystallize the competitive battle.** The proposal structures the competitive battle. Learn how to write a proposal so it defines how you want the customer to make his decision. A good proposal clearly positions the unique advantages of your value proposition and by comparison implies the competitive weaknesses of other alternatives.

WHY PROPOSE VALUE ?

★ Build the customer's desire for your solution's results.

★ Use the proposal to get to the decision-maker.

★ Make the decision easier by clarifying the issues.

★ Eliminate competitors by building commitment to your unique benefits.

HOW TO PROPOSE VALUE

The goal of your proposal is to sell your solution. This means building enough consensus among the members of the buying committee so they recommend your solution and then securing the decision-maker's commitment.

Developing and delivering the proposal is a multi-step process designed to increase your control over the customer's buying decision. During this process, you help the customer break up the large decision into a series of smaller, more specific ones, such as the technical evaluation, the financial analysis, etc. Then you orchestrate a series of events that build momentum towards the close. Throughout this process you apply your solutions selling skills to identify and resolve problems, escalate issues, and eliminate political barriers to making a positive decision. You also apply your competitive intelligence to build the customer's commitment to benefits that you can uniquely offer. The proposal process is an iterative collaboration between you and the buying committee. The more you interact, the more likely it is that you will be successful.

PROPOSAL PROCESS

1.   Create Offer.

   ➤ Create a solution optimizing your value contribution.

2.   Build Sales Momentum.

   ➤ Take control of the decision-making process.

3.   Manage Risk.

   ➤ Eliminate barriers to the sale through collaborative problem solving and planning.

STEP 1: Create An Offer

Once you know what the customer wants, you create an offer that optimizes the value contribution of your solution to your customer's business. An offer combines the products and services required to ensure that the solution will deliver your value proposition within the context of the customer's business environment. It includes a technical solution proving your technology is appropriate, a financial solution justifying the monetary investment, and a value proposition verbalizing what the customer wants to achieve and how your solution is going to get him closer to his goal.

In *Blur*, a perceptive book about the Internet economy, Stan Davis and Christopher Meyer define an offer as a blurring of products and services. "The product is simply a service waiting to happen; the service is the product in action... The successful design of offers will require thinking simultaneously about what it is and what it does and even what it enables to happen."[1]

As you create your offer, consider several important factors – the life of the solution; what the customer values, and how it makes a positive contribution to your customer's business model. Creative bundling of products and services increases your ability to satisfy the prospect's need for a whole solution. For example, consider the time-horizon of the life of your solution. Products are delivered in a moment in time. Services deliver the solution over a period of time. By combining products and services into offers, you can extend the time horizon of your solution, while still providing a single event that has enough value to justify your price.

The threat of obsolescence in the technology business tends to drive customers to choose low risk over low prices, especially when the solution is supporting mission-critical strategies. Therefore, you want to create an offer that enables your solution to evolve along with the customer's business strategy. For the product buyer who cares most about price and delivery, this might be regularly scheduled upgrades or replacements. For the services buyer who cares about ongoing support, this could be a maintenance contract.

As you build your offer, consider the different kinds of value your solution creates. What proportion of the value is inherent in the product itself or in the services that make it more useful to the customer – distribution options, delivery, training, maintenance, etc? You can build tremendous value by adding elements that customize the solution so it works better in the customer's unique business environment.

---

[1] Davis, Stan & Meyer, Christopher. *Blur,* Perseus Publishing. 1998

The offer builds a vision of the 'whole solution.' A technology sale is fundamentally an intangible sale. There are many different ways to implement a business strategy, so when you create your offer, you need to consider all the factors around the successful implementation of the solution. Even if you are not selling in your offer everything required for a successful implementation, you need to show how your offer fits into the 'whole solution.'

Some technology companies offer a complete suite of products and services so they can provide their customer with "one-stop shopping." *IBM will build your solution from soup to nuts...* If your solution addresses all of the customer's needs, then you create an offer by bundling various products and services into a complete solution. Others build partnerships with vendors who provide complimentary parts of the solutions they sell. *Sun Microsystems prides itself on its extensive partner relationships.* This is called 'best-of-breed" positioning. If your solution only addresses part of the overall solution, then you need to show the customer why you fit in better than the other alternatives.

Both strategies have advantages and disadvantages. *IBM's approach means you only have one person you have to call if the solution doesn't work. Sun's approach enables you to choose from a much wider range of options.* Early adopters tend to choose "best-of-breed" alternatives because they are looking for technological superiority and faster time to market. 'Main Street' buyers tend to like one-stop shopping because it reduces the risks associated with integrating complex systems.

CREATE AN OFFER

Ask Yourself:

? What is the time horizon for the life of the solution?

? What does the customer care about most?

? What is the primary source of value?

? How does your solution support the customer's revenue model?

Develop an ROI.

The technology decision is only part of the overall decision. Another important step in the prospect's evaluation process is determining the best economic alternative. This financial decision is made by a subset of the buying committee – the financial experts and purchasing department. Since it is the job of these players to get the best deal, they tend to ignore the value you have created during the sales process. They don't care about your technological superiority, how easy it will be to implement, or any of the other benefits that the people who have to use the solution care about. They just care about money, so you need to create a compelling ROI justification for the cost of the solution.

The ability to justify your price is directly proportional to the value that you built with the prospect. In the proposal you show the customer the potential return on investment of buying your solution by documenting the economic benefits of the results of the business strategy it enables.

An effective ROI justification is critical to the technology sale because it quantifies the intangible benefits of your solution. Since technology is subject to the laws of abundance – the more it is used, the more valuable it becomes – it is pretty easy to develop a compelling ROI. If your customer's business strategy focuses on "above the line" issues – increasing revenues, building customer loyalty, entering new markets – then your ROI justification can use the incremental results generated by your solution to prove it creates wealth. If the business strategy focuses on the bottom line – lowering costs, increasing profits, improving efficiency – then your ROI argument should focus on the potential cost savings of your offer.

As you create your offer, think about how the solution supports the customer's revenue model. If your customer is a product company, show them how your solution can help build brand loyalty, which supports repeat purchasing. If your customer is a service organization, then show him how it supports the development of ongoing and interactive relationships between him and his customers. Linking your solution to how the customer earns money is a great way to demonstrate its potential ROI.

Write the proposal.

Ideally, the proposal stage is an iterative process. You build the customer's commitment to choosing your solution by involving him in the tailoring of the offer. In order to write your proposal, you need to know what your proposal strategy is going to be. Are you going to make a single offer in a written proposal or would you be better off evolving the proposal through lots of interactivity with the customer? Depending on the situation, both approaches can be effective.

PROPOSAL OUTLINE

- ☑ Executive Summary
- ☑ Solutions Summary
- ☑ Value Proposition
- ☑ Success Metrics
- ☑ Financial Justification
- ☑ Implementation Plan
- ☑ References
- ☑ Next Steps (Closing Process)

The effect of putting your proposal in writing and quoting a price is that it moves the sale forward. It states your position and gives the customer something tangible upon which he can make his decision. This approach works great when you are working with a single decision-maker who wants to make a unilateral decision quickly. Early adopters who are more concerned with time to market than building consensus tend to respond favorably to this direct approach. Another situation in which a quick proposal process is effective is when you have a clear competitive lead because it helps you close the deal faster, which reduces the chance that a competitor will be able to get into the account.

Taking a collaborative approach to creating the proposal helps you build consensus among the members of the buying committee. This approach is very effective when you are selling a complex solution that will impact many different business processes and departments in the prospect's organization. It helps you increase customer commitment to your solution by encouraging the customer's ownership of the solution. This strategy works well with early majority and 'Main Street' buyers for whom consensus is important. This approach is effective when there is no clear competitive leader because it gives you a chance to build competitive differentiation as you work with the customer's buying committee.

Keep your pricing 'soft.' Another advantage of an iterative approach is that it lets you use soft pricing until the final offer is clear. As soon as you put a price in writing your ability to evolve the proposal in response to the prospect's changing needs is greatly reduced, so you want to be pretty close to a final offer before you actually quote a price. One of the advantages of building an offer that combines products and services into a solution is that it leaves you lots of room for "evolving" your pricing as the proposal evolves, so you don't get boxed into a price you quoted too early.

As you write your proposal, keep in mind whom you are addressing. The target of your proposal is the decision-maker, although it is likely that he will never actually read it. The secondary target is the other members of the buying committee – stakeholders, financial analysts, technical experts, etc. – each of whom will read the proposal with a very specific agenda. Balancing their needs in a single document is challenging.

Most decision-makers have very limited attention spans. They are busy people and rely on their experts to make smart recommendations. However, they aren't willing to abdicate the responsibility for the decision completely, so you need to make a very concise and convincing pitch on the first page of your proposal. Open your proposal by succinctly stating the prospect's business strategy – what they are trying to accomplish; your value proposition – how your solution will help them do it better, cheaper, or faster; and 5-7 value statements around key needs. Each value statements should address the compelling need to buy for the other influential members of the decision-making team.

STEP 2: Build Sales Momentum

Over 30% of technology decisions end up with no decision being made [2] It is easy to do nothing. The proposal process is the part of the sales cycle where you have to drive the sale forward. You need to take control, or someone else will, so once you have your proposal written, you need deliver it in a way that builds sales momentum.

Strategize the proposal delivery process.

Many salespeople make the mistake of submitting a proposal too soon. Prospects ask for proposals when they don't want to spend their time in discovery interviews. If you write a proposal before you understand the customer's compelling needs and issues, you can't structure it in a way that will win the business. Sales superstars work accounts until everyone is ready for the proposal. If you are asked to submit a proposal too early, you must convince the customer that you can't write it until you have completed your discovery. Don't submit a proposal before you are sure that you know what the customer needs; that your solution will work, and the key players are convinced of the value of your offer.

An effective proposal strategy creates excitement and moves customers forward in their buying cycle. A proposal is not just a document. It is a series of events designed to present and refine your offer. While each event has a slightly different purpose and produces a different outcome, each one should move you closer to closing the deal. The technical demo builds competitive differentiation. The executive presentation builds the decision-maker's understanding of your value proposition. A site visit builds that customer's confidence in the viability of your solution.

To figure out which events you need, break the buying decision down into decision-making milestones— the technical evaluation, the financial analysis, the risk assessment, and the strategic decision. What smaller decisions does the prospect need to make before he can make the final decision? Usually there will be economic, technical, functional, and implementation planning decisions. Once all the events have been closed successfully, all the smaller decisions add up to closing the deal.

Then schedule events to propose your solution within the context of each of the smaller decisions that need to be made.

- To support the technical decision-making process, you might schedule a competitive pilot, a series of demos, or customer education seminars.
- The economic decision could be made during a corporate visit, a financial review meeting, or on an executive call where your financial experts meet with the customer's CFO or Controller.
- Arranging site visits with other satisfied customers or meeting with your implementation consulting team can encourage a positive functional or implementation planning decision.

Keep in mind that the purpose of each of these events is to close on a specific part of the decision. Each event should have a specific purpose, which attracts people to the event. *"The purpose of a pilot is to determine which solution delivers the best performance..."* Manage each event by clearly stating the purpose of the beginning of event — *"You will see in this pilot that the Sun platform delivers ..."* — and close the event by asking for commitment to the purpose — *"Now that you have seen the superior performance of the Sun StorEdge server, will you recommend it as the best storage platform for your new CRM solution?"*

As you close, enlist the event participants in the larger sales process by securing their agreement to support the decision internally. Then make sure they have the information they need to clearly present your proposal in a way that builds value, so they can sell your alternative internally.

Build credibility at the demo.

The demo is when you gather the technical and functional evaluators in a room and show them how your solution works. The purpose of the demo is to prove the solution will deliver what you are promising by specifically showing how it solves problems and satisfies needs. During the demo you need to walk the evaluation team through the Value Map you have built during discovery and show how their business strategy translates into technical needs and how your solution satisfies those needs. By linking functionality and features to tactical needs and then showing how they add up to strategic results, you create a vision of success.

It is very important that you explicitly state the benefits of each part of the solution that you demo and the value it creates. Just because a benefit is obvious to you, it may not be to everyone else. Most likely the people who are making the decision do not have the expertise required to translate the features of your offer into the business benefits it delivers. Benefits are most powerful when they specifically show how the features of your solution solve specific problems or satisfy specific needs. Since there is a mixed audience at a demo, you need to personalize the benefits of each feature for the people who care about it. You personalize a benefit by explicitly explaining how it satisfies the need or solves a problem that a key stakeholder cares about. — *So, Mr. VP of Sales, you can see how the proven reliability of the Sun 9200 server will enable you to launch your one-to-one marketing campaign on a global scale...*

EVALUATE BENEFITS

Ask Yourself:

? Does the benefit statement explain how your functionality will help the customer accomplish their objectives?

? Are the benefits specific enough so the prospect understands its value?

? Are the benefits personalized?

Then you build the value of the benefit by relating it to other benefits and showing how they add up to making a strategic contribution to the successful implementation of the business strategy. You need to show how the whole is greater than the sum of the parts and at the same time clearly demonstrate the benefits of each part. This requires significant upfront planning, especially when you have a heterogeneous audience. It may even require that you schedule several demos, each one focusing on the needs of the various constituents served by the solution.

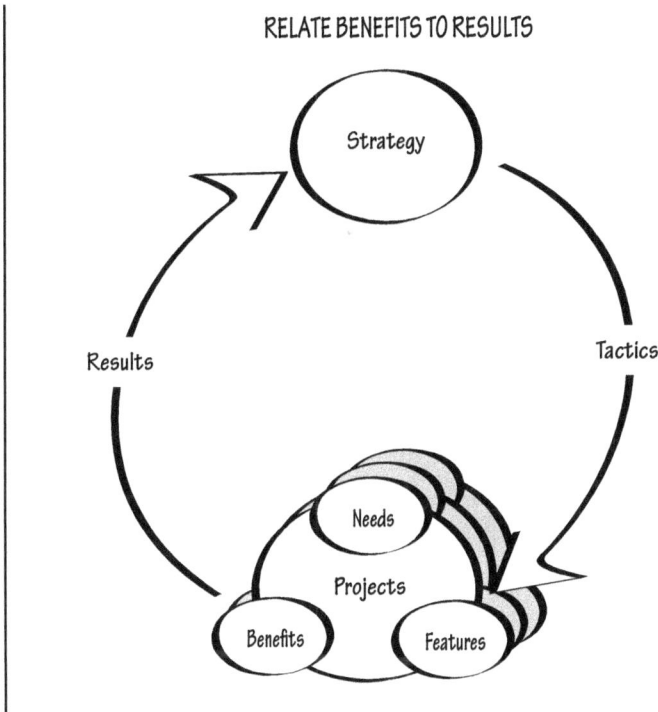

RELATE BENEFITS TO RESULTS

The demo is also a good time to clarify why your solution is superior to competitive solutions and to reinforce the importance of your differentiators to the successful implementation of their business strategy. If you have done a good job of raising the customer's pain around areas where you have unique differentiation, then the demo is a good time to invite competitive comparison. The trick at this point is to prove your competitive superiority without trashing the competition.

The proposal process is designed to winnow out the field of competitors to one or two choices. The sales objective for a demo is to pass the evaluation and be one of companies that make the short lis, so you close a demo by asking the prospect to include you in the final, decision-making presentation.

Propose value at the executive presentation.

The purpose of the executive presentation is to propose your offer directly to the decision-maker and key stakeholders. Since executives care less about how the solution works and more about what it enables, they tend to get bored during demos. Therefore, it is to your advantage to schedule an executive presentation after the demos have been made, and you have the approval of the technical evaluators.

During an executive presentation your primary goal is to get the decision-maker to accept your value proposition. Since you already have the technical blessing of the evaluation team, you can focus on the business issues that the executive cares about. It is your chance to demonstrate the economic value of the solution. In the executive presentation you prove your value by presenting the economic justification of the solution. This should include an explanation of how the solutions support the prospect's business strategy and the ROI they can expect to achieve by implementing the solution.

If you have earned enough credibility as a problem solver during the discovery process, you will be able to set up the executive presentation as a "working meeting." By inviting the executives to provide feedback on your working proposal at this time, you will be able to fine-tune the final proposal in a way that builds their commitment to your solution. This approach also lets you focus the executives on how they can manage the risk associated with the decision.

At the end of the executive presentation, ask the decision-maker for commitment to key aspects of the proposal that has been agreed to in the meeting. Commit to reworking the aspects of the proposal that are still perceived as concerns. Then close by asking for a closing meeting where the final decision will be made.

Use events to build sales momentum.

Months can pass between the initial presentation of your proposal to the executive team and the closing meeting. During that time you build sales momentum by scheduling events designed to build the customer's confidence. How you build their confidence depends a lot on the customer's technology adoption profile. If the sale is to an early adopter, you lower the customer's risk by showing him how committed your company is to their success. By connecting the customer's stakeholders and technical experts with the technical and consulting talent inside your company, you build his confidence that his innovative business strategy will be successful. If the sale is to an early majority customer, arranging for visits to other customer sites where the solution has been successfully implemented builds the confidence they need to choose your solution.

Events to consider when designing a proposal delivery strategy include:

- Site visits with other customers who have successfully implemented your solution. These visits build your credibility because they provide the prospect with a third party endorsement of your solution.
- Corporate visits that showcase your technological vision and financial stability. These visits help you sell higher because you bring your customer's executives to your corporate headquarters where they meet your company's executives.
- Executive calls when you take your senior management out to meet with the customer's executives. These meetings help you call higher in the customer's organization. They also are the perfect forums for the business conversations required to build value and win the deal.
- Financial calls where you discuss the pricing, financing, and return on investment with the financial gatekeepers. In this call you explain your pricing, propose financial options, and make sure that the deal works from a financial perspective.

Communicate progress to everyone involved.

Since every events doesn't include all the members of the buying committee, you need to continually communicate your growing success throughout the proposal process. Each time you close on a specific aspect of the sale, make sure that everyone involved in the decision hears about it. The interim closes must be communicated so they will add up to the final decision. The more closes you make, the more sales momentum you build. Everyone wants to be associated with a winner, so often promoting your growing success helps enlist new supporters.

Orchestrating this complex series of events requires that you apply your solutions selling knowledge to the account. You need to constantly reevaluate the political power behind the decision so you can manage it to your advantage. You also need to build the emotional sale. The decision will not get made until someone high up really wants it badly. This requires building their emotional commitment to the successful vision you are promising.

Take control of the sale.

At the proposal stage, the gloves come off. Lower level people who are stalling the sale with mundane issues don't count anymore. You need to appeal to the executive who has the power to make the decision. If you have not been able to get to the decision-maker during the discovery process or the demo, you can use your proposal process to set up a meeting between the customer's decision-maker and your company's executives. You need to apply what you have learned about the political sale at this point to figure out how to make sure that you present a compelling offer to the decision-maker.

Hopefully, you have been negotiating throughout the sales process. Every time the prospect has asked you for something, you have asked for something in return. For example, in discovery you traded the consulting advice of your technical engineers for information about the prospect's needs and issues. If you have negotiated wisely, the prospect has already reaped benefits from your requests. Thanks to the discovery interviews, the prospect has a much better understanding of their needs and the benefits of various approaches to satisfying them. You have created a history of fair exchange, which becomes a key selling strength as you move closer to the close.

The proposal phase of the sales process is all about power. During this stage of the buying process you need to exert your influence so you have increasing control. Account control enables you to eliminate competitors and build momentum towards the close. Without this power, you cannot win. Your source of power at this stage comes from the goodwill you have built by negotiating in a positive way throughout the sales cycle. If you haven't negotiated with the customer up until now, the customer will take control of the buying process, and you will have to resort to large concessions to stay in the running. If you have consistently negotiated back and forth, you will have created a greater perception of value, and the prospect will have become dependent on your advice. Use this power to your advantage as you orchestrate the events in the proposal phase. *Don't agree to a corporate visit until the decision-maker commits to attend. Don't present your ROI justification to a financial analyst; insist that the controller attends the meeting.* Exercising your right to negotiate increases the probability that your proposal events will close successfully.

STEP 3: Manage Risk

During the proposal process you need to eliminate any outstanding barriers to the sale. As they get closer to making a decision, customers become increasingly focused on the risks associated with the decision, so you need to lower their concerns by resolving outstanding issues, developing an implementation plan, and eliminating alternatives.

In the rational decision-making process most organizations use, there are three major steps in making a decision – setting criteria, evaluating alternatives, and assessing risk. In their evaluation phase, buying committees do a good job of the first two steps, but they tend to ignore the risk factors. Then, as they get closer to making the decision, they increasingly focus on what could go wrong – how difficult it will be to implement the solution or change management issues. They become increasingly concerned about implementation issues – service, maintenance, technical support, customer service, responsiveness, cancellation clauses, warranties, capacity, etc. Although handing these concerns is a negotiating nightmare, these questions are good news. It means that customer is serious about buying, and your solution is still in the running.

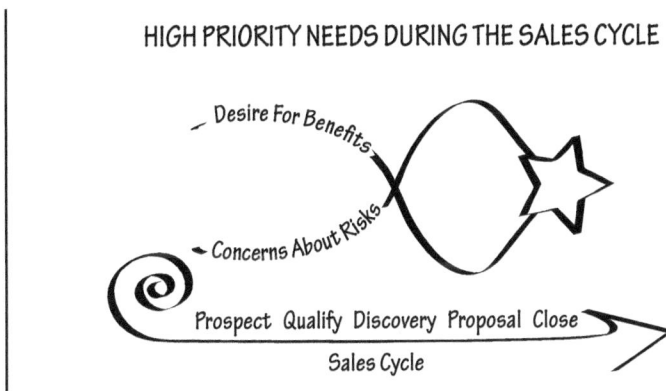

HIGH PRIORITY NEEDS DURING THE SALES CYCLE

Desire For Benefits

Concerns About Risks

Prospect Qualify Discovery Proposal Close

Sales Cycle

Resolve outstanding issues.

People are generally afraid to make decisions. They perceive decisions as final events, not part of an ongoing process. Decisions make people accountable. You can point to a decision and evaluate it. You can blame problems on bad decisions and the people who made them, so to encourage the customer to make a decision, you need to eliminate as much of perceived risk as possible. When customers are afraid to make a decision, they will not make one.

There are two kinds of risk – organizational and political. People will talk about organizational risks and actually do something to prevent. – *What if the solution doesn't work? The implementation will cost the earth and take forever? If we build it, will they come?* The second kind of risk, political risk, people don't want to discuss because it is personal – *What if the decision is unpopular? Are we rocking the boat too much? Will my vote anger my boss?* As a salesperson you need to reduce both kinds of risk.

Organizational risks are managed through constructive problems solving, improved planning, and clear communications. Usually they are not very hard to identify because people are not afraid to communicate these valid concerns. Often the perceived risks will be first communicated as objections, misunderstandings, or competitive traps. You can use your sales skills to help clarify the customer's concerns and your product and business knowledge to allay them.

Political risks are more difficult to manage because people are reluctant to discuss them and to tiptoe around theses kinds of problems. However, as a salesperson you need to raise and resolve the issues. As an outsider you have the power to handle sensitive political concerns.

Use risk management activities to sell up the organization. Unsolved problems must be escalated. Most employees don't want to be the messenger of bad news. By offering to escalate the issue or build cross functional agreement over key issues, you are providing a valuable service to the customer. You are also positioning yourself for a meeting with the decision-makers in the role of a consultant who is concerned about their success. Smart move.

Resolving problems creates sales momentum. Problems create lots of anxiety and negative energy. Solving them converts that energy into positive momentum towards the final decision, so make sure you communicate the resolution of each issue to the entire decision-making team. Explain what the problem was and the negotiated resolution in a way that builds the credibility of your solution.

Develop implementation plan.

Another factor that slows down a sale is when the customer doesn't understand how to implement the solution. Creating an implementation plan that establishes firm parameters of time, cost, and responsibility helps move the sale forward. Helping customers understand what it will really take to successfully implement the solution builds their confidence that it can be done.

It is important to remember that you and your sales team have a lot more experience in implementing your solution than the customer does. Most likely they are doing this for the first time, so they don't know what to expect. Try to set up meetings between the functional executives responsible for the project with your implementation consultants, so they can create a preliminary plan. It is also helpful to put them in contact with reference accounts that have recently implemented your solution, so they get an "unbiased" opinion about the reality of implementing the solution.

Another benefit of getting everyone involved in implementation planning is that it helps you eliminate alternative scenarios. These alternatives might be competitive vendors or completely different ways of enabling the business strategy. The more choices the customer has, the less control you have over the account. If during the implementation planning you can focus the customer increasingly on your approach and build their commitment to what differentiates your solution, then you will be eliminating competitive alternatives at the same time. The fewer the choices, the easier it will be to make the decision.

WHAT YOU NEED TO KNOW TO PROPOSE VALUE

A proposal puts your promises in writing. You lose the fuzziness of verbal communications. It is the first step of the contracting process, so it is important that it is concise, accurate, and current. The proposal crystallizes your value proposition in a way that compels the prospect to buy your solution, so solutions-specific information about how your solution works, builds value, and compares to competitive alternatives is critical.

■ **Value Building Strategies** help you verbalize and tailor your solution's value proposition. Since they create a clear logic flow between the customer's strategic business objectives and how your solution works, they are very useful in helping you clearly communicate your value proposition. Your Value Map helps you understand all the factors involved in implementing a business strategy. It organizes typical problems and technology needs by strategy. This information can be very useful when you are creating an offer because it expands your perception of the deal. It is hard to keep the customer's big picture in your head when you are focused on selling your solution. Value building strategies force you to consider your proposal from the customer's point of view. Value Building Strategies also document the kinds of issues customers must resolve before they can make a decision. This information

PROPOSING COMPETENCIES

★ Be able to propose your solution so it builds the customer's perception of its value.

★ Be able to articulate the business benefits of the technology and how it supports the customer's business strategy.

★ Be able to articulate the key differentiators of the solution.

★ Be able to tailor the solution's value proposition to the specific customer needs.

★ Be able to demonstrate how the solution supports the customer's business strategy.

★ Be able to demonstrate your competitive advantage around key customer needs or issues.

★ Be able to build the customer's perception of value through effective competitive positioning.

★ Be able to propose the solution within the context of the buyer's technology adoption profile.

★ Be able to identify and articulate change management issues and solutions.

★ Be able to build and present an ROI justification for the proposed solution.

★ Be able to work the political relationships in the account to build customer commitment to the solution.

★ Be able to write a proposal that includes all appropriate and relevant information.

helps you anticipate and resolve problems. Since many potential problems remain hidden until you specifically bring them up, this information can be very useful as you work with the customer to reduce their sense of risk.

■ **Competitive Intelligence.** A proposal documents your competitive advantage. Your positioning should center on your competitive differentiation. Your proposal needs to help the customer understand why your solution is the best choice. Use your Competitive Map to focus your unique differentiation, which helps you both build your competitive advantage and eliminate competitive options.

Your Competitive Map also helps you plan and deliver your demo. The technical evaluation team is the people most interested in how your solution compares to competitive alternatives. They are the target audience of your demo, so it is a good time to build competitive advantage around your technological superiority. Besides, once they have declared you the winner, the rest of the decision-makers won't care as much about how you stack up against the competition.

■ **Solutions Selling** A Solutions Map helps you anticipate and resolve political issues because it documents not only the official decision-making process and players, but the unofficial power structure, too. When you propose your solution, you need to use that understanding of the political landscape to ensure your offer appeals to the people who count.

An understanding of the customer's decision-making process also helps you figure out how to build sales momentum. You can use this information to figure out which smaller decisions will be made in advance of the final decision. It also helps you figure out who to include in the smaller decisions and how to close them. Building the sale and making the decision easier by breaking it up into a series of smaller ones help build your control over the account. Finally, solutions selling knowledge helps you build an effective communications plan. As we have discussed, it is critical to communicate all of your successful closes, resolved issues, and decisions made to the entire decision-making team. Don't count on customers doing it on their own. Solutions selling intelligence ensures that the right people will know what is happening.

PROPOSE VALUE PROCESS SUMMARY

What	How	Information Required
1. Create an Offer Create a complete solution that optimizes your value contribution	1.1 Create offer	Understand the scope and benefits of various services that you can use to increase the value of the solution Knowledge of partnership opportunities and other ways to expand the offer beyond your part of the solution
	1.2 Develop ROI	Financial expectations of the successfully implemented strategy Estimated cost of implementation Quantification of solution's benefits Expected ROI and payback period
	1.3 Write proposal	Value Map Solutions Map Decision making roles, responsibilities, political relationships and value drivers Description of the solution Pricing, terms and negotiation limits Competitive pricing
2. Build Sales Momentum Take control of the decision-making process	2.1 Strategize delivery	List of key events in the decision-making process List of events you can offer - demo, technical seminars executive presentations, site visits, corporate visits, executive sales call, financial workshops
	2.2 Communicate progress	Solutions Map
3. Manage Risk Eliminate barriers to the sale through collaborative problem solving and planning	3.1 Resolve outstanding issues	Value Map Competitive Map Solutions Map
	3.2 Develop implementation plan	Implementation requirements Fulfillment capabilities

TAKE ACTION

The purpose of any proposal activity is to move you one step closer to closing the deal. It should either build credibility, close on a specific aspect of the decision, or communicate your success. Sales tools designed to support this process can be very useful.

■ **ROI Value Generator.** Developing an economic justification for a technology solution is critical to any sale. The most useful ROI tools are ones that calculate the economic contribution of the solution within the perspective of the customer's business strategy. At the core of the Value Generator is a set of economic models that use customer specific data to generate realistic cost saving or revenue generating scenarios.

Salespeople like these kinds of tools because they help them quantify and personalize their value proposition. However, gathering the metrics and building the models used to measure financial contribution are complex tasks requiring specialized expertise. It is usually most productive to develop this tool centrally and then teach salespeople how to use it. It is very important the ROI Value Generator is kept as simple as possible. If it is too complex, salespeople will be intimated and will not use it with their prospects.

■ **Executive Conference Visits.** Many high technology companies invest in impressive executive briefing centers early in their development. The reason they do is so they can create an impression of stability and 'bench strength'. Creating this credibility is important, especially as the market is 'crossing the chasm' and early majority customers are looking for vendors who can promise long term support.

Executive conference visits offer prospects an opportunity to meet your senior executives and to hear about your company's technological vision. Often a customer visit is a turning point in the sale because it provides a venue for the executives from both companies to meet and build a relationship.

■ **References & Site Visits.** As soon as the market begins to consolidate, references become critically important to building customer confidence that your solution will work and deliver the benefits you are promising. References take careful planning to work effectively. You need to match the situation as closely as possible for them to be credible. For most companies this means matching company size and industry.

Also, if you match how they use the technology to enable their business strategies you can increase their appreciation of the results.

When matching references it is very important to consider the customers' technology adoption profiles. Early majority buyers won't buy your solution until they can see proof that it has worked for someone else who had the same implementation concerns that they do. Therefore, you need a list of reference accounts that will share the results of their solution with other prospects. In a perfect world this would be a straightforward task. However, in the real world it is very difficult to amass a library of early success stories.

The problem with references is that they tend to be abused. Smart salespeople jealously guard them for good reasons. Nothing threatens the hard-earned confidentially of an account relationship faster than having one of your prospect's competitors call them up and ask them how they used your technology. So be careful about sharing references and keep control over who can access the account directly.

CONCLUSIONS

- **Take control.** The sales cycle comes to a head when you propose the solution. At this point you know what the customer is trying to accomplish, his needs and issues, and what will compel him to make a decision. Your proposal provides a way to actualize their strategy.

- **Minimize risks.** Submitting a formal proposal intensifies the customer's concerns about the risks associated with the decision. Since the proposal defines the cost and implementation plan, it tends to focus the customer on what could go wrong. You need to allay his concerns by resolving outstanding issues, collaborating on an implementation plan and eliminating competitive alternatives.

- **A proposal is a series of events, not just a document.** The proposal gives you a chance to schedule events that build excitement and desire to make the decision. By closing on each event you are building moment toward the final close.

- **Be explicit.** Up until the proposal is submitted, everything is vague. The proposal not only crystallizes your promise but the promises that the prospect has made, too.

- **Position yourself against the competition.** The proposal organizes the competitive battle. It clearly positions your unique value proposition, which implies that competitive weakness of the competition. Your proposal defines how you want the customer to make his decision.

- **Identify the whole solution.** As you create your proposal you need to bundle together the products and services required to ensure that the solution will deliver your value proposition within the prospect's business environment. Therefore, you need to ensure that your proposal identifies all the factors that make up the final solution, even if your company is not supplying them all.

- **Negotiate for optimum timing.** Many salespeople make the mistake of submitting a proposal too soon. A good salesperson works the account until everyone is ready for the proposal. If you are asked to submit a proposal too early, you must convince the customer that you can't write it until you have completed your discovery.

- **Sell money.** An effective ROI justification is critical to the technology sale because it is the only way to justify the intangible benefits of your solution.

- **Keep your options open.** As soon as you put a price in writing, your ability to evolve the proposal in response to the prospect's changing needs is greatly reduced. You want to be pretty close to a final offer before you actually quote a price.

Chapter 10

Close Fast

Create Momentum & Negotiate Success

CLOSE FAST

What   Close the deal so it delivers results.

Why   During the closing negotiations it is easy to lose sight of the what
            it will take for the deal to result in an implementation that delivers
            the results everyone expects. By closing effectively, you ensure that
            your solution will live up to the promises you have made both to the
            customer and your management.

How   1. Plan the close, so you are prepared to negotiate a successful and
            profitable deal.

            2. Negotiate success, so you ensure that the final deal will deliver
            the promised results.

            3. Close the deal, so everybody feels good about their contribution
            to the decision and renews their commitment to the successful
            implementation of the solution.

So What?   A well-managed closing process ensures that you will survive the
            stressful negotiating experience with your deal, reputation, and sense
            of humor intact.

WHAT IS CLOSING?

Closing is the process of successfully negotiating and signing a contract.

During the close you carefully plan how you want to negotiate the final details and close the deal. You need to define a strategy that ensures that nothing critical gets cut from the offer during the negotiating process. You need to protect the value you have built throughout the process.

To close you access power both in your and your customer's organizations to ensure a successful conclusion. Finally you celebrate the customer's decision in a way that makes everyone feel good about it.

By the time you reach the closing phase of the sales cycle you have a single purpose. Get the contract signed. Emotionally the decision has already been made. The customer is committed to your solution and ready to start. However, there are still details that need to be resolved –price, terms and delivery… Closing is a stressful time filled with anticipation, frustration and excitement. The closing process helps you keep emotions under control and ensures that rational minds prevail.

WHY IS CLOSING IMPORTANT?

There is an excitement about the close. All your hard work is about to pay off. The decision-maker is convinced that your solution is the best. Everyone who counts is on board. The moment has arrived.

Then, all of sudden, everything changes. *New players, purchasing agents who understand neither the business strategy nor your value proposition, enter the picture. Your gatekeeper has an attack of "amnesia" and completely forgets why your solution is the best choice. The losing competitor plays dirty tricks in desperation, like cutting their price by 70%.* Before you lose control, it is time to close the deal. Fast.

■ **Ensure Your Customer's Success.** Closing negotiations are a precarious time. New people who don't understand the issues or value of the solution become involved in the decision. Mistakes are easily made. Carefully thought out plans can be sacrificed in pursuit of the best deal. It is time for you to champion the success of the project. In this chapter you will learn how careful planning and skillful negotiations can help your customers succeed, in spite of themselves.

■ **Take Control of the Process.** Seventy-five percent of all negotiations start in a stalemate. Each side waits to see what the other side is going to do. Learn how to take the initiative to lead the process, and you will gain significant advantage.

■ **Improve Profitability.** During a complex negotiation you will have many opportunities to significantly "sweeten the pot." If you have a thorough knowledge of your customer's needs and the business model of your offer, you will be able to negotiate with flexibility and style. Learn how to plan your negotiation so you end up with a profitable deal.

■ **Be Confident.** Most salespeople lack confidence when it is time to sit down at the negotiating table. This is because negotiating tactics are counterintuitive to good sales behavior. In this chapter you will learn techniques for negotiating effectively and closing fast, so you can overcome your fears.

WHY CLOSE?

★ The contract is signed.

★ The customer commits to a successful implementation.

★ You increase the profitability of the deal.

★ You negotiate with confidence.

★ You get paid!

HOW TO CLOSE FAST

The close is often the most tension-filled phase of the sales process. Your role changes from problem solver and coach to planner and negotiator. Instead of doing favors for people, you are asking people to do favors for you. Instead of saying yes, you find yourself having to say no. It doesn't feel natural.

The closing process helps you perform consistently during the emotional stress of negotiations. By planning carefully ahead of time, you can define a strategy that ensures that nothing critical gets cut from the offer during the negotiating process. Enlisting the right players to help you negotiate better and not being afraid to escalate issues help you build the power base your need for a positive outcome. Finally celebrating and communicating the buying decision help you build support and commitment for a successful implementation.

The most important thing to remember is **never undermine the value you have created during the sales process.** Don't let nasty negotiation tactics intimidate you into any action that negates the value you have carefully built. The customer has chosen your solution for some very good reasons, and most likely the lowest price is not one of them, so stand firm and get the price you deserve.

THE CLOSING PROCESS

1. Plan the Close.

   ➤ Create a negotiating strategy that delivers success.

2. Negotiate Success.

   ➤ Ensure the successful implementation of the solution.

3. Close the Deal.

   ➤ Celebrate by communicating the decision.

STEP 1: Plan the Close

Walking into a meeting to negotiate the final contract without a plan is like walking into battle without a weapon. Don't do it. Develop a plan, and stick to it.

Write the closing proposal.

Throughout the proposal stage you have collaborated with the customer to create a final offer that optimizes the potential value contribution of your solution. Even if you have consistently communicated to everyone involved in the sale what decisions have been made and why, it is very important that you summarize the offer in a final proposal. This document should cover all the topics of the original proposal – the customer's business strategy, your value proposition, key benefits, ROI justification, implementation plan, etc. It should also explain why your solution has been chosen by clearly identifying why the decision-maker has accepted your value proposition and the results your solution is expected to produce.

The closing proposal also includes the final business deal – pricing, terms, delivery dates, implementation commitments, etc. It outlines the commitments that the customer has made as part of the planning process – approval schedules, internal resources, payment schedules, etc. It is important to include in the final proposal some negotiating chips that you can use during the negotiating process. By including deliverables that 'sweeten the pot' but don't directly impact the final success of the solution, you are building negotiating power into your proposal. *For example, private labeling the order processing software, so it looks like it was developed internally.*

Define negotiation strategy.

The second step of your plan is to develop a negotiation strategy. Studies show that in 75% of all negotiations, both parties wait to see what the other party will do before they decide what to do themselves. If you take control from the start, you will gain an enormous advantage in the negotiation. Set the agenda, establish the tone of the negotiation, and you will be able to direct how the negotiation will proceed.

In your proposal you have defined your offer, which represents the in-going 'size of the pie.' In over 90% of all negotiations, people consider the deal to be a 'pie' of a certain size and work to get as much of it as they can. However, you know that the current offer reflects a compromise of a more complete solution, which could be bigger. It is equally as likely that, if you strip out some 'bells and whistles,' the solution could be a little smaller, as well. *Maybe the order processing software doesn't need a customized interface.*

Before you negotiate the final deal you need to figure out how you could make the 'pie' bigger or smaller and still have a successful outcome and profitable deal. This kind of planning will give you a big advantage during the negotiations because you know how to scale the solution up or down and still have it work. *Customizing the interface of the order processing software costs $25,000 and the impact is purely cosmetic.* The customer's professional negotiators don't have the technical expertise required to change the scope of the solution.

Knowing how to expand or shrink the solution helps you build your concession strategy, which is what you are willing to give up over the course of the negotiations. *If they want us to cut the price, we will suggest the generic version and give up the less profitable customization.* Concession strategies are very important because you will have to give up something, so the negotiator thinks he got a good deal. You just need to be sure that you don't give up anything that jeopardizes the success of the solution or makes it unprofitable for your company to fulfill the contract.

You also need to know what your 'walk-away' strategy is. Even though the buying committee has decided that they want to do business with you, a showstopper issue could come up during the negotiations that would kill the deal. *For example, if the negotiator suggests not customizing the data fields the success of the project is in jeopardy, which is a risk you can't take.* The best way to prevent this from happening is to have thought about the situation ahead of time and to be very clear on the best course of action. You need to think about the impact of walking away from the deal both from the perspective of your and the customer's company. If the customer is asking for something that makes it a bad idea to do business with him, then you need to have the courage to walk away from the deal. However, when you do, you better be able to explain to your management why you did.

You also need to be ready to explain to the customer's decision-maker why you have chosen not to sell her the solution. After all, you have promised a compelling solution, and now you are not going to deliver it. In this kind of situation a good defense is the best offense. The threat of walking often motivates the negotiator to back down, especially if you explain that on your way out you are going to explain to the decision-maker why the deal has fallen through.

As you develop your negotiation strategy, make sure that you figure out a way to keep the value of your solution visible. Have independent proof sources and market statistics at your fingertips in case you need to explain your solution's pricing. Create a chart of the value propositions that have been accepted by the key stakeholders. Ask for a copy of the financial decision-maker's recommendation that includes your ROI justification. Summarize the technical evaluators' rationale for choosing your solution onto one page. Gather all the value proof sources you can, so you can pull them out during the negotiations and use them to your advantage.

Put on your negotiating hat.

Negotiating is counterintuitive to selling. In selling, the customer is always right. Your job is to give customers what they want. Negotiation requires a different way of thinking. You need to satisfy the customer without sacrificing their success or your profitability in the process. Don't let your belief in being responsive and customer-focused result in costly negotiation errors, especially under the natural tension created by the close.

Most salespeople aren't effective negotiators because they're too willing to do whatever it takes to make the sale. Your unconscious, natural reaction in negotiations is often the opposite of the best negotiating behavior. For example, when the customer asks you for information, you tend to provide too much detail. A good negotiator provides just the information that customer needs to move the deal forward. If the customer requests a concession on price, you are most likely to give too much away too soon in hopes that you can close the deal quickly. Good negotiators concede reluctantly and make sure that they get concessions of equal value in return.

To close the deal to everyone's satisfaction you need to negotiate with power. If the customer expresses discomfort or indicates he is unhappy with certain details, then you need to stay with the tension until an agreement can be reached. This is hard to do, especially since you have spent the past few months collaborating closely building the solution. Your natural tendency is to create an alternative solution quickly. Don't forget that the people who count – the decision-maker and stakeholders – have already agreed on what you are proposing. Therefore, don't give in to someone whose job it is to make you sweat.

Enlist the right players.

Never go into the negotiating meeting alone. Good negotiators are aware of the intangible perceptions of who has greater power and higher status. They use this power and status to influence in the final outcome. Ideally you want to take the most powerful stakeholder from the customer's organization into the meeting with you. Use this person to explain the value and benefits of the solution.

If you think the customer is going to ask you to make a lot of concessions, it is helpful to have a 'professional negotiator' representing your company. You need to walk a fine line between being a helpful sales executive and a tough negotiator. This is especially important for account managers in large companies, who often only have a limited number of accounts. They have worked hard to build a close relationship with the customer and are reluctant to take any action that would anger them. Savvy purchasing managers take advantage of this behavior and ask for large discounts or other financial concessions, so bring along a hired gun.

It is also important to identify upfront who is your and your customer's 'higher authority,' who is someone not in the room with the power to overturn a decision. This is a useful person for you to have in case you find yourself negotiated into a corner, and you need a way to get out of it gracefully. It is also important to know who the customer's higher authority is and this person's relationship to the decision-maker. If the decision-maker has more power than this person, you are fine. If he doesn't then you may need to forewarn him that potential conflicts may arise.

Step 2: Negotiate Success

When closing a deal, your most important objective is to keep customers from making last minute decisions that will compromise the success of the solution. Let their negotiating team win some points. Make concessions according to your plan. Play the game, but don't let the negotiations jeopardize the solution's potential success.

Present final proposal.

The big day has arrived. It is time to present the final proposal and close the deal. This meeting may or may not include the decision-maker and the buying committee. If they are there, you can keep the meeting focused on the value proposition, resolving any outstanding issues, and signing the contract. If they are not there and you are faced with a room full of negotiators, you need to be ready to bargain.

Invariably these will be some tense moments. Someone will stop talking. Threats will be made. They will try to convince you that your competitor can do just as good a job as you can, or they will they will make some lowball offer and then give you the silent treatment.

Use your negotiating skills to fight back. Make sure you get something for everything you give up. Use your stakeholder allies to reinforce your value propositions with their negotiators. Be confident in your power. After all, you have the decision-maker's endorsement on your side. It is the negotiators' job to make the deal work.

Play fast. It is in everyone's best interest to close the deal as quickly as possible. If small concessions will result in a faster close, it may be worth it to make them. Keep the ball moving down the field.

Beware of commodification.

The most likely negotiating tactic your customer will try is to ask you to discount your price. Up until the close, price has most likely not been a big issue.

Early in the sale, prospects aren't very concerned with price because they don't know what they want to do yet. During the evaluation phase they are preoccupied with functionality and capabilities. During the proposal phase, you thought you resolved any outstanding cost issues during your ROI justification meeting. And now, at the close, price comes up as an issue.

Thanks to 'value amnesia' customers suddenly forget why they selected you after an exhaustive search. They tell you that they have several solutions to choose from, and they can't tell the difference among them. They think they would like to go with you, but your competitor has offered to discount their price to a point where it would be 'fiscally irresponsible' to choose you. So what do you do?

Don't give into this negotiating ploy. The second you give in on price during negotiations, you negate the value you have built during the sales process. Discounting sends the wrong message about your solution's value. When you discount, customers always think that they should have asked for more or that the product isn't really worth what you have led them to believe.

Now is the time to pull out your list of differentiating advantages and walk the negotiators through your value proposition step-by-step. Make sure you punctuate each major point by referencing the key stakeholder, who believes this part of the solution is critical to the success of the business strategy. *The CFO is the one who is insisting on customized data fields for the order entry software.* Even better yet, have as many of the stakeholders in the room as you can, so they can make the point for you.

Undoubtedly these counter-tactics will frustrate the professional negotiators who are asking you for the price reductions. After all, they don't care about how well the solution works; they just need to show that they have negotiated the best deal for their company. So, after you have demonstrated that you have the power of their executives behind you, make some other concession. Offer better terms or an additional service that is easy for you to provide. You can also resolve some other issue that doesn't erode the profitability of your sale, like faster delivery or a longer payment schedule, in their favor. Be creative, and let them win some points. **Just don't let them erode the value you have built!**

Escalate outstanding issues.

There may come a moment when you reach an impasse. The customer has asked you to make a compromise on something that is critical to delivering the expected results. It is time to stop the meeting and escalate issues to the decision-maker.

The decision-maker is the person who is least sensitive to the price of the solution. He has already decided that the benefits of the results outweigh the proposed costs. What the decision-maker cares about is that the project is a success. A lower price doesn't lower the risk of the project.

Fight hard for your customer's success. One thing that often happens in the closing negotiations is that services or functionality critical to the success of the implementation are cut in order to make the final price acceptable to both parties. This happens because the final details have been taken out of the hands of the people who actually know what it will take to implement the solution and put into the hands of professional negotiators – e.g. the lawyers, purchasing department, or technology buyers. Be on your guard not to let this happen, because if it does and the solution doesn't deliver, it will be your problem, not theirs.

Fortunately, it will also be the problem of the decision-maker and the key stakeholders. If you feel that the integrity of the solution is being compromised at the negotiating table, don't hesitate to escalate the problem to the decision-maker. A simple phone call explaining what is happening and the potential negative impact on the success of the project should be enough to resolve the problem. After all, the decision-maker has already made her decision and she doesn't want some staff negotiator to mess it up.

There is a magic to sales momentum. During the proposal process everyone has invested a lot of energy in making the decision. You have built a lot of excitement around the solution. Results have been promised. Everyone is ready for action.

Negotiating always seems to take forever. Your lawyers need time to review the contract. Their lawyers need to make a few changes. Another meeting has to be scheduled... Everyone will find a reason to stall the sale. Don't let it happen.

Use your political power in the account to keep the ball moving. Entice the stakeholders and decision-maker to light a fire under their negotiating team. Use your manager to make sure that your side doesn't slow things down. Make promises. Take secretaries out to lunch, whatever it takes to close. Fast.

STEP 3: Close the deal

The deal is done. It is time to pop the champagne and give everyone a pat on the back. Celebrating your success encourages commitment to implementing the solution.

Close the decision-maker.

When negotiations are completed and contract is approved, schedule a closing meeting with the decision-maker. Use the meeting to reiterate the value proposition, sign the contract, and celebrate the process. Celebrating the process is important because it recognizes everyone's hard work and encourages the buying committee to feel good about their decision. It helps put the conflicts that arose during the process behind everyone. It reminds everyone why they chose your solution and refocuses them on the future.

The success of your technology solution relies on the customer embracing the solution and the changes that it brings. Spend some time and money helping everyone feel good, and the likelihood that your solution will be successfully implemented increases.

Celebrate success.

Follow up on your closing meeting by communicating the decision inside your and your customer's organization. Explain to everyone who was involved in the decision what was decided and why. Everyone likes to be associated with success, so thank everyone individually for his or her contribution to the process.

Use this opportunity to remind them of the commitments they have made, the importance of their role in ensuring the successful implementation of the solution, and, consequently, the success of the business strategy. By linking people's contribution to strategic results, you are motivating them to take ownership in success of the solution.

If during the negotiating process any key concessions were made that might negatively impact the potential contribution of the solution, then make sure that you set new expectations. Taking this action accomplishes two things. First, it helps the customer set realistic expectations for results, so no one gets blamed for an impossible situation. Secondly, now that the customer's project team owns the problem, they might be able to quickly turn the situation around, and what was taken out of the plan might be put back in.

Get the ball rolling. Once the contract is signed, your job is not over. You need to make sure that there is a smooth hand-over between the sales and the implementation and customer support teams. Make sure that customer expectations are met; orders are shipped; services delivered on time, etc.

CLOSING COMPETENCIES

★ Be able to successfully close and negotiate a deal.

★ Be able to negotiate the contract to your company's advantage.

★ Be able to obtain pricing and cost estimate approvals quickly during negotiations.

★ Understand pricing and policies.

★ Be able to sell support as part of the solution to increase the probability of success.

WHAT YOU NEED TO KNOW TO CLOSE

■ **Independent Research and Competitive Price Lists.** During negotiations you will often be asked to justify the pricing and terms of your proposal. The reason most customers ask these kinds of questions is because they are trying to gauge whether your pricing is 'fair.' This is an attempt to put rational judgment around the emotional value you have created during the sales process. The easiest way to address this issue is to be able to point to 'industry standards.' When customers can compare your pricing to your competitor's price list or to market research documenting the true costs of implementation, then they feel better about spending the money. Therefore, it is important to have access to as much information as possible about what it really costs to implement your category of technology solution.

■ **Real-time Access to Account Fulfillment Information.** Many high tech companies are creating sales management portals that enable their sales teams' visibility into the ERP systems that manage the production, fulfillment, and delivery of the company's product and services. These 'sales dashboards' enable sales teams to easily access the resources they need to manage their accounts. It is especially useful when these sales tools include detailed information about the contribution of the products and services that make up the solution's offer. When salespeople better understand the cost structure of what they are selling, they can create more profitable offers and negotiate more effectively.

CLOSE FAST PROCESS SUMMARY

What	How	Information Required
1. Plan the Close Create a negotiating strategy that delivers success	1.1 Write closing proposal	Earlier proposals Solutions Map ROI justification Implementation plan
	1.2 Define negotiation strategy	Negotiation guidelines Concession strategy Walk away strategy
2. Negotiate Success Ensure the successful implementation of the solution	2.1 Present final proposal	Final proposal
	2.2 Escalate outstanding issues	Solutions Map Relationship of decision maker to negotiating team
3. Close Deal Celebrate by communicating the decision	3.1 Close the decision maker	Personal preferences of the decision-maker and buying committee
	3.2 Celebrate success	Implementation plan Final terms of the contract How to facilitate handing over the account to technical support, customer service, or the implementation team

CONCLUSIONS

- **Negotiating is counterintuitive to selling.** Most salespeople aren't effective negotiators because they're too willing to do whatever it takes to make the sale. Your unconscious, natural reaction in negotiations is often the opposite of the best negotiating behavior.

- **Don't underestimate your power.** To close the deal to everyone's satisfaction you need to negotiate with power. The people who count – the decision-maker and key stakeholders – have already agreed on what you are proposing, so don't give in to someone whose job it is to make you sweat.

- **Don't discount your price.** The most likely negotiating tactic your customer will try is to ask you to discount your price. During the close they may forget why they selected you after an exhaustive search. Don't give in to this negotiating ploy. The second you give in on price during negotiations you negate the value you have built.

- **Negotiate success.** One thing that often happens in the closing negotiations is that services or functionality critical to the success of the implementation are cut in order to make final price acceptable to both parties. Do not let this happen. If it does and the solution doesn't deliver the expected results, it will be your problem, not theirs.

- **Escalate issues.** If you feel that the integrity of the solution is being compromised at the negotiating table, don't hesitate to escalate the problem to the decision-maker. The decision-maker is the person who is least sensitive to the price of the solution. What the decision-maker cares about is that the project is a success. A lower price doesn't lower the risk of the project.

- **Take the initiative.** Studies show that in 75% of all negotiations, both parties wait to see what the other party will do before they decide what to do themselves, so if you take control from the start, you will gain an enormous advantage in the negotiation.

- **Know how to scale the solution.** In over 90% of all negotiations, people think of the value in a negotiation as a pie of a certain size. However, most technology offers reflect a compromise of a more complete solution. If you know how to scale the solution up or down and still have it work, you will have a unique, negotiating advantage.

- **Have a fall back plan.** Knowing how to expand or shrink the solution helps you build your concession strategy, which is what you are willing to give up over the course of the negotiations. You also need a 'walk-away' strategy.

- **Keep the value of your solution visible.** Gather all the value proof sources you can, so you can pull them out during the negotiations and use them to your advantage.

- **Never go into the negotiating meeting alone.** Take the most powerful stakeholder from the customer's organization into the meeting with you. Use this person to explain the value and benefits of the solution. Identify upfront who is your and your customer's 'higher authority.' If the decision-maker has more power than this person, you are fine. If not, forewarn your decision-maker, so he is prepared for potential conflicts.

- **Celebrate the process.** Recognize everyone's hard work and help the buying committee to feel good about their decision. By linking people's contribution strategic results you are motivating them to take ownership in the success of the solution.

Chapter 11

Make It Happen

Where You Go From Here

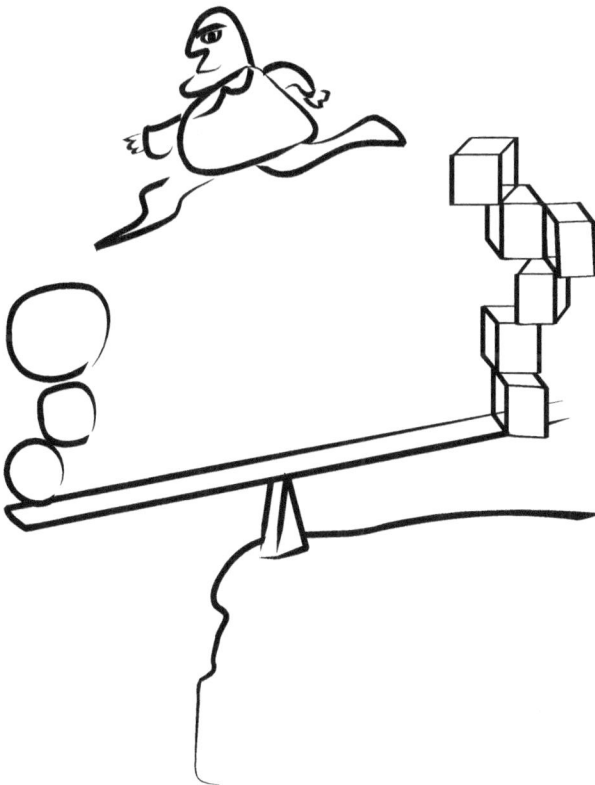

MAKE IT HAPPEN

What   Create a system to support ongoing sales force development.

Why   Content and competency management systems are essential to the
            successful implementation of strategic, go-to-market initiatives.

How   1. Develop sales ready content, so you deliver a consistent message
            to the market and accelerate the company's learning curve.

            2. Use competencies to drive the learning process, so your sales
            teams have practical, useful information that is easy to apply to
            the sales process.

            3. Use metrics to provide feedback, so you can create
            an environment of continuous improvement.

So What?   Market adoption of your technology solution can only be achieved when
            there are thousands of conversations happening around the world.
            Content and competency management systems ensure that these
            conversations happen consistently and productively.

Sell Results: *What Every Technology Salesperson Needs to Know* is about the information you need to sell successfully. The ideas presented in this book are not revolutionary. Many companies have done this before. It is not 'rocket science,' so, why isn't this information at your fingertips?

Most high tech companies don't do a good job providing their salespeople with the information they need to become sales superstars. Why not? Because, it is hard to do. Instead, they offer generic sales methodologies, market analysis, or technical product knowledge training. Since the product and market knowledge and the sales methodologies are not integrated into the sales training courses and sales tools, it is up to each individual salesperson to invent his own approach to selling the new technology solutions. Most large technology companies choose to reinvent the wheel thousands of times as each salesperson creates a unique set of sales tools – marketing materials, questioning strategies, competitive traps, proposals – to manage the sales process. This approach is very unproductive. However, companies can get away with this approach when they are selling mature technologies or have incredibly smart salespeople. (Don't forget the sales legends....)

However, when you are trying to sell new technologies into emerging markets, this 'do-it-yourself' approach can have disastrous consequences. In the time it takes for the sales force to get up to speed, the market will likely pass you buy. The way to prevent lost opportunities caused by slow learning curves is to make a commitment to building and maintaining a content management system around your core messaging, product and market knowledge, and competitive intelligence.

No one said this was going to be easy.

There are many issues around building and maintaining high-quality content, such as:

- **Building good content is hard.** It is difficult to find qualified content developers. Furthermore, building consensus around the content among key constituencies – marketing, sales and engineering – is often difficult and political. However, consensus is critical to the smooth execution of strategy in the marketplace.
- **Content needs to be creatively interpreted and applied to the sales cycle** before it is useful and productive. Creating useful, practical sales tools to sell value over a lengthy and complex sales cycle requires a skill set that most salespeople don't have. Furthermore, maintaining the accuracy and consistency of the content

across all the deliverables that use it – sales tools, training, promotional materials, etc. – is very time consuming and costly.

■ **Maintaining the evolution of your value proposition** for a new technology in an emerging market is challenging. As technology markets mature, sales-related content changes in response to the evolving technology adoption profile of the market. Supporting the evolution of the content is critical to capturing market share up the technology growth curve.

Companies need to figure out how to make selling innovative technologies into emerging markets easier. If you know who to call on, how to capture their attention, what questions to ask, and how to put together a solid offer, you are much more likely to do it. Furthermore, if someone gives you a set of sales tools that help position the value of the new solution to the early adopter, you are much more likely to pick up the phone and call them.

Technology companies need to build a core source of information and tools that make it easier to sell new technologies into emerging markets. Then they need to offer a field development process that encourages use of the information. To help you become a sales superstar, your company needs to do three things:

1. Develop 'sales ready' content.
2. Use sales competencies to guide how the content is packaged, so it is easy to assimilate into the sales process.
3. Drive the use of the information by tracking metrics that provide individuals and organizations with feedback on their progress.

MAKE IT HAPPEN

1. Develop Sales Ready Content.

    ➤ Ensure consistent messaging and accelerate learning.

2. Use Competencies to Drive Learning Process.

    ➤ Ensure that the content is useful and practical.

3. Use Metrics to Provide Feedback.

    ➤ Create an environment of continuous improvement.

STEP 1: Develop Sales Ready Content

'Sales ready' content is the information you need to successfully sell technology. In this book you have learned that to sell technology you must present the customer with the right information at the right time. Developing customer commitment is a complex process of managing their learning and decision-making processes around the technology solution. You must associate key facts in the customer's mind in order to increase the customer's perception of need, urgency to buy, and competitive advantage. 'Sales ready' content helps you manage the content critical to the sales process and apply it ways that move the sales forward.

Good content brings the perspectives of multiple disciplines – engineering, business, sales, marketing, etc. – to consensus around a credible, easy-to-communicate message of technological empowerment. In order to build an effective content management system, you must not only define the content models and deliverables, but the content development and management process, too. It is critical to clearly define

CONTENT DEVELOPMENT PROCESS

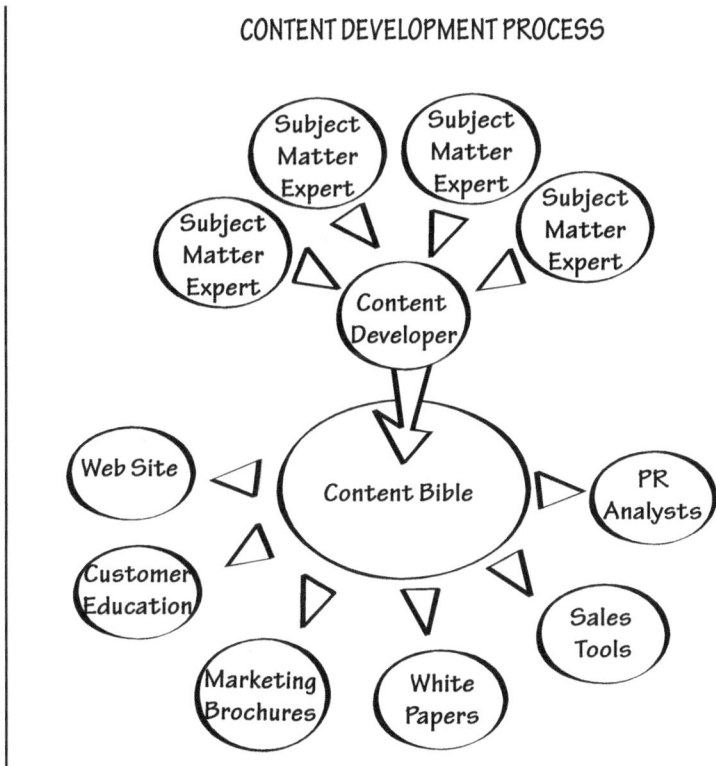

the roles and responsibilities of the various players who support a cross-functional, content management system.

A content developer drives the content modeling process. This person is someone who is highly skilled in writing, communicating, and building consensus around key issues. A content developer is a cross-functional generalist with significant sales or sales engineering experience, who understands not only what information is critical to success, but also the key information relationships required to facilitate the sales process.

The content developer's works with Subject Matter Experts (SME's) to gather relevant information concerning the market, technology, solution, sales process, etc. He then refines the content so it is useful to the field sales organization, customers, value chain partners, and marketplace. This process usually requires discussions with multiple SME's.

The content modeling process is designed to integrate the messages of multiple disciplines into a single, easy-to-understand message that the salesperson can use to educate his customer. One of the great challenges in building a content management system is that you have a wide range of 'experts' who each have a slightly

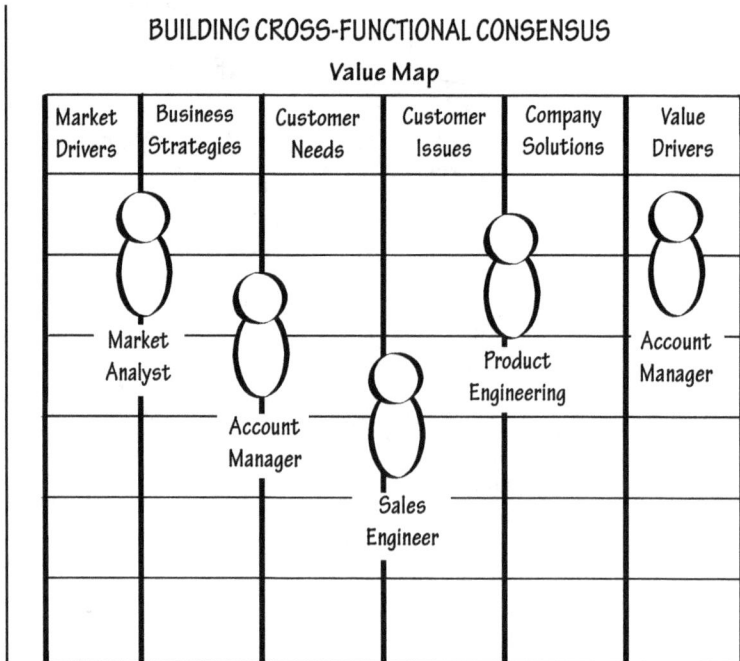

BUILDING CROSS-FUNCTIONAL CONSENSUS
Value Map

Market Drivers	Business Strategies	Customer Needs	Customer Issues	Company Solutions	Value Drivers
Market Analyst				Product Engineering	Account Manager
	Account Manager				
		Sales Engineer			

different perspective about the 'truth.' Each expert expresses herself differently and represents a different perspective. They often feel they are right, and their colleagues don't understand the complexity of the situation. The truth – e.g. the information that is most useful to the salesperson – often lies in a compromise that brings the perspectives together.

A good content management development system aligns these perspectives and builds consensus, so a single message can be communicated to the field, market, and customer. This is very important, because without consensus, the field, and, consequently, the market, get conflicting messages. Conflicting messages undermine market credibility.

Another essential requirement for a content management system is that it clearly establishes ownership for the content and the deliverables that apply the content to the sales process. Content includes all aspects of product knowledge, business applications, technology adoption, competitive alternatives, etc. Content is not the deliverables that salespeople use to sell –brochures, white papers, sales presentations, etc – it is the core information itself.

This is a confusing point. Most people think content is a training program, marketing brochure, or customer education web site. This is because content is

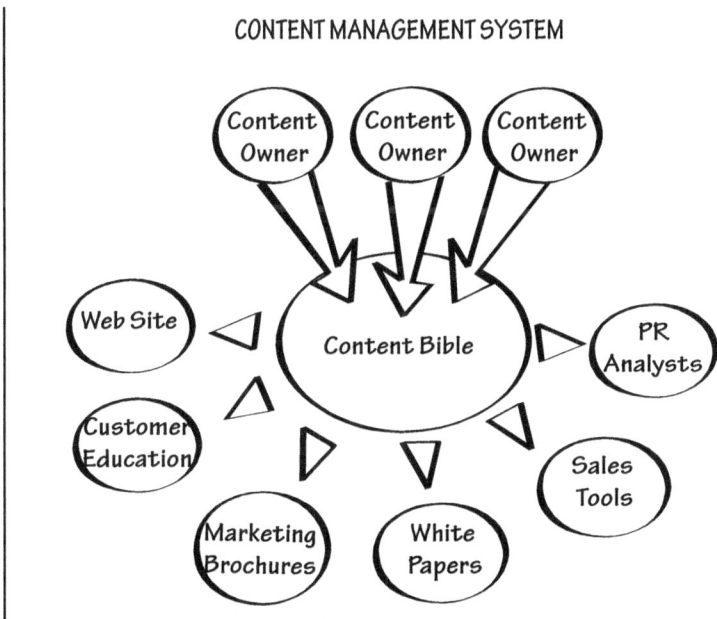

CONTENT MANAGEMENT SYSTEM

developed as part of the process of developing the deliverables. It shouldn't be. Content should be developed by the core intelligentsia of the company. Once the content is developed and everyone agrees that it is correct, accurate and timely, then deliverables that use the content as its source should be created.

In a well-designed content management system, the appropriate ownership is assigned for both the content and the deliverables. The system ensures that the 'experts' have control over the base content and that their messages are accurately interpreted in the information deliverables that are disseminated to the field and the customer. Learn more about content management at www.sellresults.com.

CONTENT MANAGEMENT KEY SUCCESS FACTORS

☑ Establish clear roles and responsibilities.

☑ Build cross-functional consensus.

☑ Empower content ownership.

☑ Maintain the quality of content over time.

Benefits of a 'sales ready' content management system

■ **More credibility in the marketplace.** The primary benefit of good content management is that it creates a consistent source of accurate, current information about the technology and what it enables. Because there is a single source of content that everyone can access to produce the many deliverables required to support a global sales effort, the company can create a consistent message. Consistent messaging builds credibility in the marketplace.

■ **Improved sales productivity and organizational responsiveness.** If content is not developed centrally, than it has be created by everyone who responds to the customer – every salesperson, every sales engineer, strategic marketing, product marketing, sales training developer, etc. This is an incredibly unproductive use of resources. When you centralize content into a single source, everyone's job becomes much easier. As a salesperson you don't have to make up the value selling strategies; you only have to apply them to your customers' situation. Furthermore, a centralized source of timely content helps improve organizational responsiveness to market evolution, increased competition, or changes in business strategy.

■ **Better, more focused, use of key resources.** A content management process makes more efficient use of valuable, overworked subject matter experts (SME's). There is a core group of experts – senior executive strategists, top salespeople, experienced sales engineers, product marketing managers – who own the core ideas and principles that guide the technology organization. These are very busy people. A content management system leverages their expertise and optimizes their contribution to the enterprise. It also gives them control over the core messaging that is disseminated to the marketplace in a myriad of ways.

■ **A more coordinated sales and marketing strategy.** The fastest way to implement a go-to-market strategy through a field sales organization is to provide it with knowledge that helps them use their skills more effectively. Skilled salespeople lacking the critical information they need to apply their skills are unproductive. By integrating solutions content into high-level thinking strategies, you can shape salespeople's thinking and behavior. By making their job easier, you encourage them to implement your strategy.

WHY CREATE 'SALES READY' CONTENT MODELS?

★ Increase market credibility through consistent messaging.

★ Improve sales productivity.

★ Respond faster to market changes.

★ Leverage your experts.

★ Improve implementation of go-to-market strategies.

Step 2: Use Competencies to Drive Learning Process

Good content isn't enough. The content needs to be creatively interpreted so it supports the sales process. To increase the utility of your content, you must figure out what the salesperson has to do at each step of the sales cycle to be successful and apply the 'sales ready' content to the situation. This process enables you to build sales and marketing tools that actually work.

The success of a high tech sales organization directly depends on how quickly it can respond to change. Getting a sales organization to respond, however, is a huge challenge. Most high tech sales organizations are large and global. Getting 8,000 people around the world to quickly change their behavior is not easy, especially since salespeople tend to be independent thinkers, who hate being taken out the of the field for formal training events. The faster the sales team can recognize change and turn it into new sales opportunities, the better.

High-performance sales organizations solve this problem by applying the principles or competency management to developing their salespeople. Competency-based development enables a sales team to quickly build the skills and knowledge they need to successfully implement the organization's sales and business strategies. This makes the sales organization more responsive to change and, consequently, more successful.

COMPETENCY DRIVES RESULTS

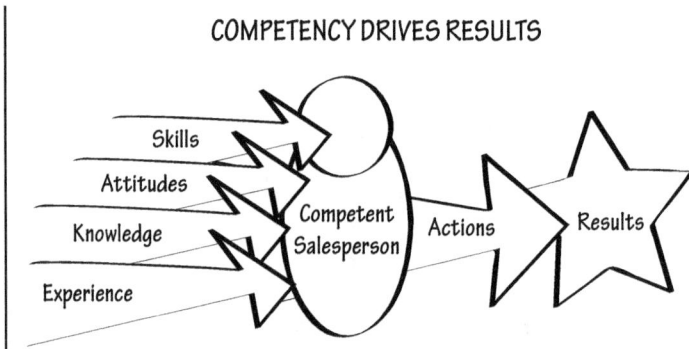

A competency is the ability to apply skills and knowledge to accomplish job related tasks. For example, competencies listed in the Section 2 of this book include:

- *Be able to estimate the potential profitability of the account.*

- *Be able to articulate the key differentiators of the solution.*

- *Be able to sell support as part of the solution to increase the probability of success.*

Sales competencies tend to fall into three categories:

- Professional skills competencies are skills required to perform a job that can be applied to any situation – *the ability to establish executive relationships at the very top of the customer organization.*

- Technology expertise competencies are knowledge required to perform a job – *the ability to explain the basic structure of TCP/IP and how it maps to the OSI model.*

- Sales process competencies integrate technical expertise and professional skills and apply them to the sales process, – *the ability to conduct a discovery interview to uncover a manufacturer's need for wireless solutions.*

SALES COMPETENCY ANALYSIS

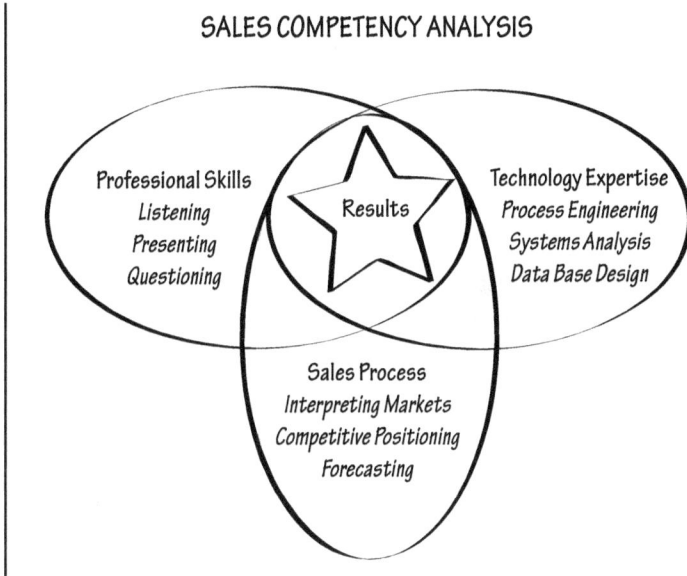

Selling technology solutions is a complex job. An analysis of a high-tech sales team results in the identification of hundreds of competencies. In each chapter in Section 2 of this book, you will find lists of the sales competencies required to successfully implement each step of the sales cycle.

You can use these competencies to analyze what you need to do to deliver results. First, clarify the results that you have to deliver in support the company's strategic business objectives. *If company wants to grow reliably, the sales force needs to be able forecast accurately.* Then create a list of things that you need to be able to do to deliver those results *In order to forecast accurately you need to be able to correctly predict how long it will take to close a deal.* These are the competencies you need to be successful. Finally, create a list of skills knowledge and attitudes you must develop in order to become competent. *Being able to predict the length of the sales cycle requires that you have good qualification skills so you are sure you are working with a serious prospect. You must be honest with yourself, so you don't make unrealistic* promises. *You need to understand the customer's compelling reason to buy, so you know if you will be able to build sales momentum. It also helps to have closed a few deals in the recent past, so you can use your experience to make an educated guess.*

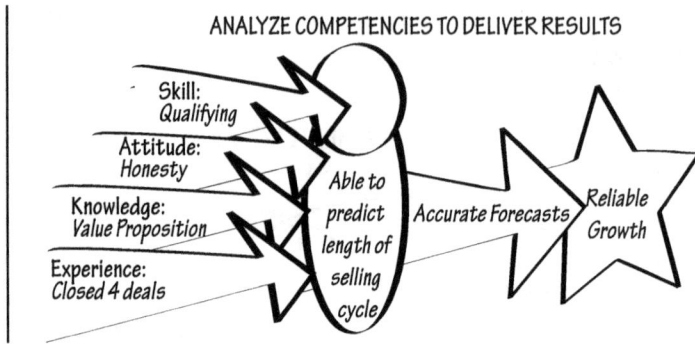

ANALYZE COMPETENCIES TO DELIVER RESULTS

Skill: Qualifying
Attitude: Honesty
Knowledge: Value Proposition
Experience: Closed 4 deals
Able to predict length of selling cycle
Accurate Forecasts
Reliable Growth

Competency-based, sales force development initiatives use competency assessments and job descriptions to personalize the learning process, so it is more efficient. Every salesperson comes to his current job with a unique set of experience, knowledge, and skills. A competency management system tailors the universe of skills and knowledge that you need to sell to the unique requirements of your background, experience, and situation. Since this approach recognizes the unique requirements of each individual salesperson in a wide variety of selling situations, it accelerates the learning curve. Your learning experiences are more productive and efficient, so positive results are achieved faster and the company's strategic goals are realized sooner.

A competency management system enables:

■ Sales managers to determine whether they have the talent necessary within the organization to meet their business objectives. It also helps them to quickly redeploy their talent to address new business opportunities.

■ Salespeople to effectively identify areas they need to develop; work with their managers to decide which competencies to focus on; build personalized development plans that link competency needs to learning opportunities, and track their progress against the plan.

■ Sales support – training, marketing, management, etc. – to prioritize development projects and measure the effectiveness of their training programs, marketing materials and sales tools.

COMPETENCY ANALYSIS

Ask Yourself:

? Considering the company's new business strategy, what results do they expect me produce?

? What do I need to do to deliver these results?

? What skills, knowledge, experiences and attitudes do I need to develop to be able to take the actions required to deliver the results?

Benefits of Competency-based Sales Training Solutions

- **Get up to speed faster.** Competency-based learning directly links learning activities to the sales process. By practically applying the content to the steps of the sales process, it is easier to assimilate the new information into established sales behaviors. Integrating learning with doing is the best way to build and reinforce competency development and speed time to competency.

- **Practical application encourages use.** When sales tools and training classes accommodate field reality, they are much more readily accepted and used. Competency-based development starts with a thoughtful analysis of what motivates the salesperson to take responsibility for his learning process. By recognizing that one solution does not meet the needs of all salespeople, a competency-based learning system designs flexibility, consensus building, field-testing, and cross-functional communication into the development process.

- **Faster response to market change.** Competency-based learning improves organizational responsiveness because it is easier to develop new learning solutions faster. By adopting a process built on a centralized content model, you can facilitate the development process and enable a wider group of people to participate in this process. Separating the content development from the course development process enables everyone to do their job better – Subject Matter Experts focus on getting the content right, and developers focus on creatively treating the content to accomplish the learning objectives.

- **Faster response to customers.** Personalized, just-in-time learning enables salespeople to respond more quickly to customers. Although developing core skills and technical expertise is important to the long-term success of any sales organization, access to immediate, accurate, useful information and sales tools is often when most learning happens. When learning becomes an integral part of "getting the job done," it results in faster response to customers' needs.

■ **Better informed, organizational decisions.** Competency-based learning usually includes a fully integrated, automated assessment process as part of the system. Good assessments provide sales management with important intelligence about what the field is able to do. It provides them with ongoing feedback about the current level of competency of the field, what they understand, and what they don't. This vital information helps sales executives make better, strategic decisions and fine tune their go-to-market strategies.

WHY USE COMPETENCY-BASED DEVELOPMENT?

★ Get up to speed faster

★ Practical application encourages use

★ Increase responsiveness to market change

★ Enable faster response to customers

★ Make better informed, strategic decisions

STEP 3: Use Metrics to Measure Progress

A competency is a combination of skills, knowledge, and attitudes that add up to the ability to get the job done. If you have the right skills, knowledge, and attitudes, then it's highly probable that you will deliver the results expected of you. This is a great theory, but, like most theories, it is tough to put into practice.

Your job is to deliver results. First and foremost, you have to make your numbers. Everything else – growing your account, communicating effectively, building relationships, etc. – is secondary. However, the only way you are going to accomplish your business goal is by making sure that the 'everything else' gets done. Seems a bit of a paradox, doesn't it?

In a competency management system, you track results rather than activity. Whether you get an advanced business degree, pass a placement test, or attend seminars is inconsequential. What really matters is if you can demonstrate the competencies required to produce the results expected of you.

To do this you need to set up a feedback system that will keep you on the right track. You need to figure out what the daily things you need to do to succeed are. What are the milestones you need to track so you are confident that they will add up to selling your quota by the end of the year? You need to create a set of metrics that provide you with quantifiable feedback on your level of competency, because, if you are competent, you will achieve results.

> For example, a core competency for any salesperson is the ability to forecast accurately. The skills and knowledge required to forecast accurately include the ability to:
>
> ★ Understand how quickly a market is emerging and how the market's momentum will drive demand for the new technology.
>
> ★ Calculate and generate an appropriate number of prospects with the correct technology adoption profile.
>
> ★ Qualify accounts quickly and determine the length of the sales cycle and probability of closure.
>
> ★ Determine the prospects' compelling reason to buy, their decision-making process, and style and degree of urgency for a solution.
>
> ★ Assess the competitive environment in order to minimize the impact of competitive losses on the forecast.

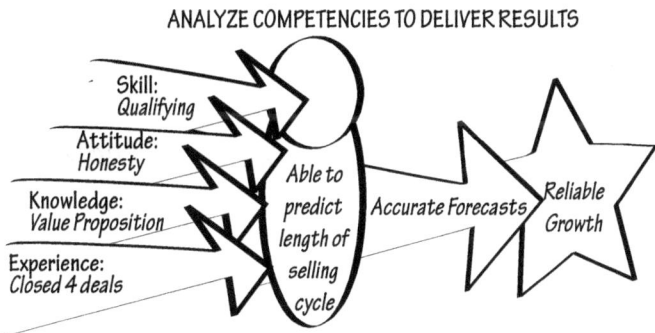

ANALYZE COMPETENCIES TO DELIVER RESULTS

Skill: Qualifying
Attitude: Honesty
Knowledge: Value Proposition
Experience: Closed 4 deals
Able to predict length of selling cycle
Accurate Forecasts
Reliable Growth

In this example you know what is expected of you – *90% accuracy on your forecast* – and what you need to do to deliver these results, which is the ability to demonstrate list of behaviors described above. However, what you don't know is how to track your performance in a way that provides you with feedback about what you are doing well and where improvement in a particular skill or knowledge area will help you deliver more consistent results.

The most obvious metric would be to *compare the number of accounts you close to your forecast.* While this metric does provide you with gross feedback on your performance, it doesn't really tell why you are not performing well if you are not. On the other hand, *if you compare the average length of your sales cycle to the average sales cycle for the rest of the company,* you learn much more about what you are doing right. This is a better metric because it gives you specific feedback on your ability to qualify an account, sell the solution, and create urgency. It also tells you how good you are at predicting how quickly a market is emerging. If you understand market energy, you will be in the right place at the right time, and consequently your sales cycles will be shorter. Another interesting metric might be to *track your competitive wins.* If you are good at assessing the competitive environment, you will focus your sales efforts on your company's 'sweet spots.' These are deals you are more likely to win because you have an inherent competitive advantage. Therefore, your forecast will probably be more accurate.

Developing metrics that measure progress is more of an art than a science. However, a good set of metrics will not only help you take control of your development process, it can also send a powerful message back to corporate headquarters. If a metric that compares competitive wins to losses is increasing, then sales management should be looking at the cause for this growth. Is the problem that the salespeople are afraid to compete? Probably not. More likely the salespeople in the field don't have the market information or competitive intelligence they need to compete. A good set of metrics can provide both the salesperson and sales management with the information they need to successfully implement strategy and produce results.

WHY USE METRICS?

★ Learn what you don't know.

★ Provide quality feedback.

★ Create a system of continuous improvement.

★ Take control of your future.

★ Make better informed decisions.

CONCLUSIONS

- **Content is king.** Most high tech companies do not effectively provide their salespeople with the information they need. Technology companies need to build a core source of information and tools that make it easier to sell the new technologies into emerging markets.

- **Content + Process = Success.** 'Sales ready' content is the information you need to successfully sell technology. It helps you manage the information critical to the sales process and apply it ways that move the sales forward.

- **Consensus is critical to credibility.** Good content brings the perspectives of multiple disciplines – engineering, business, sales, marketing, etc. – to consensus around a credible, easy-to-communicate message. Without consensus, the field and, consequently, the market get conflicting messages. Conflicting messages undermine market credibility.

- **Someone needs to care.** A content management system must clearly establish appropriate ownership of both the content and the deliverables.

- **Don't reinvent the wheel.** If content is not developed centrally then it has be done by everyone who has to respond to the customer – every salesperson, sales engineer, strategic marketing, product marketing, sales training developer etc. This is an incredibly unproductive use of resources.

- **Leverage your experts.** A content management process makes more efficient use of valuable, overworked subject matter experts by leveraging their expertise and optimizing their contribution to the enterprise.

- **Competency management accelerates change.** The success of a high tech sales organization directly depends on how quickly it can respond to change. Getting a sales organization to respond, however, is a huge challenge. High-performance sales organizations solve this problem by applying the principles of competency management to developing their salespeople. Competency-based development enables a sales team to quickly build the skills and knowledge it needs to successfully implement the organization's sales and business strategies.

- **Make learning part of getting the job done.** Competency-based learning directly links learning activities to the sales process, so it is easier to assimilate the new information into established sales behaviors.

- **Practical application drives use**. When sales tools and training classes accommodate field reality, they are much more readily accepted and used.

- **Make decisions based on data, not assumptions**. Good assessments provide sales management with important intelligence about what the field is able to do, which helps them make better, strategic decisions and fine tune their go-to-market strategies.

- **Feedback fosters growth**. In a competency management system, you track results rather than activity. To do this you need to set up a feedback system that will keep you on the right track

- **Developing good metrics is art**. A good set of metrics can provide both the individual and management with the information they need to successfully implement strategy and produce results.

Acknowledgments

Many people contributed to this book in a significant way. I would especially like to thank the terrific content experts who reviewed my manuscript – Kelly Herrick, Ted Lawrence, Marty Marsh, Dave McComb, George Peabody, Jessie Rumsey, Chris Van Collie, and Pat Wallace.

I thank the my clients and sales superstars that I have worked with over the years. Without your support this book would never have been possible.

The inspiration for many of the illustrations in this book can be found in the wonderful drawings of Saul Steinberg.

Thank you.

Index